EXPLORING

# ANCIENT CIVILIZATIONS

# 11

## Index

Marshall Cavendish

Marshall Cavendish
99 White Plains Road
Tarrytown, New York 10591-9001

www.marshallcavendish.com

*Consultants:* Daud Ali, School of Oriental and African
Studies, University of London; Michael Brett, School
of Oriental and African Studies, London; John
Chinnery, School of Oriental and African Studies,
London; Philip de Souza; Joann Fletcher; Anthony
Green; Peter Groff, Department of Philosophy,
Bucknell University; Mark Handley, History
Department, University College London; Anders
Karlsson, School of Oriental and African Studies,
London; Alan Leslie, Glasgow University Archaeology
Research Department; Michael E. Smith, Department
of Anthropology, University at Albany; Matthew
Spriggs, Head of School of Archaeology and
Anthropology, Australian National University

*Contributing authors:* Richard Balkwill, Richard
Burrows, Peter Chrisp, Richard Dargie, Steve Eddy,
Clive Gifford, Jen Green, Peter Hicks, Robert Hull,
Jonathan Ingoldby, Pat Levy, Steven Maddocks, John
Malam, Saviour Pirotta, Stewart Ross, Sean Sheehan,
Jane Shuter

WHITE-THOMSON PUBLISHING
*Editors:* Alex Woolf and Steven Maddocks
*Design:* Derek Lee
*Cartographer:* Peter Bull Design
*Picture Research:* Glass Onion Pictures
*Indexer:* Fiona Barr

MARSHALL CAVENDISH
*Editor:* Thomas McCarthy
*Editorial Director:* Paul Bernabeo
*Production Manager:* Michael Esposito

**Library of Congress Cataloging-in-Publication Data**
Exploring ancient civilizations.
    p. cm.
Includes bibliographical references and indexes.
   ISBN 0-7614-7456-0 (set : alk. paper) -- ISBN 0-7614-7457-9 (v. 1 :
alk. paper) -- ISBN 0-7614-7458-7 (v. 2 : alk. paper) -- ISBN
0-7614-7459-5 (v. 3 : alk. paper) -- ISBN 0-7614-7460-9 (v. 4 : alk.
paper) -- ISBN 0-7614-7461-7 (v. 5 : alk. paper) -- ISBN 0-7614-7462-5
(v. 6 : alk. paper) -- ISBN 0-7614-7463-3 (v. 7 : alk. paper) -- ISBN
0-7614-7464-1 (v. 8 : alk. paper) -- ISBN 0-7614-7465-X (v. 9 : alk.
paper) -- ISBN 0-7614-7466-8 (v. 10 : alk. paper) -- ISBN 0-7614-7467-6
(v. 11 : alk. paper)
  1. Civilization, Ancient--Encyclopedias.
 CB311.E97 2004
 930'.03--dc21

                                    2003041224

ISBN 0-7614-7456-0 (set)
ISBN 0-7614-7467-6 (vol. 11)

Printed and bound in China

07 06 05 04 03   5 4 3 2 1

# Contents

# Time Line

| | 65,000 | 30,000 | 3500 | 3000 | 2500 | 2000 | 1500 |
|---|---|---|---|---|---|---|---|

## AFRICA

EGYPT C. 3100 BCE–395 CE

NUBIANS 3500 BCE–540 CE

## AMERICAS

CHAVÍN 1800–200 BCE

MAYA C. 1800 BCE–C. 800 CE

OLMECS 1500–350 BCE

## EASTERN ASIA

JAPAN 30,000 BCE–700 CE

KOREA 3000 BCE–935 CE

## EUROPE

CYCLADIC CULTURE C. 3200–C. 1000 BCE

MINOANS C. 3000–C. 1450 BCE

MYCENAEAN CIVILIZATION 1600–C. 1200 BCE

| 1000 | 500 | I | 500 | 1000 |
|---|---|---|---|---|

Bantu Culture c. 500 bce–600 ce

Nok Culture 500 bce–250 ce

Anasazi c. 1 ce–c. 1300 ce

Hopewell Culture c. 300 bce–c. 450 ce

Moche Culture c. 200 bce–800 ce

Zapotecs 500 bce–800 ce

China 1700s bce–618 ce

Dong Son Culture c. 800–111 bce

Angles and Saxons 410–c. 500 ce

Celts c. 1200 bce–432 ce

Etruscans 700–90 bce

Franks c. 274–c. 760 ce

Goths c. 238–507 ce

Classical Greece c. 500–336 bce

Macedonians 359–31 bce

Roman Republic and Empire 753 bce–476 ce

| 65,000 | 30,000 | 3500 | 3000 | 2500 | 2000 | 1500 |
|--------|--------|------|------|------|------|------|

**OCEANIA
AND
AUSTRALIA**

ABORIGINAL CULTURE 65,000 BCE–1788 CE

LAPITA CULTURE 1500–700 BCE

MELANESIAN CULTURE 40,000 BCE–1643 CE

**SOUTHERN
ASIA**

ARYANS C. 20,000–C. 500 BCE

INDUS VALLEY CIVILIZATION 3100–1700 BCE

**WESTERN
ASIA**

AKKADIANS 2340–C. 2150 BCE

ASSYRIANS C. 2400–C. 610 BCE

BABYLONIANS C. 2200–275 B

ELAMITES 2700–639 BCE

HITTITES C. 1900–C. 710 BCE

KASSITES 1800–1168 BCE

MESOPOTAMIA C. 5000–539 BCE

PHOENICIANS C. 2600–C. 64 BCE

SUMER C. 4500–C. 2000 BCE

| 1000 | 500 | I | 500 | 1000 |
|------|-----|---|-----|------|

Micronesian Culture c. 2500 bce–c. 800 ce

Polynesian Culture c. 1000 bce–c. 1600 ce

Gupta Empire 320–550 ce

Kushan Empire c. 170 bce–c. 240 ce

Mauryan Empire c. 321–c. 185 bce

Achaemenids 550–330 bce

Hebrews c. 1300 bce–132 ce

Huns c. 370–455 ce

Parthians c. 247 bce–228 ce

Sasanians 224–636 ce

Scythians c. 1500–c. 130 bce

# Glossary

**abacus**  A frame holding wires on which beads can be moved, used for counting and calculating.

**adze**  A tool similar to an ax, with an arched blade set at right angles to the handle, used for trimming and shaping wood.

**ahau**  A Mayan lord, part king, part high priest, who ruled over a city region.

**Akkadian**  An ancient Semitic language of Mesopotamia, used from around 2500 BCE.

**alabaster**  A white or translucent stone used for sculpture and decorative work.

**alluvial**  Describing the environment, action, and sedimentary deposits of rivers or streams.

**amber**  A hard yellow resin used in jewelry and ornaments.

**ambrosia**  Food of the gods.

**amphitheater**  An oval, open-air space surrounded by seating, used for public entertainments.

**amphora**  An ancient Greek vase, pointed at the bottom, designed to be laid on its side or buried in sand.

**amulet**  A piece of jewelry worn in ancient times to ward off bad luck.

**anesthetic**  A drug, gas, or other method of deadening all or part of the body so that it cannot feel pain.

**anoint**  Smear, usually with oil, as part of a ritual used to indicate someone's consecrated status. Kings, priests, and prophets in ancient Israel were all anointed as a sign that they had been chosen by God. The Hebrew word *messiah*, and Christ, its Greek translation, both mean "anointed."

**anthropologist**  A scholar who studies the early history of a people.

**antiquarian**  A person who collects old objects.

**antler pick**  A digging tool made from the hard, bony antlers of deer. It was used like a pick, to loosen soil and force rock and stone from the ground.

**Apennines**  A mountain range that runs down the spine of Italy.

**apostle**  One of the twelve followers of Jesus, also called disciples.

**apse**  A domed semicircular hall at the east end of a church.

**aqueduct**  A stone channel, raised on walls, columns, or arches, designed to carry water across a valley.

**Archimedes' screw**  A device used to lift water from one level to another, consisting of a large continuous screw inside a cylinder. When the screw is turned, the water is lifted inside the cylinder by the spiral threads.

**arena**  From the Latin word for "sand." Strictly speaking, the sandy floor of an amphitheater, though the word has come to mean the whole amphitheater.

**Arian**  A Christian who followed the outlawed teachings of Arius.

**aristocrat**  A member of a wealthy, landowning family, often involved in ruling a country.

**artifact**  An ancient object made by humans; often one that comes to light through historical research.

**asceticism**  Self-denial for religious reasons.

**ashram**  An Indian word for a place where teaching is received.

**Asia Minor**  A peninsula in the extreme west of Asia, roughly corresponding to Asian Turkey.

**asphalt**  An oily black substance that seeps out of the ground. When melted over a fire, mixed with sand, and then poured onto the ground, it forms a hard waterproof surface.

**astrology**  The study of the positions of the moon, sun, and other planets in the belief that their motions affect human beings.

**atoll**  A ring-shaped island made of coral, partly or completely enclosing an area of seawater.

**auroch**  A long-horned wild ox, now extinct, but thought to be an ancestor of modern domestic cattle.

**auxiliary** An irregular soldier, one who fights only when called upon.

**avatar** Human or animal form of a Hindu god.

**baptize** Immerse in or sprinkle with water as a sign that a person has been accepted into the Christian faith.

**barbarian** A member of a wild, uncivilized people. The word was coined by the Greeks to describe people whose language sounded like "bar, bar."

**bard** Poet who recited long poems from memory, usually accompanied by music.

**basilica** A large oblong building with two rows of columns and an apse (a domed semicircular section).

**bas-relief** A type of sculpture in which the design projects slightly from a flat background.

**bastion** Something providing strong defense or support, especially for a belief, a cause, or a way of life.

**besiege** To surround a city with armed forces in order to force its surrender or capture.

**bitumen** A tarlike substance extracted from rock.

**black-figure pottery** Pottery on which the outline of a picture was first painted with slip, a watered-down mixture of clay and ash. The details were then scratched through. In the firing process, the slip baked black while the rest of the pot turned red, including the scratched detail.

**blasphemy** The sin of acting or speaking in a way disrespectful to God.

**bloodletting** Ritual cutting of the body to take blood; done to mark a birth, death, or marriage or as a cleansing rite.

**bluestone** A type of hard stone that is bluish gray in dry weather.

**bodhisattva** According to Buddhist teaching, a being who has attained enlightenment but remains in the human world to help others.

**broch** A circular stone tower found in the coastal parts of northern and western Scotland and the nearby islands.

**bulla** A round amulet worn by Roman children until they came of age (boys around sixteen, girls around fourteen or fifteen).

**cairn** A mound of stones created by human activity. Some are mounds made by farmers; others are mounds over graves or burial chambers.

**calligraphy** The art of beautiful handwriting.

**cameo** A gem with a design carved in relief, especially one in which the bottom and top layers are different colors. It is the opposite of an intaglio.

**cannibalism** The practice of eating human flesh.

**canopic jar** Jar used in ancient Egypt to hold the embalmed internal organs of a mummy.

**caravan** A column of merchants traveling, usually on camels, across desert country.

**carbon dating** A dating method based on the amount of radioactive carbon left in organic objects, such as seeds.

**carnelian** Reddish stone often used in jewelry.

**caste** Class in India, according to the principles of Hinduism; for example, the Brahmins were holy men, the Kshatriyas were warriors, and the Shudras were land-owning farmers or skilled tradesmen.

**catacomb** An underground network of passages and tombs, especially those in ancient Rome.

**cella** The most sacred part of a temple or shrine, often containing the cult statue.

**cenotaph** A monument to a person who is buried elsewhere.

**chambered cairn** A type of prehistoric tomb in which the burial chamber is covered by a mound, or cairn, of stones and soil.

**chorus** A group of performers, sometimes as many as fifty, who danced and commented in song, in groups or as one, on the action of a play.

**circumcision** The Jewish custom of removing the foreskin from the penis of a baby boy.

**Circus Maximus** A U-shaped amphitheater in Rome where chariot races were held.

**cistern** A tank or vessel used for storing water.

**citadel** A fortress or stronghold built to defend a city.

**city-state** An independent state consisting of a city and its surrounding territory.

**concubine** A woman who lives with a wealthy man, especially a king, without being his wife.

**constitution** A document setting out the basic laws or principles by which a country is governed.

**creed** A formal statement of religious belief.

**crop mark** The pattern made in a field by the different way in which a crop grows over buried walls, ditches, and pits. A crop growing above a wall will have shallow roots, and it will dry out sooner than a crop growing above a ditch or a pit, where the roots can reach deeper into the ground for moisture. Seen from the air, crop marks above walls appear light in color; those above ditches and pits appear dark.

**crucifixion** A method of killing used for political rebels in the Roman Empire. The prisoner was nailed or tied to a wooden cross and left to die.

**cult** A system of religious or spiritual beliefs.

**cuneiform** A style of writing using wedge-shaped characters, usually made by a reed or other stylus pressed into a tablet of wet clay, which was then hardened in the sun or baked. The term also describes similar writing carved into material such as stone.

**cupbearer** A person who serves wine in a noble household.

**decimal** Referring to any system of counting that is based on the number ten.

**delta** An area of wet, marshy land formed by a river that breaks into several parts as it joins the sea.

**demigod** A mythical figure with one divine parent and one human parent.

**dendochronology** A dating method in which the annual growth rings of a piece of timber are matched against a master chart to produce a date that equates to the year in which the timber was felled.

**dessication** The process of drying something out.

**dharma** According to the principles of Hinduism, one's religious or moral duty.

**didgeridoo** An aboriginal musical instrument consisting of a long thick wooden pipe that the player blows into, creating a deep humming sound.

**dike** An embankment, built along the shore of a sea or a lake or beside a river, to hold back water and so prevent flooding.

**doctrine** A formal religious teaching, especially one that all adherents of a religion are expected to endorse without qualification.

**Doric column** A style of Greek column with a fluted shaft, a rounded molding at the top, and no base.

**dowry** The money or property brought by a woman to her marriage.

**duty work** Every ancient Egyptian was expected to work for the pharaoh for a set number of days each year. This work could be building work or work in the fields or clearing canals and ditches. Scribes were the only people who did not have to do duty work.

**dynasty** A succession of rulers from the same family.

**earthwork** A structure, such as an embankment or a ditch, in which earth (soil) is the main building component.

**edict** An official command or announcement.

**Egyptologist** Someone who studies the history and artifacts of ancient Egypt.

**electrum** A mixture of gold and silver that was seen by the ancient Egyptians as the most precious metal.

**embalmer** One who treats a dead body with preservative substances to stop it from decaying.

**enlightenment** Defined by Buddhists as a state of blissful peace involving freedom from ignorance and from attachment to worldly things.

**epic** A long poem describing the adventures and deeds of a legendary hero or heroes.

**Essene** A member of a Jewish group that lived a life of prayer and fasting in the desert.

**fermentation** The process of changing sugar into alcohol.

**fibula** An arch-shaped Etruscan or Roman brooch with a long pin. It was used to fasten clothing and hold it in place.

**flax** A plant with blue flowers that is widely cultivated for its seeds, which produce linseed oil, and its stems, from which fiber to make linen is obtained.

**Flood, the** The great deluge mentioned in Mesopotamian mythology and the Old Testament.

**forum** The town square in the middle of a Roman town, used for markets, political meetings, and processions.

**fossil ivory** The ancient remains of the teeth or tusks of animals.

**fresco** Wall painting where paint is applied to fresh, damp plaster.

**fuchsite** A hard dark green rock used in carvings.

**funerary temple** A temple, built near a tomb, where prayers and offerings could be made.

**galley** A long, low-lying boat, propelled by oars or sails, used in ancient times, especially in the Mediterranean.

**geometry** The study of points, lines, angles, curves, surfaces, and solids in mathematics.

**gild** Cover with gold leaf.

**gladiator** A highly trained fighter, who may have been a slave, a prisoner of war, or a volunteer.

**glaze** A shiny coating on pottery.

**glyph** A small picture, image, or sign representing a sound or idea, as in Mayan writing.

**gold leaf** Gold hammered out until it is paper thin.

**granary** A building for storing grain.

**granulation** Decoration consisting of minute granules (grains) of metal soldered to a background.

**gymnasium** From the Greek word *gymnos*, meaning "naked," an area where young men exercised, had discussions, and heard lectures.

**Hades** In Greek mythology, the underworld kingdom inhabited by the souls of the dead.

**harem** A place where rulers in the ancient world kept their many wives.

**heifer** A young cow, especially one that has never had a calf.

**Hellenistic period** The period of Greek civilization between the late fourth and first centuries BCE.

**hemlock** A poisonous plant; it was used as a method of capital punishment in ancient Athens.

**hemp** A plant whose coarse fibers can be used to make, cloth, rope, and a writing surface.

**hierarchy** A system arranged in ranks according to authority or social position.

**hieroglyph** Symbol in a system of picture writing used by the Egyptians, the Maya, and other ancient civilizations. Individual hieroglyphs could stand for objects, concepts, or sounds.

**hippodrome** An open-air stadium in ancient Greece or Rome with an oval track that was used for horse or chariot racing.

**Hittite** A member of a people who lived in the land between the Mediterranean and the Black Seas; at their most powerful they controlled an empire that reached into Syria.

**Horus** In Egyptian mythology, a sky god (the son of Isis and Osiris) who represented kingship and was usually shown as having a falcon's head.

**hull** The framework of a ship.

**hunter-gatherer** One who lives by hunting animals for their meat and by gathering wild fruits, seeds, and vegetables.

**hurling** A game similar to hockey, played with broad sticks.

**hüyük** Turkish word for an ancient settlement mound, equivalent to the Arabic word *tell*.

**ibex** A type of wild goat.

**ibis** A wading bird with a downward-curving bill.

**Indo-European** A major language group to which most languages in Europe, India, and Iran belong.

**intaglio** A gem with a design carved into it by engraving; the opposite of a cameo.

**Ionia** Part of the western Anatolian coast and islands in the Aegean Sea, mostly populated by Greeks, that formed a province of the empire of Darius.

**Ionian** A light, graceful building style using slender columns much admired and copied by the mainland Greeks and the Romans.

**irrigation** A method of bringing a supply of water to dry land, especially to help crops grow.

**Islam** The religion of Muslims, based upon the teachings of Muhammad, who lived during the seventh century CE.

**Italic** Describing the people who lived in ancient Italy before and during Roman times.

**jaguar** An animal similar to a leopard, native to central and South America.

**joust** A contest wherein two riders with lances try to unseat each other as they pass.

**kaolin** Fine white clay used in pottery and papermaking.

**keel** The V-shaped bottom of a ship.

**kiln** An oven for baking and hardening pottery.

**kohl** A black powder often used in stick form to paint around the eyes.

**lacquer** To finish wooden bowls and other containers by painting them with lacquer, liquid sap from the lacquer tree. The artist applies several coats of lacquer, which then dry to form a tough, glossy finish.

**lapis lazuli** A bright blue mineral used as a gemstone.

**latitude** An imaginary straight line around the earth parallel to the equator.

**lava** The rock produced by an erupting volcano, whether in its molten or its cooled and hardened state.

**legion** A Roman army division, consisting of between three and six thousand soldiers, or legionaries, including cavalry.

**legionary** A Roman soldier who belonged to a force of around 5,500 men, called a legion; he served in the army for between twenty and twenty-five years.

**Levant** The eastern shore of the Mediterranean, from Greece to Egypt.

**linen** A fabric made from the stems of the flax plant.

**lintel** A timber beam or stone block placed across the top of a pair of standing stones.

**longitude** An imaginary straight line around the earth from the North to the South Pole.

**Lydia** A kingdom of fabulous wealth that occcupied much of western Anatolia.

**lyre** A plucked string instrument used in ancient Greece.

**macana** A sword with a wooden handle and a sharp blade made from obsidian or flint.

**magus** A high priest of the Persians especially skilled in interpreting dreams.

**manioc** A root vegetable.

**manta** A large, colored cloak worn by women, especially in the Americas, over their head and arms.

**mantra** A word or sound repeated to aid concentration in meditation.

**map projection** A representation of the curved surface of the earth on a flat, two-dimensional map. Ancient Greek geographers devised a number of different projections to show the world.

**matriarchal** Describing a society or family in which the governing authority is held by women.

**matrilineal** Referring to the passing on of names and property through the mother rather than the father.

**maul stone** A heavy stone used as a hammer.

**Mede** A member of a nomadic people related to the Persians and speaking an Indo-European language who settled most of northern Iran, perhaps around 1300 BCE.

**meditation** The practice of training the mind and body to be less active for certain periods, especially in order to focus on religious matters.

**megalith** A very large stone used in ancient times as a monument.

**menial** Requiring little or no skill or thought; undignified.

**mercenaries** Professional soldiers paid to fight for an army other than that of their country.

**Messiah** In the Hebrew Bible, an anointed king who will lead the Jews back to the land of Israel and establish justice in the world. Christians believe Jesus was the Messiah prophesied in the Bible.

**metallurgy** The techniques and knowledge required to extract and work with metals.

**metic** A foreigner living and working in ancient Athens.

**mica** A material composed of sharp, shiny fragments found in stone and used as decoration before glass was discovered.

**mildew** A tiny fungus that forms a white coating on an object in damp conditions.

**millet** A fast-growing annual cereal plant grown for its seed and used for hay.

**milpa** An open space in a forest cleared by burning vegetation, the ash from which fertilizes the ground.

**Minerva** The Roman goddess of handicrafts, the arts, the professions, and war.

**missionary** A person who travels, usually far from home, to spread a religious faith.

**moksha** In Hinduism, a release from the cycle of death and rebirth.

**monolith** A single large block of stone.

**monotheism** The belief that there is only one God.

**mortar** A sticky mixture of sand, water, and cement used to attach bricks to one another.

**mortuary temple** A temple built near a tomb where prayers to the dead were said and offerings could be made. In the case of pharaohs (and one or two nonpharaohs), the deceased were also worshiped as gods.

**mosaic** A picture or design made from small colored pieces of stone or glass.

**mud brick** A brick made from clay, often mixed with chopped straw or grass, and dried hard by the sun. Used in dry climates for the construction of buildings.

**mummy** The body of a person preserved for burial, often by embalming.

**mural** A large picture painted directly onto a wall.

**myrrh** A pleasant-smelling gum obtained from various trees in Africa and southern Asia; it is used in perfume, incense, and medicinal preparations.

**natron** A white, yellow, or gray mineral once used in embalming and as a soap.

**nave** The main central part of a church.

**Neanderthal** Member of an extinct subspecies of human being that lived in Europe, northern Africa, and western Asia in the early Stone Age.

**necropolis** Literally, "city of the dead": a place where a great many dead people are buried and where temples and chapels are dedicated to them.

**Neolithic** Referring to the part of prehistory (the later Stone Age) marked by the establishment of settled villages, the development of farming, and the use of new types of artifacts such as polished stone axes and pottery. Neolithic culture appeared at different dates around the world, beginning around 7500 BCE in the Middle East.

**New Testament** For Christians, the second and most important part of the Bible, concerned with Jesus' life and his message of God's justice, love, mercy, and redemption.

**Nile Delta** A great triangular area in Egypt where the Nile River flows into the Mediterranean. In ancient times the Nile Delta had seven branches.

**nomad** Any one of a group of people that move from place to place seasonally in search of pasture for their herds or food and water.

**nymph** A minor goddess or spirit of nature in mythology; a nymph inhabited areas of natural beauty, such as woods, mountains, and rivers, and was traditionally regarded as a beautiful young woman.

**oasis** A stretch of fertile land in the desert.

**obelisk** A tall, square-based column with a pyramid shape at the top.

**obsidian** A type of hard, sharp volcanic glass used by many ancient civilizations to make spear tips and cutting tools.

**ocher** A natural brownish yellow powder containing rust.

**oracle** A shrine where ancient Greeks consulted a god for advice or a prophecy; also, the priestess through whom the god was thought to speak.

**ossuary** A chamber for storing human bones.

**ostracism** Exclusion of a person from a social group as a punishment.

**Ostrogoth** A member of an eastern nomadic people from the Crimea region in southern Russia who moved into the Roman world after c. 150 CE.

**pacify** Bring to a state of peace.

**pagan** Relating to an ancient, polytheistic religion (that is, one involving many gods.)

**palaestra** A square courtyard used for wrestling, weight lifting, and other sports.

**Paleolithic** Referring to a time, also called the Old Stone Age, when people used primitive, chipped-stone tools.

**pantheon** All the gods of a given culture or people.

**papyrus** A kind of reed that grew by rivers and in marshes in ancient Egypt. The stems of the reeds were beaten flat and laid over each other to make a smooth sheet that could be written upon and rolled up for storage.

**Parsee** Member of a Zoroastrian community in India that left Persia in the seventh and eighth centuries.

**pastoral** Presenting a happy image of country life.

**pastoralism** The keeping of domestic animals, such as sheep and goats, for their milk and meat.

**patriarchal** Describing a society or family in which the governing authority is held by men.

**patrician** A noble member of society.

**patron** Somebody who gives money or other support to someone else.

**peat** Partially rotted organic matter preserved in a waterlogged oxygen-free environment.

**permafrost** Permanently frozen layer of ground in low-temperature regions of the earth.

**persecution** The practice of punishing people, often killing them, because of their race or religious or political beliefs.

**Pharisee** A member of a Jewish group whose name means "interpreters." The Pharisees interpreted, or made sense of, God's laws, applying them to everyday life. They were forerunners of rabbis.

**philosophy** Literally, "the love of wisdom"; in general, the process that attempts, chiefly through reflection and speculation, to come to an understanding of the underlying nature of existence.

**pictograph** A pictorial symbol used in writing to represent a group of words.

**potassium-argon dating** A dating method based on the rate of decay of the isotope potassium 40 to argon 40.

**potsherd** A fragment of pottery, especially one found at an archaeological site.

**Praetorian Guard** The Roman emperor's personal bodyguard, numbering several thousand soldiers with two commanders.

**procurator** A Roman official who governed a province. The procurator oversaw tax collection and maintained law and order.

**prophet** A person who interprets the will of God.

**pumice** A light, porous rock formed from solidified lava.

**Punic Wars** Three wars fought between Rome and Carthage to decide which of them should be the supreme power in the Mediterranean. They spanned a 118-year period, with the third and final conflict ending in 146 BCE with the destruction of the city of Carthage.

**Punt** Ancient Egyptian name for a part of Africa not certainly identified but probably the coast of present-day Somalia.

**quipu** A counting or tallying device used by the Incas, consisting of a string with knots representing numbers.

**quoit** A ring of metal for throwing.

**rabbi** In Judaism, a religious leader and teacher.

**radiocarbon dating** A dating method that relies on the fact that carbon 14, a radioactive isotope present in all living things, decays at a known rate and thus enables fixed points in time to be calculated.

**refugee** A person seeking a safe place to live while escaping from war or persecution.

**reincarnation** A central belief of Hinduism—that, after death, a person is born again into a new body.

**relic** An object linked with the life of a holy person, often believed to retain spiritual power.

**relief** In sculpture, a design that stands out from the surface (as opposed to an etching, which is carved into a surface).

**Republic** The period of ancient Roman history between 510 and 27 BCE, when Rome was governed by elected representatives of the people, not by an emperor.

**resin** A sticky liquid that can be squeezed out of many plants and that hardens as it dries.

**resurrection** In Christian belief, the rising of Jesus from the dead after his crucifixion and entombment.

**rhetoric** The art of argument and persuasion, taught in ancient Greek and Roman schools.

**ritual** An action or series of actions used in a ceremony, generally religious.

**Sabbath** A day of rest, dedicated to God. The Jewish Sabbath lasts from before sunset on Friday until after sunset on Saturday. Sunday is the Christian Sabbath.

**sacred** Holy; having to do with God or a god.

**sacrifice** An offering to a god. A sacrifice may consist of crops but may also involve the killing of an animal or even a person.

**Sadducee** One of a group of Jewish priests who claimed to be descended from Zadok, the chief priest under King Solomon. They controlled temple worship in Jerusalem and grew very wealthy on offerings brought to the temple.

**saffron** An orange or yellow powder obtained from the saffron plant; used as a spice in cooking.

**Sanskrit** An ancient Indian language related to most of the languages of Europe, those, that is, that are members of the Indo-European group of languages.

**sarcophagus** A stone container used to hold the body of a dead person.

**sarsen** A type of hard sandstone. In Britain sarsen was used for the construction of prehistoric monuments such as Avebury and Stonehenge.

**satrap** The noble governor of a district in the Persian empire.

**scepter** A ceremonial rod carried as a symbol of power.

**scribe** A government official who could read and write. Scribes existed in many ancient civilizations, including Egypt and Israel.

**Semitic** Referring to languages related to modern Arabic and Hebrew.

**senate** A legislative body, such as that of ancient Rome.

**Seven Wonders of the World** The seven structures that ancient scholars considered to be the most remarkable in the world; they comprise the pyramids of Egypt, the giant bronze statue of the god Apollo in Rhodes, the statue of Zeus at Olympia carved by Phidias, the temple of the goddess Artemis in Ephesus, the lighthouse of Alexandria, the mausoleum of Halicarnassus, and the Hanging Gardens of Babylon.

**sexagesimal** Based on the number sixty.

**shadoof** A water-raising device used in ancient Egypt and India consisting of a suspended pivoting pole with a bucket on one end and a counterweight on the other.

**shaman** Someone believed to be able to enter the spirit world on behalf of his or her people.

**shekel** A unit of weight and coinage used by the Babylonians, Hittites, and Jews.

**shroud** The cloth in which a dead person is wrapped.

**sibyl** In ancient times, a woman believed to foretell the future by becoming the mouthpiece of the god Apollo.

**siege machine** A movable wooden tower used to attack high city walls.

**siege** The military tactic whereby an army surrounds a place and prevents anyone and anything from entering or leaving.

**silted up** Full of or obstructed with silt, a fine-grained sediment of mud or clay particles, deposited by running water.

**Sinai** A peninsula in northeastern Egypt.

**siren** In Greek legend, a beautiful woman who by singing sweetly lured sailors onto the rocks.

**Sivan** The ninth month in the Jewish civic calendar. It falls within May and June.

**smelt** Obtain metal by a process of melting the natural ore.

**soapstone** A soft rock.

**stalactite** An icicle-like hanging rock formation composed of water mixed with half-dissolved limestone.

**stela** A tall stone monument with an altar at the base, often carved with glyphs portraying animal gods and great kings and their victories.

**steppe** A grassy treeless plain, particularly of the kind found in Russia.

**stern** The rear of a boat or ship.

**stoa** In ancient Greece, a covered walkway, usually with a row of columns on one side and a wall on the other.

**strait** A narrow channel of water that joins two larger bodies of water.

**stratigraphy** Layers, or strata, of an archaeological site.

**stupa** In Buddhism, a domed shrine.

**stylus** A pointed instrument, usually a reed, used in ancient times for writing on clay.

**suckle** Feed young offspring with milk from udders or breasts.

**Sumerian** An early non-Semitic language of ancient Mesopotamia, used from around 3000 BCE.

**sutra** Buddha's teachings preserved in a written dialogue.

**synagogue** A Jewish place of worship, from a Greek word for "assembly," or "gathering."

**syntax** The rules governing the way in which words may be arranged and combined.

**tablet** An object, usually of clay or wood, made to receive an inscription.

**talent** An ancient unit of weight and money.

**tannic acid** A colorless liquid obtained from tree bark used to convert animal skins into leather.

**taro** A starchy root crop cooked as a vegetable and also ground to make a sort of bread.

**tell** A large earthen mound formed by the remains of layers of housing over a long period of time.

**Ten Commandments** In the Bible, the ten laws given by God to Moses.

**terra-cotta** Unglazed reddish brown hard-baked clay, often used to make pottery objects.

**theorem** A mathematical statement that can be proved by reasoning.

**thread pump** A screw inserted in a watertight tube, which, when turned, draws up water in the spiral of its thread.

**thresh** Separate the seeds of a harvested plant from the straw and chaff, husks, or other residue.

**Tishri** The first month of the civic Jewish year, happening within September and October.

**toga** A draped garment commonly worn by men in ancient Rome.

**torc** A large metal ring worn around the neck by the Celts. Torcs were made from metals such as bronze, silver, gold, and electrum (a mixture of silver and gold) and could be plain or decorated.

**travertine** A hard-wearing, white-colored limestone used for buildings.

**tributary** A river or stream that flows into a larger one or into a lake.

**tribute** Payment made by one state or tribe to another as a sign of submission.

**trilithon** Two upright stones supporting a third to form a kind of arch or doorway; from the Greek for "three stones."

**trireme** A ship powered by oarsmen on three levels.

**tufa** A porous rock (that is, one that contains pores through which water passes easily) with a spongy appearance.

**turquoise** A greenish blue mineral that is used as a gemstone.

**usury** The lending of money for a fee, often a large one.

**vassal** A person, nation, or group that is dominated or occupied by another ruler or nation.

**Visigoth** A member of an eastern nomadic people related to the Ostrogoths. After entering the Roman world, the Visigoths eventually settled in Gaul and the Iberian Peninsula.

**volume** In mathematics, the amount of space filled by an object.

**votive offering** An offering made to the gods in the hope of receiving a blessing or favor in return.

**Vulcan** In Roman mythology, the god of fire.

**wampum** In North America, beads used by Native Americans as money.

**writing tablet** A small, thin sheet of wood used for carrying a written message. One type of tablet was coated with wax onto which a message was scratched with a metal writing instrument called a stylus. Because the stylus scratched through the wax, it cut into the wood below and left an impression that could be read. Another type of tablet was uncoated; a reed pen was used to write directly onto it with ink.

**yaksha** An Indian spirit; a being, more powerful than a human, who serves a god.

**ziggurat** English word for *ziqqurratu*, a temple built in the shape of a stepped pyramid, found in Mesopotamian cities.

**zodiac** An imaginary belt across the sky that holds twelve special constellations used to read horoscopes.

# Resources for Further Study

All Internet addresses were functional and accurate as of July 2003.

## BIBLIOGRAPHY

### GENERAL

#### BOOKS

Geoffrey Barraclough, ed.
**The Hammond Concise Atlas of World History**
Union, NJ: Hammond, 2001.

J. Black, ed.
**Atlas of World History**
New York: Dorling Kindersley, 1999.

Colin R. Chapman
**Weights, Money and Other Measures Used by Our Ancestors**
Baltimore: Genealogical Publishing, 1996.

Margaret Ehrenberg
**Women in Prehistory**
Norman: University of Oklahoma Press, 1989.

Peter James and Nick Thorpe
**Ancient Inventions**
New York: Ballantine Books, 1994.

John Romer and Elizabeth Romer
**The Seven Wonders of the World: A History of the Modern Imagination**
New York: Henry Holt, 1995.

Jessica Salmonson
**The Encyclopaedia of Amazons: Women Warriors from Antiquity to the Modern Era**
New York: Anchor Books, 1992.

Annemarie Schimmel
**The Mystery of Numbers**
New York: Oxford University Press, 1993.

**Past Worlds: The Times Atlas of Archaeology**
Maplewood, NJ: Hammond, 1988.

### JOURNALS
**Archaeology**
The magazine of the Archaeological Institute of America, North America's oldest and largest organization devoted to archaeology, is published in six annual issues.
www.archaeology.org

### CD-ROMS
**The Oxford Classical Dictionary (3rd edition)**
Oxford University Press (Windows only)
This interactive, fully searchable version of a world-renowned publication provides clear and authorative information on all aspects of the ancient world, including substantial coverage of topics of interest to twenty-first-century students and a range of helpful features.

### AFRICA

#### BOOKS

J. Ajayi and M. Crowder, eds.
**Historical Atlas of Africa**
New York: Cambridge University Press, 1985.

J. D. Fage with William Tordoff
**A History of Africa**
New York: Routledge, 2002.

Joann Fletcher
**The Ancient Egyptian Book of Living and Dying**
London: Duncan Baird, 2002.

Joann Fletcher
**Egypt's Sun King: Amenhotep III**
London: Duncan Baird, 2000.

Joann Fletcher
**Oils and Perfumes of Ancient Egypt**
London: British Museum Press, 1998.

George Hart
**A Dictionary of Egyptian Gods and Goddesses**
Boston: Routledge & Kegan Paul, 1986.

Mark Lehner
**The Complete Pyramids**
New York: Thames and Hudson, 1997.

B. McDermott and Joann Fletcher
**Decoding Egyptian Hieroglyphs**
London: Duncan Baird, 2001.

D. Phillipson
**African Archaeology**
New York: Cambridge University Press, 1993.

Stephen Quirke and Jeffrey Spencer
**British Museum Book of Ancient Egypt**
New York: Thames and Hudson, 1992.

C. N. Reeves
**The Complete Tutankhamen**
New York: Thames and Hudson, 1990.

C. N. Reeves and R. H. Wilkinson
**The Complete Valley of the Kings: Tombs and Treasures of Egypt's Greatest Pharaohs**
New York: Thames and Hudson, 1996

G. Robins
**Women in Ancient Egypt**
Cambridge, MA: Harvard University Press, 1993.

Barbara Watterson
**The Egyptians**
Cambridge, MA: Blackwell, 1998.

Barbara Watterson
**Women in Ancient Egypt**
New York: St. Martin's Press, 1991.

R. H. Wilkinson
**The Complete Temples of Ancient Egypt**
New York: Thames and Hudson, 2000.

## JOURNALS

*KMT: A Modern Journal of Ancient Egypt*
This quarterly 88-page periodical is devoted to the culture, history, personalities, arts, and monuments of ancient Egypt and is named after Kemmet ("black land"), the Egyptians' name for their country.
www.egyptology.com/kmt

## CD-ROMS

*Egyptian Treasures in Europe*
Ten CD-ROMS are devoted to rarely seen Egyptian antiquities in European museums, with dates ranging from the predynastic period to Roman Egypt. The set was produced by the Center for Computer-Aided Egyptological Research, Utrecht, Netherlands.
www.egyptiantreasures.org

## AMERICAS

### BOOKS

Garth Bawden
*The Moche*
Cambridge, MA: Blackwell, 1996.

F. Blom and O. La Farge
*Tribes and Temples*
New Orleans: Tulane University Press, 1926.

Richard L. Burger
*Chavín and the Origins of Andean Civilization*
New York: Thames and Hudson, 1993.

Michael Coe
*The Maya*
New York: Thames and Hudson, 1999.

Brian M. Fagan
*Kingdoms of Gold, Kingdoms of Jade: The Americas before Columbus*
New York: Thames and Hudson, 1991.

Mary Miller and Karl Taube
*The Gods and Symbols of Ancient Mexico and the Maya: An Illustrated Dictionary of Mesoamerican Religion*
New York: Thames and Hudson, 1993.

Heather Pringle
*In Search of Ancient North America: An Archaeological Journey to Forgotten Cultures*
New York: John Wiley and Sons, 1996.

### JOURNALS

*Latin American Antiquity*
A quarterly journal on archaeology, prehistory, and ethnohistory in Mesoamerica, Central America, South America, and culturally related areas, published by the Society of American Archaeology.
http://www.saa.org/Publications/
     LatAmAnt/latamant.html

## EASTERN ASIA

### BOOKS

Michael Loewe and Edward L. Shaughnessy
*The Cambridge History of Ancient China*
New York: Cambridge University Press, 1999.

Patricia Buckley Ebrey
*The Cambridge Illustrated History of China*
New York: Cambridge University Press, 1996.

Patricia Buckley Ebrey, ed.
*Chinese Civilization: A Sourcebook*
New York: Free Press, 1993.

Keith Weller Taylor
*The Birth of Vietnam*
Berkeley: University of California Press, 1983.

Brian Williams
*Ancient China*
New York: Viking, 1996.

### JOURNALS

*Early China*
The journal of the Society for the Study of Early China is published annually.
http://humanities.uchicago.edu/depts/
     easian/earlychina/publications/ec_
     journal/index.htm

*Education about Asia*
This journal, produced by the Association for Asian Studies is published three times a year.
www.aasianst.org/eaa-toc.htm

## EUROPE

### BOOKS

Horace Gregory and Zhenya Gay, illus.
*Ovid: Metamorphoses*
New York: Signet, 2001.

Aubrey de Selincourt, trans., and John Marincola, rev.
*Herodotus: The Histories*
New York: Penguin Books, 1996.

Alan Fildes and Joann Fletcher
*Alexander the Great: Son of the Gods*
Los Angeles: J. Paul Getty Museum, 2002.

K. Grandsen, trans.
*Virgil: The Aeneid*
New York: Cambridge University Press, 1990.

M. Grant
*The Classical Greeks*
London: Phoenix Press, 2001.

M. Grant
*The Fall of the Roman Empire*
New York: Collier Books, 1990.

M. Grant
*The World of Rome*
London: Phoenix Press, 2000.

S. Hornblower and A. Spawforth
*Oxford Companion to Classical Civilization*
New York: Oxford University Press, 1998.

S. Hornblower and A. Spawforth
*Oxford Companion to Classical Literature*
New York: Oxford University Press, 1998.

Antony Kamm
*The Romans: An Introduction*
New York: Routledge, 1995.

Robert B. Kebric
*Greek People*
Mountain View, CA: Mayfield Publishing, 1989.

Kathleen Lines, ed., and Faith Jaques, illus.
*The Faber Book of Greek Legends*
Boston: Faber and Faber, 1983.

Philip Matyszak
*Chronicle of the Roman Republic: The Rulers of Ancient Rome from Romulus to Augustus*
New York: Thames and Hudson, 2003.

Robert Morkot
*Penguin Historical Atlas of Ancient Greece*
New York: Penguin, 1996.

Barbara Leonie Picard and Joan Kiddell-Monroe, illus.
*The* Iliad *of Homer Retold*
*The* Odyssey *of Homer Retold*
New York: Oxford University Press, 2000.

C. Scarre
*Chronicle of the Roman Emperors*
New York: Thames and Hudson, 1995.

Brian Sparkes, ed.
*Greek Civilization: An Introduction*
Malden, MA: Blackwell Publishers, 1998.

Rosemary Sutcliff and Alan Lee, illus.
*Black Ships before Troy: The Story of the* Iliad
New York: Delacorte Press, 1993.

Rosemary Sutcliff and Alan Lee, illus.
*The Wanderings of Odysseus: The Story of the* Odyssey
New York: Delacorte Press, 1996.

Margaret Williamson
*Sappho's Immortal Daughters.*
Cambridge, MA: Harvard University Press, 1995.

JOURNALS
*Journal of Roman Archaeology*
An international journal publishing book reviews, articles, and research findings in the field of Roman archaeology.
http://www.journalofromanarch.com/

*The Classical Quarterly*
A journal published by Oxford University Press and devoted to Greco-Roman antiquity. It publishes research papers and short notes in the fields of language, literature, history, and philosophy.
http://www3.oup.co.uk/jnls/list/clquaj/

## OCEANIA AND AUSTRALIA

BOOKS
Paul Bahn and John Flenley
*Easter Island Earth Island*
New York: Thames and Hudson, 1992.

Stanley Breeden
*Uluru: Looking after Uluru-Kata Tjuta, the Anangu Way*
East Roseville, NSW: Simon and Schuster Australia, 1994.

I. C. Campbell
*A History of the Pacific Islands*
St. Lucia: University of Queensland Press, 1990.

Wally Caruana
*Aboriginal Art*
New York: Thames and Hudson, 2003.

Steven Ferry
*Australian Aborigines*
Mankato, MN: Smart Apple Media, 1999.

Josephine Flood
*Archaeology of the Dreamtime: the Story of Prehistoric Australia and its People*
Sydney, NSW: Angus & Robertson, 1999.

Patrick Vinton Kirch
*On the Road of the Winds: An Archaeological History of the Pacific Islands before European Contact.*
Berkeley: University of California Press, 2000.

Robert Layton
*Uluru: An Aboriginal History of Ayers Rock.*
Canberra: Aboriginal Studies Press, 2001.

John Mulvaney and Johan Kamminga
*Prehistory of Australia*
Washington, DC: Smithsonian Institution Press, 1999.

Matthew Spriggs
*The Island Melanesians*
Cambridge, MA: Blackwell, 1997.

JOURNALS
*Australian Archaeology*
This official publication of the Australian Archaeological Association publishes, in two issues a year, articles relating to all fields of archaeological research and practice in Australia and nearby areas.
www.australianarchaeologicalassociation.com.au/australianarchaeology.html

*Asian Perspectives*
Published twice a year and devoted to the prehistory of Asia and the Pacific region, *Asian Perspectives* features articles and book reviews on ethnoarchaeology, paleoanthropology, physical anthropology, and enthnography.
http://www.uhpress.hawaii.edu/journals/ap/

## SOUTHERN ASIA

BOOKS
William Buck
*Mahabharata*
New York: Meridian, 1993.

William Buck and Shirley Triest, illus.
*Ramayana [King Rama's Way]*
Berkeley: University of California Press, 1976.

Edward Conze
*A Short History of Buddhism*
Boston: Unwin Paperbacks, 1982.

Joe Cummings and Bill Wassman, photographer
*Buddhist Stupas in Asia*
Oakland, CA: Lonely Planet Publications, 2001.

Robert Fisher
*Buddhist Art and Architecture*
New York: Thames and Hudson, 1993.

John Keay
*India: A History*
New York: Atlantic Monthly Press, 2000.

Juan Mascaró, trans.
*The Bhagavad Gita*
New York: Penguin Books, 2003.

Juan Mascaró, trans.
*The Upanishads*
Baltimore: Penguin Books, 1965.

James McIntosh
*A Peaceful Realm: The Rise and Fall of the Indus Civilization*
Boulder, CO: Westview Press, 2001.

George Michell
*Hindu Art and Architecture*
New York: Thames and Hudson, 2000.

R. K. Narayan, trans., and R. K. Laxman, illus.
*The* Mahabharata: *A Shortened Modern Prose Version of the Indian Epic*
Chicago: University of Chicago Press, 2000.

Shereen Ratnagar
*Understanding Harappa: Civilization in the Greater Indus Valley*
New Delhi: Tulika, 2001.

John Snelling
*Buddhism*
Rockport, MA: Element, 1996.

Alistair Shearer
*Buddha: The Intelligent Heart*
New York: Thames and Hudson, 1992.

## WESTERN ASIA

### BOOKS

John Westerdale Bowker
*The Complete Bible Handbook*
New York: Dorling Kindersley, 2001.

Dale M. Brown
*Mesopotamia: The Mighty Kings*
Alexandria, VA: Time Life, 1995.

Dale M. Brown, ed.
*Sumer: Cities of Eden*
Alexandria, VA: Time Life, 1994.

John Curtis et al., eds.
*Art and Empire: Treasures from Assyria in the British Museum*
New York: Metropolitan Museum of Art, 1995.

Vesta Sarkhosh Curtis
*Persian Myths*
Austin: University of Texas Press, 1993.

Stephanie Dalley, trans.
*Myths from Mesopotamia: Creation, the Flood, Gilgamesh, and Others*
New York: Oxford University Press, 1991.

Andrew George, trans.
*The Epic of Gilgamesh: The Babylonian Epic Poem and Other Texts in Akkadian and Sumerian*
New York: Penguin Books, 2003.

Gwendolyn Leick
*Historical Dictionary of Mesopotamia*
Lanham, MD: Scarecrow Press, 2003.

Gwendolyn Leick
*Who's Who in the Ancient Near East*
New York: Routledge, 1999.

Glen E. Markoe
*The Phoenicians*
Berkeley: University of California Press, 2000.

Michael Roaf
*The Cultural Atlas of Mesopotamia and the Ancient Near East*
New York: Facts on File, 1990.

### JOURNALS

*Near Eastern Archaeology*
A journal published by the American Schools of Oriental Research. It presents research and articles on the archaeology of Mesopotamia and the northern Middle East.
http://www.bu.edu/asor/pubs/nea/index.html

# PLACES TO GO

## NORTH AMERICA

### UNITED STATES
#### CALIFORNIA
**J. Paul Getty Museum**
1200 Getty Center Drive
Los Angeles, CA 90049-1687
310-440-7330
Created in 1953, this popular and well-endowed museum is housed in a re-creation of the first-century-BCE Villa dei Papiri at Herculaneum, complete with elaborate gardens. The Getty has acquired extraordinary classical collections.
www.getty.edu/museum

**De Young Museum**
75, Tea Garden Drive
San Francisco, CA 94118-4501
(Opens 2005)
415-750-7640 (The de Young Art Center, 2501 Irving Street, at 26th Avenue)
The de Young collection includes primitive pre-Columbian artifacts and art collections from Oceania, Africa, and the native cultures of the northwestern coast of America. Until the museum's brand-new building in Golden Gate Park opens in June 2005, the art education programs are run from the de Young Art Center.
http://www.thinker.org/deyoung

#### COLORADO
**The Denver Art Museum**
100 West 14th Avenue Parkway
Denver, CO 80204
720-865-5000
The Denver Art Museum is noted for its collection of primitive African, Oceanic, American, and Northwest Indian arts; Peruvian art; and Chinese, Japanese, Korean, Indian, Southeast Asian, Tibetan, West Asian, and North African art.
www.denverartmuseum.org

#### DISTRICT OF COLUMBIA
**Arthur M. Sackler Gallery, Smithsonian Institution**
1050 Independence Avenue, SW
Washington, DC 20560
202-357-2700
This gallery contains a permanent collection of Asian art, including ancient works from China, the Indian subcontinent, and Southeast Asia.
www.asia.si.edu

#### HAWAII
**Honolulu Academy of Arts**
900 South Beretania Street
Honolulu, HI 96814
808-538-3693
The academy, founded in 1927, has a general collection representing everything from ancient Near Eastern and Mediterranean arts to European and American arts.
www.honoluluacademy.org

#### ILLINOIS
**Oriental Institute Museum, University of Chicago**
1155 East 58th Street
Chicago, IL 60637
773-702-9514
This institute houses a collection of archaeology and art of the ancient Near East, Babylonia, and Egypt, of early Christian cultures, and of Islamic civilization.
www-oi.uchicago.edu

**The Field Museum of Natural History**
1400 South Lake Shore Drive
Chicago, IL 60605
312-922-9410
Founded in 1893, the Field Museum contains collections on anthropology, costumes, ethnology, geology, and Native American artifacts.
www.fmnh.org

#### INDIANA
**Indiana University Art Museum**
1133 East 7th Street
Bloomington, IN 47405
812-855-5445
This fine collection of ancient to contemporary art includes Egyptian, Greek, and Roman sculpture; coins and glass; and Far Eastern arts.
www.indiana.edu/~iuam

#### MARYLAND
**Walters Art Gallery**
600 North Charles Street
Baltimore, MD 21201
301-547-9000
Assembled by father and son, the Walters Art Gallery opened in 1931 and holds a collection of exquisite ancient and medieval treasures.
www.thewalters.org

MASSACHUSETTS
**Museum of Fine Arts**
465 Huntington Avenue
Boston, MA 02115
617-267-9300
This collection, founded in 1870, includes ancient Egyptian, Greek, and Roman collections and is famed for a Greek marble head of Aphrodite.
www.mfa.org

MICHIGAN
**The Detroit Institute of Arts**
5200 Woodward Avenue
Detroit, MI 48202
313-833-7900
Founded in 1885, this institute is renowned for its vast collection of world arts, including art of the ancient world.
www.dia.org

MISSOURI
**The St. Louis Art Museum**
Forest Park
St. Louis, MO 63110
314-721-0072
Founded in 1881, the St. Louis Art Museum contains a comprehensive collection of art from all eras of civilization.
www.slam.org

NEW JERSEY
**The Art Museum**
Princeton University
Princeton, NJ 08544
609-258-3788
This museum's comprehensive collection of world art includes many classical antiquities.
www.princetonartmuseum.org

NEW YORK
**The Brooklyn Museum**
200 Eastern Parkway
Brooklyn, NY 11238
718-638-5000
The Brooklyn Museum was founded in 1823 and has amassed comprehensive collections of Egyptian and classical arts; American arts; European and American graphics; and pre-Columbian, African, and Native American arts.
www.brooklynmuseum.org

**The Jewish Museum**
1109 Fifth Avenue
New York, NY 10128
212-423-3200
This collection numbers over 23,000 objects ranging from ancient archaeological artifacts from the eastern Mediterranean to contemporary art. A permanent exhibit, The Jewish Experience, spans 4,000 years of history and culture.
www.jewishmuseum.org

**The Metropolitan Museum of Art**
Fifth Avenue at 82nd Street
New York, NY 100028
212-879-5500
Founded in 1870 and long one of the world's major museums, the Met houses collections that cover 5,000 years of art.
www.metmuseum.org

OHIO
**Cleveland Museum of Art**
11150 East Boulevard
Cleveland, OH 44106
216-421-7340
This museum, founded in 1913, houses the arts of many cultures, including those of the ancient world.
www.clevelandart.org

**The Toledo Museum of Art**
2445 Monroe Street at Scottwood Avenue
Box 1013
Toledo, OH 43697
419-255-8000
Collections range from ancient Egypt, Greece, and Rome through contemporary Europe and America.
www.toledomuseum.org

OKLAHOMA
**Thomas Gilcrease Institute of American History and Art**
1400 North Gilcrease Museum Road
Tulsa, OK 74127
918-582-3122
This art collection captures the saga of America from prehistoric to modern times.
www.gilcrease.org

OREGON
**Portland Art Museum**
1219 South West Park Avenue
Portland, OR 97205
503-226-2811
The Portland, founded in 1892, focuses on Native American arts of the Northwest. Among its other collections are a unique collection of Cameroon art and pre-Columbian arts.
www.portlandartmuseum.org

PENNSYLVANIA
**University of Pennsylvania Museum of Archaeology and Anthropology**
3260 South Street
Philadelphia, PA 19104
215-898-4000
Founded in 1887, this museum is renowned for its ancient and primitive art, its collection of Native American gold, and the largest grouping of West African art in the Americas.
www.museum.upenn.edu

**Carnegie Museum of Art**
4400 Forbes Avenue
Pittsburgh, PA 15213
412-622-3131
This museum, founded in 1896, displays art from around the world, including ancient and classical art.
www.cmoa.org

TEXAS
**The Museum of Fine Arts, Houston**
1001 Bissonnet Street
Houston, TX 77005
713-639-7300
This museum's wide-ranging collection of world art, established in 1900, includes pre-Columbian and Native American art.
www.mfah.org

WISCONSIN
**Elvehjem Museum of Art, University of Wisconsin**
800 University Avenue
Madison, WI 53706
608-263-2246
The Elvehjem Museum has a wide-ranging collection of world art that dates back to ancient times, with fine examples of classical coins and marbles.
www.lvm.wisc.edu

CANADA
**The Royal British Columbia Museum of Anthropology**
675 Belleville Street
Victoria, BC V8V IX4
250-356-7226
A range of exhibitions depicts the accomplishments of native peoples, the achievements of early explorers and settlers, and British Columbia's natural heritage and archaeological past.
http://rbcm1.rbcm.gov.bc.ca/

**Royal Ontario Museum**
100 Queens Park
Toronto, ON M5S 2C6
416-586-5549
The Royal Ontario Museum is the largest museum in Canada and one of the world's few multidisciplinary museums combining art, archaeology, and science.
www.rom.on.ca

**The Canadian Museum of Civilization**
100 Laurier Street
P.O. Box 3100
Station B
Gatineau, PQ J8X 4H2
819-776-7000
Canada's renowned national museum of human history.
www.civilization.ca

MEXICO
**Museo Nacional de Antropología
(National Museum of Anthropology)**
Paseo de la Reforma y Calzada Gandhi
Mexico City 11560
(+52) 5-286-5195
Considered one of the world's finest museums, this famous institution houses four square kilometers of exhibits in 23 exhibition halls.
www.mna.inah.gob.mx (in Spanish)

**Museo de Antropología de Xalapa
(Xalapa Museum of Anthropology)**
Avenida Jalapa y Acueducto
Xalapa, Veracruz
(+52) 15 09 20
Presents almost 30 centuries of art and history; guards the most important collections of pre-Columbian works produced by peoples living in the present-day state of Veracruz.
www.xalapa.net/antropologia

**Teotihuacán**
31 miles (50 km) northeast of Mexico City.
Teotihuacán is one of the greatest Mesoamerican cities, has been extensively restored, and is arguably the most important archaeological site in the Americas.
http://archaeology.la.asu.edu/teo (Arizona State University's "Teotihuacán Home Page").

EUROPE

UNITED KINGDOM
**Ashmolean Museum of Art and Archaeology**
Beaumont Street
Oxford OX1 2PH
(+44) 01865 278000
One of the oldest public museums in the world, the Ashmolean, a museum of the University of Oxford, was founded in 1683. Admission to its extensive collection of art and antiquities from around the world is free.
www.ashmol.ox.ac.uk

**The British Museum**
Great Russell Street
London WC1B 3DG
(+44) 020 7323 8000
Founded in 1753, the British Museum holds one of the world's finest collections of ancient art and artifacts; access to the collections is free.
www.thebritishmuseum.ac.uk

### Skara Brae Visitor Centre
Bay of Skaill
Sandwick
Orkney
(+44) 1856 841815
The oldest and best-preserved Neolithic settlement in northern Europe.

### Stonehenge
Salisbury Plain
Wiltshire SP4 7DE
(+44) 01980 624715
Stonehenge, the world's best-known prehistoric stone monument, is located in central southern England and is managed by English Heritage.
http://www.english-heritage.org.uk/

### Roman Baths Museum
Pump Room
Stall Street
Bath
BA1 1LZ
(+44) 01225 477774
One of the world's best-preserved ancient Roman spa complexes.
www.romanbaths.co.uk

### The Fitzwilliam Museum
Trumpington Street
Cambridge CB2 1RB
(+44) 01223 332900
This museum holds magnificent collections of works of art and antiquities of national and international importance.
www.fitzmuseum.cam.ac.uk

## OTHER EUROPEAN COUNTRIES
### Musée du Louvre
75058 Paris Cedex 01
FRANCE
(+33) 0140 205151
One of Paris's leading attractions, the Louvre was founded in 1793 and incorporates works dating from the birth of the great ancient civilizations.
www.louvre.fr/louvrea.htm (English version)

### Museo Archeologico Nazionale
Piazza Museum Nazionale 18–19
Naples
ITALY
(+39) 081 292893
A building dating from the sixteenth century, this museum houses a remarkable collection of antiquities, including jewelry, papyri, and mosaics from Herculaneum and Pompeii.
www.cib.na.cnr.it/remuna/mann/mann.html

### Pergamon Museum
Am Kupfergraben Mitte
Berlin
GERMANY
(+49) 030 2090 5555
Of its vast collection of ancient artifacts, the Pergamon Museum's crowning glory is the two-story second-century-BCE altar from the Zeus temple in Pergamon, one of the world's most significant archaeological finds.
www.pergamonmeuseum.de

## AUSTRALIA

### Melbourne Museum
GPO Box 666E
Carlton Gardens
Melbourne, Victoria 3001
(+61) 13 11 02
This is the largest museum complex in the Southern Hemisphere and draws on the latest technology and interpretation methods to give visitors an insight into Australia's flora, fauna, culture, and way of life.
http://melbourne.museum.vic.gov.au

### National Museum of Australia
Lawson Crescent
Acton Peninsula
Canberra, ACT 2600
(+61) 02 6208 5000
This new museum is arranged around three themes: land, nation, and people. Children's stories, experiences, and interpretations feature throughout.
www.nma.gov.au

### Museum of Ancient Cultures
Macquarie University
Balaclava Road
North Ryde
Sydney, NSW 2109
(+61) 02 9850 7111
This museum houses many objects from the ancient Mediterranean world (Egypt, Greece, Cyprus, Israel, Palestine, Rome, Jordan, and Jericho) and includes the largest collection of papyri in Australia, decorated mummy covers, and coins.
www.museums.mq.edu.au

# INTERNET RESOURCES

**Ancient Egypt (British Museum)**
A comprehensive Web site that explores the region's geography, religion, and everyday life.
www.ancientegypt.co.uk

**The Ancient Indus Valley**
Contains 800 illustrated pages of information about the largest and least-known ancient urban civilization.
www.harappa.com

**The Asclepion**
This Indiana University Web site is dedicated to the study of ancient medicine.
http://www.indiana.edu/~ancmed/intro.HTM

**At the Tomb of Tutankhamen**
This Web site from *National Geographic* magazine allows visitors to share the excitement felt in 1923 as the tomb of Tutankhamen in the Valley of the Kings in Egypt was opened to journalists for the first time.
www.nationalgeographic.com/egypt

**BBC History**
This site includes a range of clearly written and informative articles, time lines, interactive games, and links to other BBC and non-BBC Web sites.
www.bbc.co.uk/history

**Bible History Online**
Offers links to thousands of articles and pictures covering a wide range of aspects of life in the ancient world.
www.bible-history.com

**Britannia**
This series of Web sites explores the history of the Roman army in Britain.
www.morgue.demon.co.uk

**Buddhist Art and Architecture**
Provides pictures and historical information about southern Asian sites such as Sanchi.
www.buddhanet.net/gallery.htm

**The Cave of Lascaux**
This official Web site offers a virtual tour and illustrated history of France's world-famous Paleolithic cave site. English version.
www.culture.fr/culture/arcnat/lascaux/en

**Crystalinks: Ancient and Lost Civilizations**
Provides links to hundreds of short articles on a vast range of topics relating to the ancient world.
www.crystalinks.com/ancient.html

**The Edicts of King Ashoka**
Provides an English translation of Ashoka's edicts, inscribed on rocks and pillars throughout northern India during the third century BCE.
www.cs.colostate.edu/~malaiya/ashoka.html

**Emuseum**
Created at the University of Minnesota, Mankato, this site presents information about several ancient civilizations, including China, Japan, and Latin America, as well as the early history of Minnesota itself.
http://emuseum.mnsu.edu

**Encyclopedia Mythica**
This on-line encyclopedia of the world's mythology, folklore, and legend focuses particularly on Roman mythology.
www.pantheon.org/mythica.html

**Fact Monster**
Browse the World History section for a time line that stretches back to 4.5 billion years BCE and contains links to a number of short, informative articles on a range of ancient civilizations.
www.factmonster.com

**Fifteen Ancient Greek Heroes from Plutarch's *Lives***
Provides English translations of Plutarch's key biographies of figures that include Alexander the Great, Pericles, and Solon.
www.e-classics.com

**From Jesus to Christ: The Early Christians**
This thorough, engaging, and well-illustrated companion site to a PBS *Frontline* documentary examines the early history of Christianity.
www.pbs.org/wgbh/pages/frontline/shows/religion

**Greek and Roman Science and Technology**
Includes a who's who of scientists, explanations of major technological inventions, essays on specific subjects, such as geography, mathematics, and medicine, a timeline that puts ancient scientists and their inventions in a historical context, and links to both original versions and translations of the key ancient texts.
www.swan.ac.uk/classics/staff/ter/grst/
     Home%20Page%20G&RS&T.htm

**History for Kids**
This site offers historical information from every part of the world, from distant prehistory until 1500 CE, illustrated throughout.
www.historyforkids.org

**Illustrated History of the Roman Empire**
This site contains a huge amount of information on all aspects of life in the Roman Empire, and includes maps, time lines, and pictures.
www.roman-empire.net

## Indigenous Australia
Information on this site includes information on cultural heritage, spirituality, family, land, and social justice, plus a glossary and time line (part of the Australian Museum on-line).
www.dreamtime.net.au

## Internet Ancient History Sourcebook
Provides and organizes a wide range of ancient texts for use in classrooms and includes links to other on-line collections. No images.
www.fordham.edu/halsall/ancient/asbook.html

## Internet Classics Archive
Select from a list of 441 works of classical literature (in English translation) by 59 different authors. Most are Greek and Roman works; some are Chinese and Persian.
http://classics.mit.edu

## Livius
Areas covered by a range of articles include ancient civilizations of Mesopotamia, Egypt, Rome, Greece, and Persia, as well as miscellaneous subjects.
www.livius.org

## Mesopotamia (British Museum)
This beautifully presented interactive Web site includes games that explore the geography, religion, and everyday life of Assyria, Babylonia, and Sumer.
www.mesopotamia.co.uk

## The Myth Man Presents Greek Mythology Today
This site contains a series of articles, illustrated by works of art from the Renaissance and the Pre-Raphaelite school, about all aspects of Greek mythology.
www.thanasis.com/myth.htm

## The Myth Man: Egyptian Mythology
This site offers links to a range of sites exploring Egyptian mythology.
http://egyptmyth.com

## The Myth Man: Roman Mythology
This site offers links to a range of sites exploring Roman mythology.
http://romanmyth.com

## Nubianet
This colorful site is packed with information, pictures, and interactive exhibits about the great ancient African civilizations of Nubia.
www.nubianet.org

## PBS History Online
Browse in the Ancient World section for informative and entertaining articles about a range of ancient civilizations from Alexander the Great to Ice Mummies.
www.pbs.org/neighborhoods/history

## PBS Nova Archive
Accompanies PBS's science programs and covers a range of topics from Roman Bath to giant statues on Easter Island.
http://www.pbs.org/wgbh/nova/archive/int_hist.html

## The Perseus Digital Library
A wide range of classical Greek texts and translations of ancient Egyptian papyri are brought together in a highly esteemed on-line library that also features dictionaries, secondary sources, and special exhibits.
www.perseus.tufts.edu

## Prehistoric Archaeology of the Aegean
Chronologically arranged lessons include Cycladic culture, Minoan and Mycenaean civilizations, and Troy, along with bibliography, glossary, links, and images.
http://projects.dartmouth.edu/history/bronze_age

## The Seven Wonders of the Ancient World
Take a virtual tour of the Mediterranean sites that were home to such marvels as the Hanging Gardens of Babylon and the Statue of Zeus at Olympia.
http://ce.eng.usf.edu/pharos/wonders

## The State Hermitage Museum, Saint Petersburg, Russia
This excellent official Web site of Russia's leading antiquities museum, whose collections, put together over 250 years, present the development of culture and art from the Stone Age to the twentieth century, includes some of the finest treasures of antiquity.
www.hermitagemuseum.org

## Stone Pages
The Web guide to Megalithic sites in Europe.
www.stonepages.com

## Teotihuacán: The City of the Gods
This site provides an introduction to the greatest city of ancient Mesoamerica, supported by maps, pictures, and links.
http://archaeology.la.asu.edu/teo

## Treasures from the Royal Tombs of Ur
This site accompanies a special exhibition at the McClung Museum (University of Tennessee, Knoxville) of the exquisite jewelry, pottery, and clothing that lay buried in tombs at Ur for 4,500 years.
http://mcclungmuseum.utk.edu/specex/ur/ur.htm

## World Coin Catalog
Photographs of coins from all periods of history and all areas of the world are accompanied by maps and background information.
www.worldcoincatalog.com

# RESOURCES FOR YOUNGER READERS

BOOKS

**The Aboriginal Peoples of Australia**
Anne Bartlett
Minneapolis: Lerner, 2002.

**Aborigines of Australia**
Robyn Holder
Vera Beach, FL: Rourke Publications, 1987.

**Ancient Civilizations**
Wendy Madgwick
New York: Kingfisher, 2000.

**Ancient Egypt**
George Hart
New York: Knopf, 1990.

**Ancient Greece**
Anne Pearson
New York: Knopf, 1992.

**Ancient Rome**
Sean Sheehan
Austin, TX: Raintree Steck-Vaughn, 2000.

**Ancient Rome**
Patricia Levy and Richard Hook.
Austin, TX: Raintree Steck-Vaughn, 2001.

**The Ancient World of Rome**
Patricia Levy and Sean Sheehan
Austin, TX: Raintree Steck-Vaughn, 1999.

**Atlas of the Greek World**
Peter Levi
New York: Facts on File, 1980.

**Atlas of the Roman World**
Tim Cornell and John Matthews
New York: Facts on File, 1982.

**Costume of Ancient Egypt**
P. Watson
New York: Chelsea House, 1987.

**Cultures of the Past: The Ancient African Kingdom of Kush**
P. F. Service
Tarrytown, NY: Benchmark Books, 1998.

**Cultures of the Past: The Ancient Egyptians**
E. Marston
Tarrytown, NY: Benchmark Books, 1996.

**Cultures of the Past: The Ancient Greeks**
V. Schomp
Tarrytown, NY: Benchmark Books, 1996.

**Cultures of the Past: The Ancient Hebrews**
Kenny Mann
Tarrytown, NY: Benchmark Books, 1999.

**Cultures of the Past: The Ancient Romans**
K. Hinds
Tarrytown, NY: Benchmark Books, 1997.

**Cultures of the Past: The Celts of Northern Europe**
K. Hinds
Tarrytown, NY: Benchmark Books, 1997.

**Cultures of the Past: Mesopotamia**
Pamela F. Service
Tarrytown, NY: Benchmark Books, 1998.

**Cultures of the Past: The Persian Empire**
Karen Zeinert
Tarrytown, NY: Benchmark Books, 1997.

**Cultures of the Past: The Phoenicians**
Elsa Marston
Tarrytown, NY: Benchmark Books, 2002.

**The Earliest Civilizations**
Margaret Oliphant
New York: Facts on File, 1993.

**The Egyptian News**
Scott Steedman and James Putnam
Milwaukee, WI: Gareth Stevens, 2000.

**Fishing for Islands: Traditional Boats and Seafarers of the Pacific**
John Nicholson
Saint Leonards, NSW: Allen & Unwin, 1999.

**The Greek News**
Anton Powell and Philip Steele
Milwaukee, WI: Gareth Stevens, 2000.

**Growing Up in Ancient Greece**
Chris Chelepi
Mahwah, NJ: Troll Associates, 1994.

**Houses and Homes**
Tim Wood
New York: Viking, 1997.

**The Iliad and the Odyssey Retold**
Marcia Williams
Cambridge, MA: Candlewick Press, 1996.

**Illustrated Encyclopaedia of Ancient Egypt**
Geraldine Harris and Delia Pemberton
Lincolnwood, IL: Peter Bedrick Books, 1999.

**India**
Julie Nelson
Austin, TX: Raintree Steck-Vaughn, 2002.

**Journey to the Past: Mayan Tikal**
Romano Solbiati
Austin, TX: Raintree Steck-Vaughn, 2001.

**Mesopotamia and the Fertile Crescent, 10,000 to 539 B.C.**
John Malam
Austin, TX: Raintree Steck-Vaughn, 1999.

**Myths of China and Japan**
Jen Green
New York: Raintree Steck-Vaughn, 2002.

**Oceania**
Charlotte Greig
Broomall, PA: Mason Crest Publishers, 2003.

**Oxford First Ancient History**
Roy Burrell and Peter Connolly
Oxford: Oxford University Press, 1994.

*Recovering the Tracks: The Story of Australian Archaeology*
David Horton
Canberra: Aboriginal Studies Press, 1991.

*The Roman News*
Andrew Langley and Philip De Souza
Milwaukee, WI: Gareth Stevens, 2000.

*The Sailor through History*
Roger Coote
New York: Thomson Learning, 1993.

*Slavery in Ancient Egypt and Mesopotamia*
Jacqueline Dembar Greene
New York: Franklin Watts, 2000.

*The Story of Weights and Measures*
Anita Ganeri
New York: Oxford University Press, 1996.

*The Story of Money*
Betsy Maestro and Giulio Maestro, illus.
New York: Mulberry Books, 1995.

*Technology in the Time of Ancient Egypt*
Judith Crosher
Austin, TX: Raintree Steck-Vaughn, 1997.

*Technology in the Time of Ancient Rome*
Robert Snedden
Austin, TX: Raintree Steck-Vaughn, 1998.

*What Do We Know about the Greeks?*
Anne Pearson
New York: Peter Bedrick Books, 1992.

## VIDEOS

*The Spear in the Stone*
Director: Kim McKenzie. 36 minutes, with study guide available.
About an aboriginal stone ax quarry.
Canberra: Aboriginal Studies Press, 1983.

*Making a Bark Canoe*
Director: Rodger Sandall. 20 minutes.
Canberra: Aboriginal Studies Press, 1969.

*The Wiril Canoe*
Director: Rod Adamson. 27 minutes.
Canberra: Aboriginal Studies Press, 1968.

## INTERNET RESOURCES

**BBC Schools: The Romans**
This colorful and entertaining Web site explores all areas of life in the Roman Empire, including a soldier's uniform and Caesar's bald spot. A range of puzzles, activities, quizzes, and cartoons make learning fun.
www.bbc.co.uk/schools/romans

**Other BBC Schools sites:**
**The Greeks**
www.bbc.co.uk/schools/landmarks/
   ancientgreece
**The Anglo-Saxons**
www.bbc.co.uk/education/anglosaxons

**Mark Millmore's Ancient Egypt**
This informative site includes stories of the great kings and queens, the fabulous buildings of the ancient Egyptians, interactive maps, pyramid and temple reconstructions, a hieroglyphic translator, and information about Egyptian numerals.
www.eyelid.co.uk

**Myths about Gods of Olden Cultures**
Provides information about Egyptian, Roman, and Saxon and Viking gods and links to the author's other pages, which cover topics such as days of the week, month names, and Roman numbers.
www.gwydir.demon.co.uk/jo/myths.
   htm

**Mythweb**
Engaging texts written in Latin and English are illustrated with lively cartoons on this site dedicated to the heroes, gods, and monsters of Greek mythology.
www.mythweb.com

**Thinkquest Internet Challenge Library: Archaeology, Ancient Civilizations, and History**
This library contains unique educational Web sites, created through ThinkQuest competitions and programs, built by young students for young students to use and learn.
http://www.thinkquest.org/library/
   cat_show.html?cat_id=31&cid=1

**Mummy Tombs**
News, information, and pictures of ancient and modern mummies from around the world are included on this site.
www.mummytombs.com

**Vindolanda**
An engaging multimedia presentation about the Roman fort at Vindolanda near Hadrian's Wall.
http://www.vindolanda.com

**Wallnet: Hadrian's Wall Education Website**
This colorful and engaging guide to the history of Hadrian's Wall and the people who lived and worked near the wall includes interactive tours of several forts and of the antiquities museum.
http://museums.ncl.ac.uk/wallnet/

**You Wouldn't Want to Be an Egyptian Mummy!**
Follow the step-by-step process that will turn your body into an Egyptian mummy in this innovative Web book. Not for the fainthearted.
www.salariya.com/web_books/mummy

**You Wouldn't Want to Be a Roman Gladiator!**
The Web site user becomes a barbarian fighting against the Romans who is captured, sold as a slave, and trained to become a Roman gladiator in this innovative, fully clickable Web book.
www.salariya.com/web_books/gladiator

# List of Maps and Site Plans

A number preceding a colon indicates the volume number.

Aboriginal settlement of Australia from 60,000 BCE 1: 14

Achaemenid Empire, 550–330 BCE 1: 18

Akkadians, 2340–2150 BCE 1: 30

Alexandria 1: 40

Anasazi, Hohokam, and Mogollon territories in the southwestern United States 1: 50

Angle, Saxon, and Jute invasions of Britain, c. 500 CE 1: 54

Aryans 1: 75

Ashur 2: 86

Assyrian Empire, 1800–627 BCE 2: 90

Athens 2: 100

Avebury 2: 110

Babylon 2: 112

Babylonian Empire in the time of Hammurabi (1792–1750 BCE) 2: 115

Bantu migration, c. 500 BCE – c. 300 CE 2: 123

Calah 2: 142

Çatal Hüyük 2: 151

Celtic territory in Europe 2: 153

Chang'an during the Tang dynasty (618–907 CE) 2: 157

Chavín de Huantár 3: 164

China during the Shang, Qin, and Han dynasties (c. 1700 BCE–220 CE) 3: 172

Copán 3: 209

Corinth 3: 211

Cyclades 3: 217

Delphi 3: 234

Dong Son Culture 3: 236

Dunhuang and the Mogao Caves 4: 247

Egypt during the period of the New Kingdom (c. 1550–1085 BCE) 4: 253

Elamite territory during the mid-twelfth century BCE 4: 266

Ephesus 4: 270

Erech 4: 274

Eridu 4: 276

Etruscan area of influence, c. 500 BCE 4: 278

Frankish kingdom, c. 500 CE 4: 298

Gothic kingdoms (Ostrogoths and Visigoths), c. 500 CE 4: 312

Great Wall of China 4: 316

Greek civilization in 450 BCE 5: 324

Gupta Empire at its height, c. 400 CE 5: 340

Hadrian's Wall 5: 345

Hannibal's route across the Alps and battles with the Roman army (219–202 CE) 5: 348

Hebrews 5: 355

Hittites 5: 368

Hopewell and Adena cultures 5: 372

Hunnish Empire at the time of the Battle of Châlons (451 CE) 5: 381

Indus valley civilization during the Harappan period (3100–2000 BCE) 6: 404

Japan, period of early state formation (100 BCE–300 CE) 6: 411

Korea in the third century CE 6: 441

Kushan Empire at its height (c. 150 CE) 6: 446

Lapita migration, c. 1500–1000 BCE 6: 456

Macedonian Empire under Alexander the Great and his successors (c. 323–281 BCE) 6: 468

Mauryan and Nanda Empires at their fullest extent (365–185 BCE) 7: 494

Maya civilization during the classic period (250–800 CE) 7: 498

Melanesia 7: 503

Mesopotamia under successive empires (c. 3000–610 BCE) 7: 509

Micronesia 7: 514

Minoan civilization 7: 520

Moche culture 7: 524

Mohenjo Daro 7: 528

Mycenaean Greece, c. 1550–1150 BCE 7: 545

Nok culture, sixth century BCE–third century CE 8: 566

Nubia and Egypt 8: 572

Olmecs 8: 583

Parthian Empire and Eastern Roman Empire, c. 100 CE 8: 591

Paul of Tarsus, three missionary journeys and journey to Rome, c. 46–62 CE 8: 596

Phoenicia at the height of its powers, 1100 BCE 8: 606

Polynesian migrations and settlements, 1000 BCE–1300 CE 8: 612

Roman Empire at its greatest extent, c. 120 CE 9: 656

Rome, city of, c. 300 CE 9: 665

Sasanian Persia, 224–642 CE 9: 678

Scythian territory, c. 400 BCE 9: 686

Spartan and Athenian allies during the Peloponnesian War (431–404 BCE) 9: 712

Sumer, c. 3000–c. 2000 BCE 10: 726

Valley of the Kings, location of the major tombs 10: 770

Zapotec and Olmec territory in present-day central Mexico 10: 788

# Index of Maps and Site Plans

This index includes place-names appearing in the maps and site plans. For place-names mentioned in the articles and captions, see the Geographical Index.

**Boldface** numbers preceding a colon indicate the volume number.

Abdera **9**:712
Abu Simbel **8**:572
Abydos **4**:253
Acanthus **9**:712
Achaea **9**:712
Achaemenid Empire **1**:18
Acre **8**:606
Adena **5**:372
Adena Park **5**:372
Adriatic Sea **4**:278, **7**:520, **7**:545
Aegean Sea **1**:40, **2**:100, **2**:151, **2**:153, **3**:211, **3**:217, **3**:234, **4**:270, **5**:324, **7**:520, **7**:545, **9**:712
Aegina **7**:545
Aegospotami **9**:712
Aegyptus **9**:656
Africa **2**:121
A Guardia **2**:153
Ajanta **5**:340
Akkad **2**:115
Akkadian Empire of Sargon I **1**:30, **7**:509
Akkad (possible site) **1**:30, **10**:726
Akrotiri **3**:217, **7**:545
Aleppo **1**:18
Alexandria **1**:40, **7**:494, **8**:572, **8**:591, **8**:596, **9**:656, **9**:678
  Caesarium **1**:40
  Catacombs **1**:40
  Cleopatra's Needles **1**:40
  eastern cemeteries **1**:40
  Gate of the Moon **1**:40
  Gate of the Sun **1**:40
  Island Palace **1**:40
  Mouseion Library **1**:40
  Roman Theater **1**:40
  Shrine of Pompey **1**:40
  Temple of Isis **1**:40
  Temple of Poseidon **1**:40
  Temple of Serapis and Pompey's Pillar **1**:40
  Western Cemetery **1**:40
Allen's Cave **1**:14

Alpes Maritimae **9**:656
Alps **2**:153, **5**:348
Altar de Sacrificios **7**:498
Al-Ubaid **10**:726
Amarna **4**:253
Ambracia **9**:712
Amorgos **3**:217
Amphipolis **8**:596, **9**:712
Amu Darya River **9**:686
Anafi **3**:217
Anasazi **1**:50
Anatarbus **8**:596
Anatolia **2**:151, **4**:270, **7**:545
Anatolian Plateau **5**:368
Ancyra **9**:656
Andes Mountains **3**:164, **7**:524
Andhapura **7**:494
Andros **3**:217, **9**:712
Angola **2**:121
Antimilos **3**:217
Antioch **1**:40, **6**:468, **8**:591, **8**:596, **9**:656, **9**:678
Antiochia **8**:596
Antiparos **3**:217
Antonine Wall **9**:656
Anyang **3**:172, **4**:316
Aparanta **7**:494
Apollonia **8**:596
Aquincum **9**:656
Aquitania **9**:656
Arabia **1**:18, **9**:656
Arabian Desert **2**:115
Arabian Peninsula **1**:30, **5**:355, **6**:468, **7**:509, **8**:591, **9**:656, **9**:678, **10**:726
Arabian Sea **1**:18, **1**:75, **5**:340, **6**:404, **6**:446, **6**:468, **7**:494, **9**:678
Arachosia **1**:18, **6**:468, **7**:494
Aral Sea **6**:468, **9**:686
Arausio **5**:348
Aravali Range **6**:404
Arawe Islands **6**:456
Arginusae Islands **9**:712
Argos **7**:545, **9**:712
Aria **1**:18
Arikamedu **6**:446
Armenia **1**:18, **5**:381, **6**:468, **8**:591, **9**:656, **9**:678
Arretium **4**:278

Ashur **1**:30, **2**:86, **2**:90, **7**:509, **10**:726
  building of Sennacherib **2**:86
  Inner City **2**:86
  New City **2**:86
  New Palace **2**:86
  Old Palace **2**:86
  royal tombs **2**:86
  Tabira Gate **2**:86
  Temple of Anu-Adad **2**:86
  Temple of Ashur **2**:86
  Temple of Ishtar **2**:86
  Temple of Nabu **2**:86
  Temple of Sin-Shamash **2**:86
  West Gate **2**:86
  ziggurat **2**:86
Asia **9**:656
Asia Minor **8**:591
Askalon **5**:355
Assos **8**:596
Assyria **1**:18, **2**:90, **2**:115, **4**:266, **5**:355, **5**:368, **9**:656, **9**:686
Asuka **6**:411
Asuncion Mita **7**:498
Aswan **4**:253, **8**:572
Athenian Empire **9**:712
Athens **1**:40, **2**:100, **3**:211, **3**:217, **3**:234, **4**:270, **5**:324, **6**:468, **7**:520, **7**:545, **8**:596, **9**:712
  Acropolis **2**:100
  agora **2**:100
  Areopagus **2**:100
  Odeum of Pericles **2**:100
  Olympieion **2**:100
  Parthenon **2**:100
  Pnyx **2**:100
  Theater of Dionysus **2**:100
Atlantic Ocean **2**:121, **4**:298, **4**:312, **5**:372, **5**:381, **8**:566, **9**:656
Atlas Mountains **9**:656
Attalia **8**:596
Augusta **9**:656
Aulnat **2**:153
Australia **6**:456, **7**:503
  aboriginal **1**:14

Avebury **2**:110
Augusta Vindelicorum **9**:656

Babylon **1**:18, **1**:30, **2**:90, **2**:112, **2**:115, **4**:266, **4**:274, **4**:276, **5**:355, **6**:468, **7**:509, **8**:591, **9**:678, **9**:686, **10**:726
  Ishtar Gate **2**:112
  Northern Fortress **2**:112
  Palace of Nebuchadrezzar **2**:112
  Southern Fortress **2**:112
  Temple of Ishtar of Agade **2**:112
  Temple of Marduk **2**:112
  Temple of Ninmakh **2**:112
  ziggurat **2**:112
Babylonia **4**:266
Babylonian Empire **2**:115, **7**:509
Babylonians, Kingdom of **1**:18
Bactra **6**:468
Bactria **1**:18, **5**:340, **6**:446, **6**:468, **7**:494, **8**:591, **9**:678
Baetica **9**:656
Bahrain **9**:678
Balearic Islands **5**:348
Balkan Mountains **9**:686
Baltic Sea **4**:298, **4**:312
Baluchistan **6**:404
Bampur **1**:18
Bantu culture **2**:121
Bantu homeland **8**:566
Barbalissus **9**:678
Barygaza **6**:446
Bass Point **1**:14
Bat Cave **1**:50
Bay of Bengal **1**:75, **5**:340, **6**:446, **7**:494
Bayuda Desert **8**:572
Beas River **6**:404
Becan **7**:498
Begram **6**:446
Beijing **2**:157, **3**:172, **4**:316
Belgica **9**:656
Belize **3**:209
Bellona **6**:456
Belur **5**:340
Benue River **8**:566
Beroea **8**:596

Ebla 7:509
Ecbatana 1:18, 6:468, 8:591, 9:678
Edessa 8:591, 8:596, 9:678
Edom 5:355
Edzna 7:498
Efate 6:456
Egypt 1:18, 1:40, 4:253, 5:355, 5:368, 6:468, 8:572, 8:591, 8:606, 10:770
 Lower Egypt 4:253
 Upper Egypt 4:253
Elam 1:30, 4:266, 7:509
Elba 1:30
Elbe River 4:298, 4:312
Elburz Mountains 1:18, 6:468, 9:678
El Morro 1:50
Elouae Island 6:456
El Purgatório 7:524
El Salvador 3:209
Elymais 8:591
Emerita Augusta 9:656
Emporiae 5:348
England 2:153
Entremont 2:153
Ephesus 1:18, 1:40, 4:270, 8:596, 9:656, 9:712
 agoras 4:270
 basilica 4:270
 Celsus Library 4:270
 gymnasium 4:270
 hillside houses 4:270
 Odeum 4:270
 Prytaneum 4:270
 stadium 4:270
 Temple of Domitian 4:270
 theater 4:270
 Verulanus Hall 4:270
Epidaurus 3:234, 9:712
Epirus 6:468, 9:656, 9:712
Erech 1:30, 4:266, 4:274, 4:276, 7:509, 10:726
 Anu Ziggurat 4:274
 Bit-Akitu 4:274
 Bit-Rosh 4:274
 Irigal 4:274
 Kara-indash Temple 4:274
 Mithraeum 4:274
 north gate 4:274
 Palace of Sin-kashid 4:274
 Parthian ruins 4:274
 Sanctuary of Eanna 4:274
 Temple of Gareus 4:274
 Ur Gate 4:274
 White Temple 4:274
 Ziggurat of Inanna 4:274

Eretoke 6:456
Eretria 9:712
Eridu 1:30, 4:274, 4:276, 7:509, 10:726
Eshnunna 1:30, 7:509
Euphrates River 1:18, 1:30, 2:112, 2:115, 4:266, 4:274, 4:276, 5:355, 5:368, 7:509, 8:591, 9:656, 9:678, 9:686, 10:726
Europe 6:468

Felsini 4:278
Feni Islands 6:456
Ferghana 6:446
Fiji 6:456, 7:503, 8:612
Folegandros 3:217
France 2:153
Franks, Kingdom of the 4:298, 4:312, 5:381
Fraser Cave 1:14
Fuha River 2:121

Galatia 9:656
Gandhara 1:18, 6:446, 6:468
Ganges River 1:75, 5:340, 6:446, 7:494
Ganweriwala 6:404
Gauda 7:494
Gaya 7:494
Gaza 8:606
Gedrosia 1:18, 6:468
Germania Inferior 9:656
Germania Superior 9:656
Germany 2:153
Gila 1:50
Giringara 7:494
Giza 4:253, 8:572
Gla 7:545
Glastonbury 2:153
Gortuna 8:596
Goths 4:312
Grand Canyon 1:50
Gran Quivira 1:50
Grasshopper 1:50
Grave Creek Mound 5:372
Great Chesters 5:345
Great Lakes 5:372
Great Wall of China 2:157, 3:172, 4:247, 4:316
Greece 1:18, 1:40, 2:100, 2:151, 2:153, 3:211, 3:217, 3:234, 4:270, 7:520
 classical Greece 5:324
Green Islands 6:456
Guatemala 3:209
Gulf of California 1:50

Gulf of Mexico 3:209, 5:372, 7:498, 8:583, 10:788
Gulf of Tonkin 3:236
Gumla 6:404
Gupta Empire 5:340, 6:468
Gutians 1:30, 7:509, 10:726

Hadrian's Wall 5:345, 9:656
Hadrumetum 5:348
Halab 1:30, 7:509
Halicarnassus 5:324
Hallstatt 2:153
Hannibal's route 5:348
Hanoi 3:236
Haran 1:30, 2:90
Harappa 6:404
Harran 1:18, 7:509
Hatra 8:591
Hattusha 5:368
Havana 5:372
Hawaiian Islands 8:612
Hawikuh 1:50
Hay Hollow Valley 1:50
Hebrew lands 5:355
Hecatompylos 6:468
Heraklia 3:217
Herat 1:18
Heuneburg 2:153
Hibernia 9:656
Highland Maya 7:498
Hill of Tara 2:153
Himalayas 1:75, 5:340, 6:404, 6:446, 7:494
Hindu Kush 1:75, 6:446, 8:591, 9:678
Hittite Empire 5:368
Hoa 3:236
Hohokam 1:50
Hokkaido 6:411
Honduras 3:209
Honshu 6:411
Hopewell culture 5:372
Hormuz 1:18
Housesteads 5:345
Huaca Colorada 7:524
Huns, Empire of the 5:381
Hurrians 1:30, 7:509

Iconimum 8:596
Île des Pins 6:456
India 1:18, 1:75, 5:340
Indian Ocean 3:236, 7:494
Indo-Parthian Empire (Sistan) 8:591
Indus River 5:340, 6:404, 6:446, 7:494
Indus valley 6:404

Iolcus 7:545
Ionia 1:18, 9:712
Ios 3:217
Ipsus 6:468
Ipu 4:253
Iranian Plateau 1:18
Ireland 2:153
Irish Sea 1:54
Israel 8:606
Italy 2:153
Izamal 7:498
Izumo 6:411

Japan 2:157, 3:172, 4:316, 6:411, 6:441
Jaxartes River 6:468, 8:591, 9:678
Jebel Barkal 8:572
Jerusalem 1:18, 1:40, 2:90, 5:355, 6:468, 8:591, 8:596, 8:606, 9:678
Jhelum River 6:404
Joppa 8:606
Jordan 5:368
Jordan River 8:606
Jos Plateau 8:566
Judaea 1:40, 5:355, 9:656
Judah 8:606
Jutes 1:54

Kabah 7:498
Kabul 9:678
Kadesh 5:368
Kalgan Hall 1:14
Kalibangan 5:340, 6:404, 6:446
Kamnama 2:121
Kanchipuram 7:494
Kandahar 1:18
Kandrian 6:456
Kanesh 1:30, 7:509
Kapilavastu 7:494
Karnataka 5:340
Kassites 1:30, 7:509, 10:726
Kea 3:217
Keilor 1:14
Kenniff Cave 1:14
Kerma 8:572
Keros 3:217
Khorsabad 2:90
Kibi 6:411
Kimolos 3:217
Kinai 6:411
King's Table 1:14
Kiribati 7:514
Kish 1:30, 7:509, 10:726
Knossos 3:217, 7:520, 7:545

Koguryo 6:441
Kongju 6:441
Korea 6:411, 6:441
Koshala 7:494
Koufonissi 3:217
Kunlun Mountains 3:172,
 4:316
Kushan Empire 6:446
Kushite Empire 8:572
Kwangju 6:441
Kyongju 6:441
Kythnos 3:217
Kyusho, northern 6:411
Kyushu 6:411

Labna 7:498
Lagash 1:30, 4:274, 4:276,
 7:509
La Honradez 7:498
Lake Chad 8:566
Lake Chalco 8:583
Lake Mareotis 1:40
Lake Texcoco 8:583
Lanka 5:340, 6:446
Lapita 6:456
Larsa 1:30, 2:90, 7:509
La Tène culture 2:153
Latisa 8:596
La Venta 8:583
Lesbos 5:324, 9:712
Leucas 9:712
Libya 4:253
Lima 3:164
Lindus 9:712
Loire River 4:298, 4:312
Lombards 4:298, 4:312
Londinium 9:656
Lothal 5:340, 6:404
Lowland Maya 7:498
Lubaantun 7:498
Lugdunensis 9:656
Lugdunum 9:656
Lumbini 7:494
Luolang 6:441
Luoyang 2:157, 3:172, 4:216
Lusitania 9:656
Luxor 4:253
Lycia 9:656
Lydia 1:18, 9:686
Lysimachus 6:468
Lystra 8:596

Ma'adi 4:253
Mabueni 2:121
Macedon 9:712
Macedonia 1:18, 1:40, 2:100,
 5:324, 6:468, 7:545, 9:656

Macedonians 6:468
Machaquila 7:498
Magadha 7:494
Magdalenburg 2:153
Mahisa Mandala 7:494
Maiden Castle 2:153
Makran 1:18
Malangaugerr 1:14
Mallia 7:520
Malo 6:456
Malta 5:348
Mammoth Cave 1:14
Manchán 7:524
Manching 2:153
Manchuria 3:172, 4:316,
 6:441
Mantinea 9:712
Marañón River 7:524
Mari 1:30, 7:509
Mariana Islands 7:514
Marietta Harness 5:372
Marksville 5:372
Marquesas Islands 8:612
Marshall Islands 7:514
Mathura 7:494
Mauretania Caesariensis 9:656
Mauretania Tingitana 9:656
Maurya Empire 7:494
Maya 7:498
Mayan Empire 3:209
Maya-Toltec 7:498
Mazun 9:678
Media 1:18, 6:468, 8:591,
 9:686
Media Atropatene 8:591
Mediterranean Sea A:3, 1:18,
 1:40, 2:90, 2:115, 2:151,
 2:153, 3:217, 4:253, 4:298,
 4:312, 5:324, 5:348, 5:355,
 5:368, 5:381, 6:468, 7:509,
 7:520, 7:545, 8:572, 8:591,
 8:596, 8:606, 9:656, 9:678,
 9:686, 10:726, 10:770
Melanesian culture 7:503
Melita 8:596
Melos 3:217, 7:545
Memphis 1:18, 1:40, 2:90,
 4:253
Menalaion 7:545
Menindee Lake 1:14
Meroe 8:572
Mersin 1:30, 7:509
Merv 1:18, 6:468, 8:591
Mesa Grande 1:50
Mesopotamia 1:18, 2:115,
 6:468, 7:509, 8:591, 9:656,
 9:678, 10:726

Messina 8:596
Methone 9:712
Mexico 3:209
Miamisburg 5:372
Micronesian culture 7:514
Miletus 5:324, 7:520, 7:545,
 8:596, 9:712
Miller 5:372
Mimbres Valley 1:50
Minoans 7:520, 7:545
Miriwun 1:14
Mississippi River 5:372
Mitla 10:788
Mitylene 9:712
Moab 5:355
Moche culture 7:524
Moesia 9:656
Moesia Inferior 9:656
Moesia Superior 9:656
Mogollon 1:50
Mohenjo Daro 6:404, 7:528
 college 7:528
 granary 7:528
 great bath 7:528
 stupa 7:528
Mongolia 2:157, 3:172, 4:247,
 4:316
Monte Albán 8:583, 10:788
Mont Lassois 2:153
Morelos 8:583
Mound City 5:372
Mount Newman 1:14
Mount Sinai 5:355
Muziris 6:446
Mycenae 7:520, 7:545
Mycenaean civilization 7:545
Mykonos 3:217
Myra 8:596, 9:656
Mytilene 5:324, 8:596

Nad-l Ali 1:18
Nakum 7:498
Namibia 2:121
Nanda Empire 7:494
Nanking 2:157, 3:172, 4:316
Napata 8:572
Naranjo 7:498
Narbo 9:656
Narbonensis 9:656
Navan 2:153
Nawamoyn 1:14
Naxos 3:217
Ndora 2:121
Neapolis 4:278, 8:596
Nebas 7:498
Neo-Assyrian Empire 7:509
Nepal 5:340

Newark 5:372
New Britain 6:456
New Caledonia 6:456, 7:503,
 8:612
New Guinea 1:14, 3:236,
 6:456, 7:503, 7:514
New Ireland 6:456
New Zealand 8:612
Nicomedia 9:656
Nicopolis 8:596, 9:656
Niger River 8:566
Nile River 2:121, 4:253,
 5:368, 8:572, 8:591, 10:770
Nineveh 1:18, 1:30, 2:90,
 4:266, 7:509, 9:686, 10:726
Nippur 1:18, 1:30, 4:266,
 4:274, 4:276, 7:509, 10:726
Nisa 8:591
Nishapur 9:678
Niuatoputapu 6:456
Nobi 6:411
Nok 2:121, 8:566
Noricum 9:656
North Sea 1:54, 4:298, 4:312,
 9:656
Notium 9:712
Nubia 4:253, 8:572
 Lower Nubia 8:572
 Upper Nubia 8:572
Nubian Desert 8:572

Oaxaca 8:583
Oaxaca Valley 10:788
Oescus 9:656
Ohio Hopewell 5:372
Olmec heartland 8:583
Olmecs 10:788
Olympia 3:211, 3:234, 5:324
Olympus 7:545
Orchomenus 7:545
Orontes River 8:606
Ostrogoths, kingdom of the
 4:298, 4:312, 5:381
Oxus River 6:446, 8:591,
 9:678

Pacatnamu 7:524
Pacific Ocean 1:50, 3:164,
 3:236, 6:411, 6:456, 7:498,
 7:503, 7:514, 7:524, 8:583,
 8:612, 10:788
Paekche 6:441
Palenque 7:498, 8:583
Palestine 4:253, 8:591, 8:606
Palmyra 6:468
Pañamarca 7:524
Pannonia Inferior 9:656

Pannonia Superior **9**:656
Papaloápan River **8**:583
Paphos **8**:596, **9**:656
Paramonga **7**:524
Paros **3**:217
Parthia **1**:18, **6**:468, **9**:686
Parthian Empire **8**:591, **9**:656
Pasargadae **1**:18
Pataliputra **5**:340, **6**:446, **7**:494
Paul of Tarsus, journeys **8**:596
Pella **1**:18, **9**:712
Peloponnese **2**:100, **3**:211, **3**:234, **5**:324, **7**:520, **9**:712
Pergamum **8**:591
Perge **8**:596
Persepolis **1**:18, **8**:591, **9**:678
Persian Empire **9**:712
Persian Gulf **1**:18, **1**:30, **2**:90, **2**:115, **4**:266, **4**:274, **4**:276, **6**:468, **7**:509, **8**:591, **9**:678, **10**:726
Persis **1**:18, **6**:468, **8**:591
Peru **3**:164
Perusia **4**:278
Petroglyph Canyons **1**:50
Phaistos **7**:520, **7**:545
Pharos
    island of **1**:40
    lighthouse **1**:40
    Temple of Isis **1**:40
Philippi **8**:596
Philippine Islands **7**:514
Philistia **5**:355
Philistines **8**:606
Phocaea **9**:712
Phoenicia **4**:253, **5**:355, **8**:606
Phrygia **6**:468, **9**:686, **9**:712
Phylakopi **7**:545
Picts **5**:381
Piedras Negras **7**:498
Pisa **4**:278
Plateau of Iran **1**:75
Plateau of Tibet **7**:494
Points of Pines **1**:50
Polynesian migrations **8**:612
Ponape **7**:514
Pontus **6**:468
Populonia **4**:278
Porter **5**:372
Portsmouth **5**:372
Potidaea **9**:712
Prachya **7**:494
Pratisthana **7**:494
Prayaga **7**:494
Ptolemaic Empire **6**:468
Ptolemais **8**:596

Puebla **8**:583
Pueblo Grande **1**:50
Pundra **7**:494
Punjab **5**:340
Puntutjarba **1**:14
Purushapura **6**:446
Pusilha **7**:498
Puteoli **8**:596
Puyo **6**:441
Pylos **7**:520, **7**:545, **9**:712
Pyrenees **5**:348

Quirigua **7**:498

Raetia **9**:656
Rajagriha **7**:494
Ravenna **9**:656
Ravi River **6**:404
Red River **3**:236
Red Sea **1**:18, **2**:90, **2**:115, **2**:121, **4**:253, **5**:355, **5**:368, **6**:468, **8**:572, **8**:591, **10**:770
Rennell **6**:456
Rhegium **8**:596
Rhine River **2**:153, **4**:298, **4**:312
Rhodes **7**:520, **7**:545, **8**:596, **9**:712
Rhone River **5**:348
Rio Bec **7**:498
Rio Grande **1**:50
Rocky Mountains **1**:50
Roman Empire **9**:656
Roman Republic **9**:656
Rome **2**:153, **4**:278, **5**:348, **8**:596, **9**:656, **9**:665
    Aventine Hill **9**:665
    Baths of Caracalla **9**:665
    Baths of Constantine **9**:665
    Baths of Diocletian **9**:665
    Baths of Titus **9**:665
    Baths of Trajan **9**:665
    camp of the Praetorian
        Guard **9**:665
    Capitoline Hill **9**:665
    Circus Maximus **9**:665
    Colosseum **9**:665
    Emporium **9**:665
    Esquiline Hill **9**:665
    Forum Romanum **9**:665
    imperial forums **9**:665
    imperial palace **9**:665
    Mausoleum of Augustus
        **9**:665
    Mausoleum of Hadrian
        **9**:665
    Palatine Hill **9**:665

Pantheon **9**:665
    Stadium of Domitian **9**:665
    Temple of Claudius **9**:665
    Temple of Hadrian **9**:665
    Temple of Jupiter **9**:665
    Temple of Saturn **9**:665
    Temple of Serapis **9**:665
    Temple of Trajan **9**:665
    Temple of Venus and Rome
        **9**:665
    Temple of Vesta **9**:665
    Theater of Marcellus **9**:665
Roonka **1**:14
Rusellae **4**:278

Saguntum **5**:348
Sahara Desert **2**:121
Saitobaru **6**:411
Salamis **8**:596
Salonae **9**:656
Samapa **7**:494
Samaria **2**:90
Samoa Islands **6**:456, **8**:612
Samun Dukiya **8**:566
Sanchi **5**:340, **6**:446
San Lorenzo **8**:583
Santa Cruz Islands **6**:456
Santorini **3**:217, **7**:520
    *see also* Thera
Saqqara **4**:253
Sardinia **4**:278, **5**:348, **9**:656
Sardis **1**:18, **2**:90, **8**:596
Sarmatians **9**:686
Sarmizegetusa **9**:656
Sarnath **7**:494
Sasanian Empire **9**:678
Sasanians **5**:381, **9**:678
Sattagydia **1**:18
Saxons **1**:54, **4**:298, **4**:312
Sayil **7**:498
Schinoussa **3**:217
Scotland **2**:153
Scythia **6**:468
Scythians **8**:591, **9**:686
Sea of Crete **3**:217
Sea of Galilee **8**:606
Sea of Japan **6**:411, **6**:441
Sea of Marmara **9**:712
Sechura Desert **7**:524
Segusio **9**:656
Seibal **7**:498
Seip **5**:372
Seleucia **6**:468, **8**:591
Seleucus, Empire of **6**:468
Semna **8**:572
Serifos **3**:217
Serpent Mound **5**:372

Shandong Peninsula **6**:441
Shanghai **2**:157, **3**:172, **4**:316
Shatavahana **6**:446
Shikoku **6**:411
Sicilia **9**:656
Sicily **5**:347
Sidon **1**:18, **2**:90, **8**:596, **8**:606
Sierra Madre Occidental **1**:50
Sifnos **3**:217
Sikinos **3**:217
Silk Road **2**:157, **3**:172, **4**:247
Silla **6**:441
Sinai **8**:572
Sinai Peninsula **8**:606
Sindhu **7**:494
Sinkiang **3**:172, **4**:247, **4**:316
Slavs **4**:298, **4**:312
Smyrna **8**:596
Snaketown **1**:50
Society Islands **8**:612
Sogdia **8**:591
Sogdiana **1**:18, **6**:446, **6**:468, **7**:494
Sohano Islands **6**:456
Soleb **8**:572
Solomon Islands **6**:456, **7**:503
South Africa **2**:121
South America **7**:524
South China Sea **3**:236
Spain **2**:153
Sparta **3**:211, **3**:217, **3**:234, **5**:324, **8**:596, **9**:712
Spartolus **9**:712
Sphacteria **9**:712
Squawkie Hill **5**:372
Stanegate **5**:345
Suevi **4**:298, **4**:312, **5**:381
Sulaiman Range **6**:404
Sumer **2**:115, **7**:509, **10**:726
Surashtra **7**:494
Surparaka **7**:494
Susa **1**:30, **2**:90, **2**:115, **4**:274, **4**:276, **6**:468, **7**:509, **8**:591, **10**:726
Susiana **1**:18
Sutlej River **6**:404
Suvarnagiri **7**:494
Syracusa **8**:596
Syria **1**:30, **2**:115, **2**:151, **4**:253, **5**:355, **5**:368, **6**:468, **7**:509, **8**:591, **8**:606, **9**:656, **9**:678, **9**:686, **10**:726
Syrian Desert **1**:30, **7**:509, **8**:606, **9**:656, **10**:726
Syros **3**:217

Tahiti **8**:612
Talgai **1**:14
Tanis **2**:90
Tarnralipu **7**:494
Tarquinii **4**:278
Tarraco **9**:656
Tarraconensis **9**:656
Tarsus **1**:30, **2**:90, **7**:509,
   **8**:596, **9**:656
Taruga **2**:121, **8**:566
Tarunga **2**:121
Tasmanian land bridge, lost
   **1**:14
Taurus Mountains **1**:18, **1**:30,
   **2**:151, **7**:509, **10**:726
Taxila **6**:446, **6**:468, **8**:591,
   **9**:678
Tazumal **7**:498
Tell 'Uqair **1**:30, **7**:509
Tennessee River **5**:372
Teotihuacán **3**:209, **8**:583
Teotitlan del Valle **10**:788
Than **3**:236
Thar Desert **6**:404, **7**:494
Thasos **9**:712
Thebes, Egypt (present-day
   Luxor) **1**:18, **2**:90, **4**:253,
   **8**:572
Thebes, Greece **3**:211, **3**:234,
   **5**:324, **7**:520, **7**:545, **9**:712
Thera **3**:217, **7**:520, **7**:545
   *see also* Santorini
Therassia **3**:217
Thessalonika **6**:468, **8**:596,
   **9**:656
Thessaly **2**:100, **5**:324, **7**:545,
   **9**:712
Thrace **1**:18, **2**:100, **5**:324,
   **6**:468, **7**:545, **9**:686, **9**:712
Thracia **9**:656
Tiber River **4**:278, **9**:665
Tibet **2**:157, **3**:172, **4**:247,
   **4**:316, **5**:340
Ticinus **5**:348
Tigris River **1**:30, **2**:115,
   **4**:266, **4**:274, **4**:276, **5**:355,
   **5**:368, **7**:509, **8**:591, **9**:656,
   **9**:678, **9**:686, **10**:726
Tikal **3**:209, **7**:498
Tingis **9**:656
Tinos **3**:217
Tiryns **7**:520, **7**:545
Tonalá River **8**:583
Tonga Islands **6**:456, **8**:612
   Ha'apai Group **6**:456
   Tongatapu Group **6**:456
   Vava'u Group **6**:456

Tonggou **6**:441
Tonto **1**:50
Topoc Maze **1**:50
Trasimene **5**:348
Trebbia **5**:348
Trempaleau **5**:372
Tremper **5**:372
Tres Zapotes **8**:583
Troas **8**:596
Troy **7**:520, **7**:545
Turkey **2**:151, **2**:153
Turkmenistan **8**:591
Turner **5**:372
Tutub **1**:30, **7**:509
Tuvalu **6**:456
Tuzigoot **1**:50
Tyras **9**:686
Tyre **1**:18, **1**:40, **2**:90, **8**:596,
   **8**:606
Tyrrhenian Sea **4**:278

Uaxactun **7**:498
Ucayali River **7**:524
Ugarit **1**:30, **7**:509, **8**:606
Ujjain **5**:340, **7**:494
Upper Swan **1**:14
Ur **1**:30, **2**:90, **4**:216,
   **4**:266, **4**:274, **7**:509,
   **10**:726
Ural River **9**:686
Urarth **9**:686
Uttarar Patha **7**:494
Uxmal **7**:498

Vahavasi **7**:494
Valley of the Kings **4**:253,
   **10**:770
Vandals **5**:381
Vandals, kingdom of the
   **4**:298, **4**:312
Vanga **7**:494
Vanuatu **6**:456, **7**:503
Vapheio **7**:545
Varanasi **5**:340, **6**:446
Veii **4**:278
Vetulonia **4**:278
Vidisha **7**:494
Vietnam **3**:236
Vindhya Mountains **1**:75
Vindolanda **5**:345
Visigoths, kingdom of the
   **4**:298, **4**:312, **5**:381
Viti Levu **6**:456
Volaterrae **4**:278
Volga River **9**:686
Volsinii **4**:278
Vulci **4**:278

Wales **2**:153
Walkunder Arch **1**:14
Wallsend **5**:345
Walnut Canyon **1**:50
Watom **6**:456
Western Desert **8**:572
Western Roman Empire **5**:381
White Nile **8**:572
Willandra Lakes **1**:14

Xianyang **2**:157, **3**:172, **4**:316
Xpuhil **7**:498
Xtampak **7**:498
Xunantunich **7**:498

Yamato **6**:411
Yamuna River **6**:446
Yangtze River **3**:172, **4**:316
Yap Islands **7**:514
Yaxha **7**:498
Yayoi culture **6**:411
Yellow River **3**:172, **4**:316
Yellow Sea **3**:172, **4**:316, **6**:441
Yelwa **8**:566
Yucatán Peninsula **8**:583
Yule **6**:456

Zagros Mountains **1**:30, **4**:266,
   **6**:468, **7**:509, **10**:726
Zakros **7**:545
Zama **5**:348
Zapotecs **10**:788
Zohak **1**:18

# Biographical Index

Page numbers in *italic type* refer to illustrations. **Boldface** numbers preceding a colon indicate the volume number.

Aaron **7**:536
Abraham **5**:355, **6**:427, **8**:638
Absalom **3**:225
Achaemenes **1**:18
Achilles **1**:25, **5**:393, **8**:581, **8**:605, **10**:759
Actaeon **5**:334
Adad-nirari II **2**:90
Adapa **4**:277
Aegeus **5**:334
Aegisthus **1**:25, **4**:246
Aeneas **1**:22, **9**:664
Aeolus **8**:581
Aeschylus **1**:25, **4**:245, **4**:246, **5**:330
Aesop **9**:700
Aetius **2**:103–104, **5**:383, **5**:384
Agamemnon **1**:24–25, **4**:246, **5**:393, **10**:758
Agesilaus II **9**:716
Agni **1**:76, **1**:77, **5**:364, **5**:*364*
Agnodice **10**:782
Agricola, Gnaeus Julius **10**:731
Agrippa, Marcus **2**:108, **2**:*109*
Agrippina, Julia (the Younger) **1**:26–27, **3**:195, **7**:493, **7**:557, **9**:653, **10**:782
Agrippina, Vipsania (the Elder) **1**:26, **1**:27
Ahab **10**:765
Ahasuerus **10**:787
Ahmose I **1**:46
Ahriman **1**:28, **10**:795
Ahura Mazda **1**:28–29, **3**:222, **8**:600, **10**:787, **10**:795, **10**:797
Ajashatru **8**:594
Ajax **8**:581
Akhenaten **1**:45, **1**:46, **4**:254, **6**:437, **7**:555, **7**:556, **8**:589, **10**:762
Aksapadama Gautama **5**:396
Alaric **3**:212, **4**:313, **4**:314, **4**:315
Alcibiades **5**:*337*
Alcinous **5**:393
Alexander the Great **1**:19, **1**:37–39, **1**:47, **1**:68, **2**:113, **2**:117, **2**:120, **3**:221, **4**:271,

**5**:325, **5**:*339*, **5**:358, **5**:398, **6**:417, **6**:*468*, **6**:469, **6**:470, **7**:494, **7**:495, **7**:532, **7**:*533*, **8**:601, **8**:607, **8**:608, **9**:687, **9**:688, **10**:758, **10**:764, **10**:773, **10**:775
Almudj **6**:433
Alcyoneus **5**:*332*
Amar-Sin **9**:695
Amaterasu **1**:42–43, **6**:412, **6**:413
Ambrose **2**:105
Amenemhat I **10**:743
Amenemhat III **8**:589
Amenhotep III **1**:44–45, **1**:46, **6**:461, **8**:589, **10**:*743*
Amenhotep (son of Hapu) **1**:45
Amenpanufer **10**:772
Amitrochates *see* Bindusara
Ammianus Marcellinus **5**:381
Ammut **2**:127, **3**:230, **4**:255
Amulius **9**:648, **9**:649
Amun **1**:45, **1**:46–47, **3**:229, **4**:261, **4**:263–264, **4**:290, **5**:349, **5**:350, **10**:743
Amun Kematef **1**:46
Amun Ra **1**:46, **4**:263
Amyitis **7**:554
Amyntas II **8**:604
Amyntas III **1**:67
Anahita **1**:29
Anaxagoras **5**:326, **5**:336, **8**:598
Anaximander **2**:96, **4**:304, **8**:629
Anaximenes **5**:336
Andromeda **5**:335
Anicetus **1**:27
Ankhesenpaaten (Ankhesenamen) **3**:*198*, **7**:555, **10**:762
Antiochus of Syria (Antiochus IV) **5**:358, **5**:359, **6**:417
Antoninus Pius **5**:344, **6**:475
Antony, Mark **1**:56–57, **2**:107, **2**:108, **3**:196–197
Anubis **2**:127, **3**:229, **4**:255, **4**:265, **7**:489
Anu **2**:119, **4**:307
Aphrodite **1**:24, **5**:333, **5**:334, **8**:637, **9**:675
Apollo **1**:25, **3**:211, **3**:219, **3**:234, **4**:273, **4**:292, **5**:333, **7**:543, **9**:*668*
Apollonius **8**:630

Apuleius **6**:465
Aquila, Tiberius Julius **6**:462
Arachne **2**:99
Arcadius **4**:271
Archimedes **8**:580, **9**:682, **9**:683
Ardashir (Artaxerxes) **9**:678–679
Ardavan **9**:*679*
Ares **2**:98, **5**:333, **7**:492
Ariadne **5**:335
Arinna (Wurusemu) **5**:370
Aristarchos of Samos **2**:97, **8**:624
Aristophanes **2**:101, **5**:330, **9**:707
Aristotle **1**:37, **1**:67–69, **2**:96, **4**:304, **5**:336, **5**:338, **5**:339, **5**:398, **6**:461, **7**:532, **8**:579, **9**:652, **9**:654, **9**:707
Arius **4**:312–313
Arjuna **6**:473, **8**:631
Arrian **3**:221, **5**:398
Arsaces **8**:591
Arta **1**:28
Artabanus **3**:223
Artaxerxes I **1**:19, **8**:601
Artaxerxes II **1**:19
Artaxerxes III **1**:19
Artemis **3**:219, **4**:270, **5**:333, **5**:334, **7**:492, **9**:*668*
Artemisia **10**:749
Aryabhata **5**:341
Asclepius **4**:272, **4**:273, **5**:352
Ashoka **2**:84–85, **2**:136, **4**:251, **7**:495, **7**:497, **7**:517, **8**:595, **9**:672–673
Ashurbanipal **2**:88–89, **2**:91, **2**:95, **4**:266, **4**:268, **4**:307, **6**:461, **8**:565
Ashurnasirpal **1**:72
Ashurnasirpal II **2**:86, **2**:*87*, **2**:92, **2**:116, **2**:142
Ashur-uballit I **2**:91
Asklepios **6**:468
Astarte **8**:609
Astyages **3**:220
Aten **1**:45, **1**:46, **4**:254, **10**:762
Athanasius, bishop of Alexandria **3**:186
Athena **1**:20, **1**:21, **1**:79, **2**:98–99, **5**:*332*, **5**:333, **5**:393, **7**:551, **8**:581, **8**:*582*, **8**:637, **9**:*704*, **10**:779

Atossa **10**:786
Attila the Hun **2**:103–104, **4**:314, **5**:382–384
Atum **4**:263
Augustine of Hippo **2**:105–106, **3**:185
Augustus (Octavian) **1**:22, **1**:23, **1**:41, **1**:56, **2**:107–109, **3**:190, **3**:196–197, **4**:284, **4**:306, **7**:485, **8**:608, **9**:652, **9**:657, **9**:659, **9**:665, **9**:666
Aurelian **4**:312, **10**:791
Ausonius **4**:251
Ay **10**:762, **10**:763

Baal Hamon **2**:150, **8**:609
Bacchus **4**:*297*, **8**:637
Bahram II **9**:678
Bahram V **9**:679
Ban Zhao **10**:782
Barak **3**:233
Bassus, Junius **8**:*638*
Batiatus, Lentulus **9**:713
Bel **6**:478
*see also* Marduk
Belshazzar **2**:125–126
Bes **4**:261, **4**:*263*, **7**:489
Bindusara **7**:495, **7**:496
Bleda **2**:103
Bodhidharma **2**:138
Bolon Tzaicat **7**:502
Boudicca **2**:129–130, **7**:493
Brahma **5**:366–367, **5**:*395*
Brhadratha **7**:495, **7**:497
Briseis **5**:393
Britannicus **1**:27, **3**:195, **7**:557, **10**:*780*
Brutus **2**:107, **2**:141
Bucephalus **1**:37
Buddha (Siddhartha Gautama) **1**:71, **2**:131–133, **2**:134, **3**:182–183, **3**:222, **4**:248, **4**:251, **5**:342, **6**:447, **6**:448, **8**:638, **9**:672, **9**:673
Budha Gupta **5**:341
Buluk Chaptan **7**:502
Burnaburiash II **6**:437
Burrus, Africanus **1**:27, **7**:557

Caesar, Julius **1**:22, **1**:56, **2**:107, **2**:139–141, **2**:146, **2**:154, **2**:155, **3**:189, **3**:190, **3**:196, **3**:212, **5**:361, **9**:652, **9**:653, **9**:657, **9**:659, **9**:700, **9**:714, **10**:753, **10**:758,

Caesar, Julius *(cont.)*
**10**:775
Caligula (Gaius Caesar
Augustus Germanicus) **1**:26,
**1**:27, **2**:147–148, **3**:194
Calixtus **3**:*185*
Calypso **5**:393, **8**:582
Cambyses **1**:18
Cang Jie **5**:379, **5**:380
Cartimandua **7**:493
Cassandra **1**:25
Cassius **2**:107, **2**:141
Catiline (Lucius Sergius
Catalina) **3**:189, **3**:190,
**3**:*190*, **9**:659
Cato the Elder **9**:669
Cato the Younger **9**:653,
**9**:*654*
Catullus **9**:663
Celer **9**:649
Cerberus **3**:230
Ceres **9**:668
Chanakya **7**:494
Chandragupta **5**:341
Chandra Gupta I **5**:341,
**8**:595, **10**:775
Chandra Gupta II **5**:341,
**6**:434, **8**:595, **9**:670
Chandragupta Maurya
**7**:494–496
Chang Heng **9**:685
Changsu **6**:445
Chang Taoling *see* Zhang
Daoling
Chaos **5**:332
Charon **3**:230, **3**:*231*
Charvaka **5**:397
Charybdis **5**:393, **8**:582
Cheng **2**:157, **3**:167–168,
**3**:*167*, **3**:173, **3**:174, **3**:175,
**3**:204–205, **4**:316, **4**:318,
**10**:775, **10**:778
Childeric **4**:298, **4**:299
Chiron **4**:273
Chlodwig *see* Clovis I
Chosroes I **9**:679, **9**:680
Chosroes II **9**:679
Chrysippus **5**:338
Cicero **2**:105, **2**:141, **7**:*544*,
**9**:*654*, **9**:*659*
Cimon **1**:74, **8**:598
Circe **5**:393, **8**:582
Claudius **1**:26–27, **2**:148,
**3**:194–195, **3**:*194*, **7**:493,
**7**:557, **9**:657, **10**:780,
**10**:782
Cleis **9**:674

Cleisthenes **2**:100
Cleitus **1**:38
Clement of Alexandria **3**:185
Cleopatra **1**:41, **1**:56–57,
**2**:108, **2**:140–141, **2**:146,
**3**:196–197, **3**:*196*, **6**:469,
**6**:470, **8**:605, **9**:*663*, **10**:781
Clotilda, Saint **4**:299
Clovis I **4**:298, **4**:299, **4**:314
Clytemnestra **1**:25, **4**:246
Commodus **6**:476
Conchobor **7**:550, **7**:552
Confucius **1**:48–49, **3**:173,
**3**:181, **3**:203, **3**:205, **3**:*205*,
**4**:250, **6**:455
Constantine **1**:41, **2**:145,
**3**:184, **3**:186, **3**:202,
**3**:207–208, **6**:418, **9**:657,
**9**:660, **9**:666, **10**:740,
**10**:794
Constantine III **1**:54
Constantinus II **9**:679
Copernicus **2**:97
Coronis **4**:273
Crassus, Marcus **2**:139, **2**:141,
**3**:189, **9**:714
Criton **8**:610
Croesus **3**:235, **4**:270
Cronus **5**:332, **10**:793
Cuchulainn **7**:550, **7**:552
Culann the Smith **7**:552
Cupid **7**:*549*
Cyaxares **2**:87
Cybele **7**:544, **9**:650
Cyclops, Polyphemus the
**5**:393, **5**:394, **8**:581
Cynisca **9**:716
Cyrus the Great **1**:18, **1**:19,
**2**:120, **2**:125, **2**:126,
**3**:220–221, **3**:235, **6**:417,
**6**:478, **7**:554, **8**:600, **9**:687,
**9**:688, **10**:786

Danae **10**:794
Dang Thi Sach **10**:760
Daniel **3**:231
Dante Alighieri **1**:23
Darius I **1**:18, **1**:19, **1**:38,
**3**:222–223, **9**:687, **9**:688,
**10**:786, **10**:797
Darius III **1**:19, **10**:787
David **3**:224–225, **3**:*224*,
**5**:356, **5**:357, **6**:416, **6**:428
Deborah **3**:232–233, **3**:*232*,
**10**:782
Demeter **4**:292, **5**:333, **7**:493,
**9**:668

Democritus **5**:336
Devanampiya Piyadasi **2**:84–85
Diana **4**:270, **7**:492
Dido of Carthage **1**:22, **2**:149,
**2**:150
Dimpimekug **3**:228
Dio Cassius **2**:129, **2**:130,
**3**:202, **5**:359
Diocletian **9**:657, **9**:659
Diogenes **3**:171, **5**:*339*
Diomedes **2**:98, **2**:99
Dionysus **4**:244, **4**:*246*, **4**:282,
**4**:297, **5**:333, **7**:489, **7**:492,
**7**:543, **8**:605, **8**:637
Djoser **4**:258, **8**:626, **10**:748
Domitian **9**:666
Draco **3**:215, **9**:709
Drusilla **1**:27
Dumuzi **4**:275, **6**:410

Ea **2**:119, **4**:276, **4**:277,
**6**:477
Echo **9**:651
Eleazer ben Yair **7**:487, **7**:488
El **8**:609
Elijah **10**:765
Ellil (Enlil) **1**:34, **2**:119,
**4**:307
Empedocles **5**:339
Enheduanna **9**:677, **10**:730
Enki **6**:409, **6**:410
Enkidu **4**:307
Eostre **1**:55
Epicurus **5**:*338*, **9**:653
Eratosthenes of Alexandria
**1**:41, **4**:304, **4**:305
Erectheus **1**:21
Ereshkigal **7**:550
Eros **5**:332, **5**:334
Esarhaddon **2**:88
Eshmunazar **8**:*609*
Euclid **1**:40–41, **9**:682
Eupalinos of Megara **1**:66,
**5**:389
Eupolis **9**:707
Euripides **2**:101, **4**:245, **5**:330,
**6**:461
Europa **10**:793
Eusebius **3**:208
Ezekiel **5**:357, **7**:554

Fabiola **10**:782
Fabulus (Famulus) **7**:*558*
Fa Hsien **5**:342, **8**:595
Faunus **9**:650
Faustina **6**:476
Frija (Frigg) **1**:55, **2**:145

Gadatas **2**:126
Gaea (Gaia) **4**:288, **5**:332,
**7**:551
Galba, Servius Sulpicus **7**:558
Galen, Claudius **5**:354
Ganesha **5**:367
Gaozu **2**:157, **2**:158, **3**:168,
**6**:467
Garuda **9**:670
Geb **4**:264
Gessius Florus **7**:487
Gildas **1**:54
Gobryas **2**:126
Goliath **3**:224
Gordian III **9**:679
Gu Kaizhi **1**:74

Hadrian **1**:65, **3**:212,
**5**:343–344, **5**:345–346,
**5**:359, **6**:475, **9**:666
Hakhamanish **1**:18
Hamilcar Barca **5**:347
Hammurabi **2**:115, **2**:117,
**2**:119, **3**:213, **3**:214, **4**:266,
**4**:267, **5**:370, **7**:509, **9**:701,
**10**:753
Hannibal **5**:347–348, **6**:471,
**9**:657, **10**:774, **10**:775
Hanuman **8**:631
Hapi **4**:254, **4**:263
Harishena **9**:670, **9**:671
Hasdrubal **5**:347
Hathor **2**:97, **4**:264, **8**:636,
**8**:637
Hatshepsut **5**:349–350, **7**:486,
**7**:493, **10**:781, **10**:*782*
Hattusilis III **5**:369
Hector **5**:393, **10**:759
Helena (mother of
Constantine) **6**:418
Helen of Troy **1**:24, **5**:392,
**10**:758
Helios **8**:582, **9**:668
Henutmehyt **2**:128
Hephaestion **1**:39
Hephaestos **1**:70–71, **5**:333
Heraclitus **4**:271
Heraclius **9**:679, **9**:680
Hera **3**:215, **5**:326, **5**:333,
**5**:335, **8**:588, **9**:651, **10**:793
Herakles (Hercules) **5**:335,
**6**:447, **6**:468, **7**:492, **7**:537,
**8**:587, **10**:793
Hermes **5**:328, **5**:333
Hermod **7**:551
Hero of Alexandria **10**:736
Herod the Great **5**:359, **6**:418

Herodotus **1**:18, **1**:19, **2**:112, **3**:200, **3**:220, **3**:223, **5**:353, **5**:362, **5**:362–363, **5**:389, **5**:391, **8**:571, **8**:606, **9**:686, **9**:689, **10**:786, **10**:787
Hesiod **6**:463, **10**:794
Hesperus **9**:675
Hestia **3**:169, **5**:333
Hetepheres **8**:627
Hieron I **4**:279, **8**:580
Hillel **6**:431
Hipparchus **4**:305, **8**:625, **9**:684
Hippocrates **5**:326, **5**:352, **5**:*354*, **9**:*682*
Hiram **9**:693, **10**:764
Homer **3**:170, **4**:288, **5**:324, **5**:325, **5**:328, **5**:332, **5**:392–394, **6**:451, **8**:629
Honorius **3**:202, **4**:315
Horace **2**:109, **9**:663
Horemheb **7**:556, **10**:762
Horus **2**:127, **4**:263, **4**:264, **4**:265, **5**:351, **5**:399
Hostilian **5**:391
Huangdi (Huang-ti) **5**:379–380
Hulla **5**:371
Humbaba **4**:307
Hunefer **2**:127
Hwanung, Prince **6**:442, **6**:443
Hypatia **1**:41, **10**:78
Hystaspes **10**:797

Ibbi-Sin **9**:696
Imhotep **1**:45, **4**:258, **8**:626, **10**:748
Inanna **4**:275, **4**:307, **6**:409, **7**:550, **7**:551, **8**:637
Indra **1**:76, **1**:*77*, **1**:78, **5**:364
Inshushinak **4**:268, **4**:269
Iphigenia **1**:25, **4**:246
Isaac **8**:*638*
Isaiah **3**:231
Ishtar **1**:33, **1**:36, **2**:87, **2**:120, **2**:142, **4**:275, **4**:307, **6**:409–410, **8**:564, **9**:696, **10**:730
Isis **4**:264, **4**:265, **8**:636, **8**:637, **9**:650
Ixion **3**:215
Izanagi **1**:42

Jacob **5**:355
Jael **3**:233
Jaimini **5**:396
James, Saint **8**:597

Janus **9**:669
Jason **5**:335
Jehoiachin **7**:553
Jeremiah **7**:554
Jerome, Saint **2**:105, **3**:185
Jesus Christ (Jesus of Nazareth) **2**:105, **3**:184–185, **3**:186–187, **3**:188, **3**:207, **3**:227, **3**:230–231, **4**:250, **4**:293, **6**:419–421, **8**:596, **8**:638, **9**:669, **10**:740
Jezebel **10**:765
Jimmu Tenno **1**:43
John, Saint **8**:597
John the Baptist **6**:420
Jordanes **4**:312
Joseph **6**:419
Josephus, Flavius **6**:425–426, **6**:430, **7**:487–488
Joshua **6**:414
Judas Iscariot **6**:420
Julia, Caesar's daughter **2**:109, **2**:141
Julian **4**:299, **9**:679
Jupiter **1**:47, **2**:146, **8**:637, **9**:648, **9**:668, **9**:*683*, **10**:793
Justinian **5**:339, **8**:576, **9**:655
Juvenal **3**:193

Kajula Kadphises **6**:447
Kalidasa **5**:342, **6**:434–435
Kali Ma **10**:781
Kanada **5**:396
Kanishka **6**:446, **6**:447, **6**:448
Kapila **5**:396
Kautilya *see* Chanakya
Khepri **4**:263
Khonsu **4**:291
Khshayarsa *see* Xerxes
Khufu **4**:258, **4**:309, **4**:311, **8**:626, **9**:*692*, **10**:748
Khumbannumena **4**:267
Kidin-Khutran **4**:267
Kiya **10**:762
Klio **1**:*23*
Kong Qiu (Kong Fuzi) *see* Confucius
Krishna **4**:291, **5**:367, **6**:473, **8**:631
Kronos **8**:587
Kumara Gupta **5**:341
Kumuradevi **5**:341
Kunti **6**:*474*
Kurigalzu I **6**:437
Kurigalzu II **6**:438
Kutir-Nahhunte I **4**:267
Kwanggaet'o-wang **6**:445

Laertes **5**:394
Lakshmana **8**:*632*
Lakshmi **5**:367, **9**:670
Lao-tzu (Laozi) **3**:*180*, **3**:181, **6**:453–455
Larthia Seinti **4**:279
Lechares **4**:292
Leda **10**:793
Lei Zu **5**:379
Leo I, Pope **2**:104, **5**:384
Leonidas (architect) **8**:*587*
Leonidas **9**:*711*
Lepidus, Marcus Aemilius **1**:56, **2**:107, **2**:108
Licinius **3**:208
Liu Bang *see* Gaozu
Liu Hsin **9**:684
Liu Hsiu **6**:466–467
Liu Xiang **10**:782
Livia Drusilla **2**:*108*, **2**:109, **7**:*484*
Livilla **1**:*27*
Livy **5**:348
Lleu Llaw Gyffes **7**:550
Lucretia **4**:279
Lucretius **7**:544
Lugalbanda **4**:275
Lygdamis **5**:362
Lysippus **9**:*707*

Maecenas **1**:23
Magnentius **4**:298, **4**:299
Mahavira **5**:398
Maimonides, Moses **3**:214
Manichaeus (Mani) **9**:678
Manu **4**:252
Marcellinus, Ammianus **5**:381
Marcellus **2**:108
Marcus Aurelius **3**:216, **5**:354, **6**:475–476, **9**:653
Marduk **2**:113, **2**:119, **2**:125, **2**:146, **4**:290, **5**:368, **6**:477–478, **7**:551, **7**:553, **7**:554, **9**:669, **9**:691, **10**:727, **10**:787
Marinatos, Spyridon **3**:218
Marius **9**:659
Mark, Saint **1**:41
Maro, Publius Vergilius *see* Virgil
Mars **7**:492, **7**:*549*, **9**:648
Mary Magdalene **6**:421
Mary, mother of Jesus **6**:419
Mausolus of Caria **5**:363, **10**:749
Maxentius **3**:207
Ma Yuan **10**:761

Medea **5**:335, **10**:798
Medusa **2**:98, **5**:335
Megabazus **3**:223
Megasthenes **7**:496, **7**:497, **8**:594
Melpomene **1**:*23*
Melqart **8**:609, **10**:764–765
Menander **8**:595
Menas **1**:37
Mencius **1**:49, **3**:181, **3**:*181*, **3**:204
Menelaus **5**:392, **10**:758
Menes **4**:253
Meng-tzu (Mengzi) *see* Mencius
Menkaura **4**:309, **4**:311
Menna **9**:*701*
Mentuhotep II **1**:46
Menvra **4**:280
Mercury **2**:146
Merneptah **8**:589
Meryt **7**:*508*
Mesehti **4**:260
Messalina **10**:*780*, **10**:782
Metis **2**:98, **10**:793
Mezzulla **5**:371
Micah **3**:225
Milo of Kroton **9**:718
Min **4**:292
Minerva *see* Athena
Ming Ti **9**:*705*
Minos **6**:439
Minotaur **5**:335, **6**:440
Mithra **1**:29, **6**:447
Mithras **8**:*636*, **8**:637, **9**:650
Mithridates (of Pontus) **2**:141
Mithridates II **8**:593
Mitra **1**:76
Modestinus **7**:485
Moses **3**:214, **5**:355, **5**:357, **6**:429, **7**:*519*, **7**:536–538, **8**:634, **9**:677
Mursilis I **5**:368
Mursilis II **5**:369
Mushhushshu **6**:477
Mut **4**:261, **4**:290
Muwatallis **5**:368, **5**:369
Myron **1**:71

Nabodinus **2**:125, **7**:554
Nabopolassar **2**:113, **2**:117, **7**:553
Nabu **2**:142, **7**:553
Nakht **5**:*377*
Namarrgon (Namarrkun) **6**:433

Nanna **6**:409
Nanna-Suen **9**:677
Napirasu **4**:*267*
Naram-Sin **1**:31, **1**:32, **1**:34
Narcissus **9**:651
Narmer **4**:253
Nebuchadrezzar I **6**:478
Nebuchadrezzar II **2**:113,
    **2**:114, **2**:117, **2**:125, **5**:356,
    **6**:417, **7**:509, **7**:510,
    **7**:553–554
Nefertari **4**:*256*, **4**:*265*, **4**:*301*,
    **8**:633
Nefertiti **4**:*254*, **7**:555–556,
    **10**:762, **10**:781
Neferure **5**:349
Nemesis **8**:637
Neoptolemus **7**:*518*
Nephthys **4**:264
Neptune **10**:793
Nerik **5**:370–371
Nero (Lucius Domitius
    Ahenobarbus) **1**:26–27,
    **2**:129, **3**:186, **3**:195, **3**:201,
    **6**:425, **7**:493, **7**:532,
    **7**:557–558, **8**:597, **9**:653,
    **10**:732, **10**:782
Nespanetjerenpere **3**:*229*
Nespawershepi **4**:262
Ngalyod **6**:433
Nicomachus **1**:67
Nike **8**:587
Nimrod **8**:564, **8**:565
Ninigi **1**:43
Ninkasi **4**:295
Ninurta **2**:142
Nitocris **2**:125
Noah **7**:511, **8**:565
Nut **4**:263, **4**:264, **10**:*772*

Octavian *see* Augustus
Odaenathus **10**:791, **10**:792
Odin **2**:145, **7**:550, **7**:551
Odoacer **4**:313
Odysseus **2**:98, **5**:392,
    **5**:393–394, **7**:550,
    **8**:581–582
Oisin **7**:550
Olympias **1**:37, **8**:605
Orestes (Agamemnon's son)
    **1**:25
Orestes (governor of
    Alexandria) **1**:41
Origen **3**:185
Orpheus **7**:551
Osiris **2**:127, **3**:229–230,
    **4**:264, **4**:265, **4**:288, **4**:301,

**7**:550
Ouranos **5**:332, **7**:551
Ovid **5**:332, **5**:335, **9**:651

Pallas Athene *see* Athena
Papa **7**:551
Paris **1**:24, **5**:392, **10**:758
Parmenides **5**:339
Parvati **5**:342, **5**:367
Pashedu **1**:71
Patanjali **5**:396
Patrick, Saint **2**:155
Patroclus **5**:393, **10**:759
Paul of Tarsus **3**:185, **3**:212,
    **8**:596–597, **9**:701
Pausanias **8**:605
Pazuzu **2**:92
Peisistratos **9**:710
Penelope **5**:393, **5**:394, **8**:582
Periander **3**:212
Pericles **1**:20, **1**:21, **2**:102,
    **8**:598–599
Persephone **3**:230, **5**:333,
    **5**:*334*
Perseus **2**:98, **5**:335
Peseshet **10**:782
Peter, Saint **3**:187, **5**:383,
    **5**:384, **8**:597
Phidias **1**:20, **1**:21, **8**:587
Philip III (Philip Arrhidaeus)
    **6**:469
Philip II of Macedon **1**:37,
    **1**:68, **5**:325, **6**:469,
    **8**:604–605
Philippus I **9**:679
Philo of Byzantium **2**:114
Philodemus of Gadara **5**:361
Piankhy **8**:576
Pisistratus **6**:461
Piso, Lucius Calpurnius
    **5**:361
Plato **1**:67, **2**:102, **2**:106,
    **4**:301, **5**:326, **5**:327, **5**:329,
    **5**:336, **5**:337, **5**:339, **7**:522,
    **8**:609, **8**:610–611, **8**:629,
    **9**:652, **9**:655, **9**:707, **9**:708
Plautius, Aulus **3**:194
Plautus **9**:663
Pliny the Elder (Gaius Plinius
    Cecilius Secundus) **1**:71,
    **1**:74, **6**:423, **9**:685
Pliny the Younger **8**:616
Plotinus **9**:655
Plutarch **1**:57, **3**:197, **7**:495,
    **9**:683
Pluto **3**:230, **10**:793
Pollio, Marcus Vitruvius **1**:59

Polycletus the Younger **4**:273
Polygnotos of Thasos **1**:74
Polyphemus, the Cyclops
    **5**:393, **5**:394
Pompey the Great **2**:139,
    **2**:140, **2**:*141*, **3**:189, **5**:359,
    **6**:469, **9**:714
Pontius Pilate **6**:421
Poseidon **1**:21, **2**:98, **3**:212,
    **5**:333, **10**:793
Prasutagus **2**:129
Priam **7**:*518*, **10**:758, **10**:759
Priscus **5**:38
Prometheus **10**:794
Pseudo-Xenophon **9**:702
Psyche **5**:334
Ptolemy, Claudius (of
    Alexandria) **2**:96–97, **4**:305,
    **4**:306, **6**:470, **8**:624–625
Ptolemy (Cleopatra's brother)
    **2**:141
Ptolemy I **6**:462
Ptolemy II **1**:40
Ptolemy III **1**:40, **6**:462
Ptolemy Soter **1**:40
Ptolemy XII **3**:196
Ptolemy XIII **3**:196
Ptolemy XIV **3**:196
Pu-Abi **3**:228, **10**:747
Pushyamitra Shunga **7**:497
Pyramus **9**:651
Pythagoras **2**:96, **2**:97, **4**:304,
    **8**:579, **8**:629–630, **9**:682
Pythia **3**:234
Python **3**:234

Qin Shi Huangdi *see* Cheng
Quetzalcoatl **10**:742
Quirinus **9**:649

Ra **1**:45, **1**:46, **4**:254, **4**:262,
    **4**:263, **4**:264
Rama **8**:631, **8**:632
Rama Gupta **5**:341, **9**:670
Ramses II **4**:255, **5**:369, **7**:556,
    **8**:576, **8**:633–634
Ramses III **5**:389, **7**:517,
    **8**:589, **9**:716
Ramses VI **10**:*772*
Rangi **7**:551
Ravana **8**:631, **8**:632
Remus **9**:648–649, **9**:657,
    **9**:664
Renenutet **4**:288
Rhea **5**:332, **8**:587, **9**:650,
    **10**:793

Rhea Silva **9**:648
Romulus **7**:537, **9**:648–649,
    **9**:657, **9**:664
Roxana **1**:39
Rufus, Lucius Verginius
    **10**:732
Rugila **2**:103, **5**:382

Sabinus, Nymphidius **7**:558
Sagburro **4**:275
Salem **6**:416
Sammonicus, Serenus **6**:462
Samudra Gupta **5**:340, **5**:341,
    **9**:670–671
Sappho **9**:674–675
Sargon of Akkad **1**:30–31,
    **1**:32, **1**:*33*, **7**:509,
    **9**:676–677, **10**:727
Sargon II **2**:91, **2**:92, **2**:94,
    **2**:143, **4**:*308*, **9**:690
Saturn **8**:625, **9**:650
Saul **3**:224, **5**:356
Scipio Africanus **5**:348, **10**:775
Scylla **5**:393, **8**:582
Sebeknefru **10**:781
Sekhmet **8**:575
Seleucus **6**:470, **6**:471, **7**:554,
    **8**:594
Seleucus Nicator **7**:494–496
Seneca **1**:27, **5**:389, **7**:557,
    **9**:653, **9**:654, **9**:655, **9**:661
Sennacherib **1**:*58*, **2**:91, **2**:93,
    **2**:117, **8**:564, **8**:565,
    **9**:690–691
Sennedjem **4**:259
Sennefer **7**:*508*
Senustris III **8**:573
Serapis **1**:41
Seshat **10**:*785*
Setanta *see* Cuchulainn
Seth **4**:264, **4**:265
Sethlans **4**:280
Shamash-shum-ukin **2**:88
Shalmaneser I **2**:91, **2**:142
Shalmaneser III **2**:143
Shamash **2**:120, **3**:213
Shamshi-Adad I **2**:91
Shankara **5**:397
Shapur I **9**:678, **9**:679, **10**:792
Shapur II **9**:679
Shimon Bar Kokhba **5**:344,
    **5**:359
Shiva **5**:342, **5**:366, **5**:367,
    **8**:635, **8**:638
Shu **4**:264, **8**:575
Shulgi **4**:266, **6**:409,
    **9**:695–696, **10**:729, **10**:769

Shutruk-Nahhunte **6**:438
Siculus, Diodorus **2**:156
Siddhartha Gautama *see*
  Buddha
Siduri **4**:308
Silva, Flavius **7**:487
Silvanus **4**:298
Sin **2**:125
Sirius **2**:144
Sisera **3**:23
Sita **8**:631
Skanda Gupta **5**:340, **5**:341,
  **5**:342
Smenkhkare **7**:556, **10**:762
Smoking Frog **10**:745
Sneferu **8**:626, **8**:627, **10**:748
Sobek **4**:262
Sobekemsaf II **10**:772
Socrates **1**:69, **2**:101, **5**:325,
  **5**:326, **5**:336–337, **5**:339,
  **7**:517, **8**:610, **9**:707–708
Solomon **5**:356, **6**:416, **6**:428,
  **9**:693
Solon **2**:100, **9**:674,
  **9**:709–710
Sophocles **2**:101, **4**:245, **5**:330,
  **5**:332
Sosigenes of Alexandria **2**:146
Sosurim **6**:445
Spartacus **2**:141, **9**:657, **9**:702,
  **9**:713–714
Stephen, Saint **8**:596
Strabo **4**:305, **7**:492
Suddhodhana **2**:131
Suetonius **1**:27, **2**:107, **2**:109,
  **2**:148, **3**:195
Suetonius Paullinus **2**:130
Sulla **9**:659
Sun Tzu **10**:775
Surus **5**:347
Susano-wo **1**:42
Su Ting **10**:760
Syrus **8**:624

Tacitus **3**:215, **7**:558,
  **10**:731–732
Tadius, Spurius **1**:71
Tanit **2**:150, **8**:609
Tarhun **5**:370
Tarquin (Tarquinius Superbus)
  **4**:279, **9**:650, **9**:656, **9**:657
Taru **5**:370
Tawa **1**:51
Taweret **4**:264
Tefnakht **8**:576
Tefnut **4**:264, **8**:575
Teiresias **2**:99

Telemachus **5**:393, **5**:394,
  **8**:582
Terminus **9**:650
Tertullian **3**:186
Teshub **5**:370
Teumman **8**:*565*
Teutates **9**:*667*
Thales **5**:336, **8**:629
Themis **10**:793
Theocritus **1**:41
Theodora **8**:576
Theodoric the Great **4**:313,
  **4**:314, **9**:*706*
Theodosius I **1**:41, **3**:184,
  **3**:235, **6**:462, **8**:588, **8**:638,
  **10**:794
Theodosius II **2**:103, **5**:382,
  **5**:*383*
Theon **8**:624
Theseus **5**:334–335, **7**:492
Thespis **7**:489
Thisbe **9**:651
Thor **1**:55, **2**:145
Thorismund **2**:*104*
Thoth **2**:127, **4**:262, **4**:265,
  **6**:449
Thucydides **8**:599
Thutmose **7**:555
Tiamat **6**:477
Tiberius **2**:108, **2**:147, **7**:*484*,
  **7**:485
Tiglath-Pileser I **2**:87, **2**:91
Tiglath-Pileser III **1**:72
Tinia **4**:280
Tir **1**:55
Titus **9**:666
Tiy **8**:590
Tjuiu **5**:*377*
Tollund Man **7**:539
Trajan **5**:343, **8**:603, **9**:666
Trung Nhi **10**:760–761
Trung Trac **10**:760–761
Tsuki-yomi **1**:42
Tu Fu **9**:647
Tushratta **1**:44
Tutankhamen **1**:47, **3**:*198*,
  **4**:301, **7**:*485*, **7**:555, **7**:556,
  **10**:744, **10**:762–763,
  **10**:*784*
Tuthmosis I **5**:349, **7**:486
Tuthmosis II **5**:349, **7**:486
Tuthmosis III **5**:349, **5**:350
Tuthmosis IV **9**:*701*
Tyr **2**:145

Ulam-Buriash **6**:436, **6**:437
Ulfilas **4**:313

Uni **4**:280
Untash-Gal **4**:267, **4**:269
Ur-Nammu **9**:695, **10**:729,
  **10**:768, **10**:769
Utnapishtim **4**:308
Utu **4**:275, **6**:40
Uzume **1**:42

Valens **4**:313, **4**:314
Valerian **9**:659, **9**:679, **10**:792
Valmiki **8**:631
Varuna **1**:76
Venus **2**:120, **7**:*549*
Vercingetorix **2**:139
Verus, Lucius **6**:475, **6**:476
Vespasian **3**:201, **6**:425, **6**:426,
  **9**:666, **10**:731
Virgil **1**:22–23, **2**:109, **5**:332,
  **9**:663
Vishnu **5**:366–367, **6**:473,
  **8**:631, **8**:638, **9**:670
Vishtaspa **10**:797
Vitiges **1**:59
Voltumna **9**:650
Volturnus **9**:650
Vulcan **4**:319

Wahballet **10**:791
Wang Mang **6**:467
Wei Fu-Jen **10**:782
Woden **1**:55, **2**:145
Wu Di **3**:173, **3**:175, **3**:206

Xenophanes **5**:336, **5**:337,
  **5**:339
Xenophon **2**:126, **5**:325
Xerxes **1**:18, **1**:19, **1**:28, **1**:29,
  **8**:601, **8**:608, **10**:786–787
Xi Wangmu **3**:179
Xunzi **1**:49, **3**:204

Yasodhara **2**:131
Yax K'uk Mo' **3**:209
Yax-Pac **3**:210
Yax Pasah **3**:210
Yazdagird III **9**:679, **9**:680
Yellow Emperor *see* Huangdi
  (Huang-ti)
Yosef ben Mattityahu *see*
  Josephus, Flavius
Yu Huang Shang Di **3**:179

Zarathustra **1**:28, **10**:795–796,
  **10**:797
Zarpanitum **6**:477
Zedekiah **7**:553, **7**:554
Zeno **9**:652

Zenobia **10**:791–792
Zeus **1**:21, **1**:47, **1**:71, **2**:98,
  **3**:215, **5**:326, **5**:332, **5**:333,
  **5**:334, **5**:335, **5**:359, **6**:417,
  **6**:468, **7**:506, **8**:587, **8**:588,
  **8**:637, **9**:648, **9**:668, **10**:779,
  **10**:793–794
Zeus-Ammon **1**:47, **8**:605
Zhang Daoling **6**:455
Zhang Heng **3**:179
Zheng *see* Cheng
Zoroaster *see* Zarathustra

# Index of Civilizations and Peoples

Page numbers in *italic type* refer to illustrations. **Boldface** numbers preceding a colon indicate the volume number.

aboriginal culture **1**:14–17, **6**:432–433, **6**:*451*, **7**:506, **10**:766–767, **10**:779
Achaemenids **1**:18–19, **3**:220, **8**:600, **10**:786–787
Adena culture **5**:372, **5**:373
Akkadians **1**:30–36, **4**:275, **7**:509, **7**:510, **8**:577, **9**:677, **10**:727
Alans **5**:383
Algonquins **7**:531
Alizones **9**:686
Amorites **1**:36, **2**:86, **10**:728
Anasazi **1**:50–53
Angles **1**:54–55
Anglo-Saxons **2**:155
Aryans **1**:75–78, **5**:364, **7**:519, **9**:705, **10**:798
Assyrians **2**:90–95, **2**:117, **4**:266, **4**:267, **4**:268, **5**:356, **5**:357, **5**:369, **5**:371, **6**:438, **7**:553, **8**:564, **8**:565, **10**:764, **10**:774, **10**:775, **10**:795
Athenians **2**:100–102, **3**:223, **8**:598
Aztecs **10**:741, **10**:789

Babylonians **1**:58, **2**:90, **2**:91, **2**:95, **2**:96, **2**:115–120, **2**:144, **2**:145, **3**:213–214, **3**:222, **4**:290, **5**:356, **5**:357, **6**:430, **6**:477–478, **7**:509, **7**:551, **7**:553–554, **8**:577, **8**:578, **8**:579, **8**:580, **8**:617–618, **9**:682, **9**:684, **9**:685, **9**:691, **10**:764
Bantu culture **2**:121–124, **8**:566
Basket Maker culture **1**:50–53
Britons **1**:54, **2**:129, **5**:346, **10**:775
Burgundians **4**:298, **4**:299

Canaanites **3**:233, **6**:416
Carthaginians **2**:149, **2**:150, **5**:347, **6**:471
Celts **2**:129, **2**:153–156, **4**:278, **4**:279, **4**:292–293, **7**:493, **7**:531, **7**:539, **9**:658, **9**:667, **9**:687, **9**:688
Chavín **3**:164–166, **10**:734
Chinchorro **5**:386, **7**:540
Chinese **1**:47, **2**:157–158, **3**:167, **3**:172–179, **3**:181, **3**:183, **3**:237, **4**:247–248, **4**:291, **6**:411, **7**:518, **8**:617, **10**:760–761
Ciconians **5**:393, **8**:581
combware peoples **6**:441, **6**:443
Crow Indians **7**:491
Cycladic culture **3**:217–219

Dong Son culture **3**:236–238
Dorians **7**:518, **7**:548, **9**:711

Egyptians **1**:18, **1**:40, **1**:44–47, **1**:56, **2**:88, **2**:89, **2**:122, **2**:127, **2**:140, **4**:253–260, **5**:369, **6**:469, **8**:589, **8**:*618*, **8**:622, **8**:633–634, **10**:743, **10**:762, **10**:770
Elamites **1**:30, **1**:32, **2**:88, **4**:266–269, **6**:437, **6**:438, **6**:478, **8**:*565*, **9**:676, **9**:695, **10**:727
Essenes **3**:226, **6**:425, **6**:430, **6**:431, **6**:479
Etruscans **2**:154, **4**:278–281, **5**:388

Franks **4**:298–299, **4**:313
Frisians **1**:54, **1**:55

Goths **3**:212, **3**:235, **4**:312–315, **5**:383
Greeks **2**:98–102, **2**:104, **2**:109, **2**:139, **2**:149, **2**:154, **2**:155, **3**:193, **3**:211, **3**:215–216, **3**:223, **3**:234, **5**:324–331, **6**:470–471, **7**:518, **8**:581, **8**:587, **8**:595, **8**:604
Gupta Empire **5**:340–342, **5**:365, **5**:367, **6**:434, **6**:447, **8**:594, **8**:595, **9**:670–671
Gutians **1**:36, **10**:727, **10**:728

Halstatt Culture **2**:154, **2**:155
Han dynasty **1**:47, **2**:157, **3**:173, **3**:174, **3**:175, **3**:176, **3**:178, **3**:181, **3**:205, **3**:237, **4**:247, **4**:304, **4**:316, **4**:318, **5**:376, **5**:381, **6**:442, **6**:466–467, **10**:761
Harappan culture **6**:405, **7**:528, **8**:*635*
Hebrews **3**:214, **5**:355–359, **6**:416–417, **7**:536–538, **7**:543, **7**:553, **8**:565, **9**:690, **9**:691
*see also* Israelites; Jews
Hellenistic period **2**:159, **3**:230, **5**:338, **6**:470–471, **8**:565, **8**:639
Helots **9**:711, **9**:712
Hittites **5**:368–371, **6**:436, **6**:437, **8**:633, **8**:639, **9**:*691*
Hohokam people **1**:50, **1**:51, **1**:52
Hopewell culture **5**:372–374
Hopi **1**:50
Hsiung-Nu **6**:446, **6**:447
Huns **2**:103–104, **4**:313, **4**:314, **5**:381–384, **8**:571
Hyksos people **10**:743

Iceni **2**:129
Ife **8**:568
Incas **8**:577
Indus valley peoples **1**:75–77, **3**:192, **5**:364, **5**:388–389, **6**:404–408, **7**:519, **7**:528–529
Inuit **7**:506
Iroquois **7**:491, **7**:531
Israelites **2**:91, **3**:224, **3**:232, **3**:233, **5**:355, **7**:554, **8**:634
*see also* Hebrews; Jews

Japanese **6**:411–413
Jebusites **3**:224, **6**:416
Jews **2**:125, **2**:126, **2**:144, **3**:184, **3**:185, **3**:220, **3**:225, **3**:226, **5**:356, **5**:358–359, **6**:416–417, **6**:425–426, **6**:430, **7**:487–488, **7**:536–538, **7**:553, **7**:554, **8**:596–597, **10**:773
*see also* Hebrews; Israelites

Jomon culture **6**:411, **6**:412, **6**:413
Jutes **1**:54, **1**:55

Kassites **6**:436–438
Koreans **6**:411, **6**:441–445
Kurgan culture **6**:450
Kushan Empire **6**:446–448

Lapita culture **6**:456–458, **7**:504, **8**:612, **8**:613, **9**:694
La Tène culture **2**:*154*, **2**:155
Lydians **3**:220, **7**:531

Maccabees **5**:357, **5**:*358*, **5**:359, **6**:417
Macedonians **6**:468–471, **9**:688
Massagetes **9**:687, **9**:688
Mauryan Empire **2**:84, **5**:340, **7**:494–497, **8**:594–595, **9**:644, **9**:672
Maya **2**:131, **3**:209–210, **7**:498–502, **8**:585, **10**:745–746, **10**:754
Medes **1**:18, **1**:19, **1**:58, **2**:87, **2**:91, **2**:95, **2**:125, **2**:143, **3**:220, **3**:239, **8**:564, **8**:565
Melanesian culture **7**:503–505
Merovingians **4**:299
Mesoamerican culture **1**:65, **4**:244, **4**:249
Mesopotamians **1**:30–36, **2**:90, **2**:96, **2**:115, **2**:119, **3**:192, **4**:266, **4**:268, **4**:274, **4**:286, **4**:307–308, **5**:356, **6**:436, **7**:509–513, **9**:676–677, **9**:679, **9**:688, **9**:695, **9**:714, **10**:733, **10**:756, **10**:768
Messenians **9**:711
Micronesian culture **7**:514–516, **10**:755
Minoans **3**:218, **3**:219, **6**:439–440, **7**:520–523
Mitanni people **2**:90
Mixtecs **7**:*534*, **10**:788, **10**:789
Moche culture **1**:*72*, **7**:524–527, **9**:*703*
Mogollon people **1**:50, **1**:51, **1**:52
Mycenaean civilization **3**:219,

**5**:324, **7**:522, **7**:545–548, **10**:748, **10**:793

Nabataeans **8**:602
Neanderthal **3**:198, **3**:228, **3**:229, **3**:239, **4**:294
Neolithic **2**:10, **2**:151, **2**:152, **2**:156, **2**:159, **3**:191, **3**:198, **3**:237, **4**:285, **4**:287, **4**:294, **5**:387, **6**:452, **7**:491, **8**:622, **9**:692, **9**:697–698, **10**:737
Neuri **9**:686
Nok culture **8**:566–569
Nubians **8**:572, **8**:572–576, **8**:627

Olmecs **1**:52, **4**:300, **6**:451, **7**:518, **8**:583–586
Ostrogoths **1**:59, **4**:270, **4**:313, **4**:314, **4**:315, **4**:319, **5**:384, **9**:*706*

Parsees **10**:795, **10**:*796*, **10**:799
Parthians **2**:87, **8**:591–593
Pazyryk culture **7**:539
Persians **1**:18–19, **1**:20, **1**:28–29, **1**:38, **2**:100, **2**:113, **2**:117, **2**:120, **2**:125, **3**:220, **3**:222–223, **3**:235, **5**:325, **5**:357, **5**:358, **7**:510, **7**:517, **8**:564, **8**:565, **8**:598, **8**:608, **10**:775, **10**:792
Pharisees **5**:357, **6**:425, **6**:431, **6**:479
Philistines **3**:224, **3**:225, **5**:356
Phoenicians **2**:150, **4**:290, **8**:606–609, **9**:692, **10**:755, **10**:757, **10**:764–765, **10**:774
Picts **1**:54, **7**:493
Pitjantjatjara **10**:766
Polynesian culture **7**:517, **7**:551, **8**:612–614, **8**:614
Pueblo peoples **1**:50–53

Qin dynasty **2**:157, **2**:158, **3**:167–168, **3**:173, **3**:175, **3**:204–205, **4**:316, **4**:317, **4**:318

Romans **1**:22, **1**:56–57, **2**:103, **2**:104, **2**:107, **2**:109, **2**:129–130, **2**:139, **2**:147, **2**:149, **3**:185, **3**:194, **3**:207, **3**:239, **4**:288, **4**:312, **5**:343,

**5**:357, **5**:359, **5**:360, **8**:597, **8**:603, **8**:606, **8**:608, **8**:615–616, **8**:637, **9**:654, **9**:656–663, **9**:664–666, **10**:791, **10**:792
Sabines **9**:649
Sadducees **5**:357, **6**:425, **6**:431, **6**:479
Saka **9**:686, **9**:687
Samnites **5**:360, **8**:615
Sarmatians **9**:687, **9**:688
Sasanians **1**:29, **4**:271, **6**:446–447, **9**:678–680, **10**:795, **10**:798
Saxons **1**:54–55
Scythians **1**:19, **3**:223, **9**:686–689
Sealand dynasty **6**:436, **6**:437
Sea People **5**:369, **5**:371, **7**:517
Seleucid Empire **5**:357, **8**:591, **10**:765
Shang dynasty **3**:172, **3**:173, **3**:175, **3**:177, **3**:178, **4**:291, **5**:380, **7**:543, **9**:700, **10**:784
Spartans **1**:18, **8**:599, **10**:786
Steppe nomads **8**:570–571
Sui dynasty **2**:158, **3**:173, **3**:174, **4**:247, **4**:316, **4**:318
Sumerians **1**:30, **1**:33, **2**:115, **2**:119, **2**:120, **3**:192, **3**:221, **3**:228, **4**:266, **4**:274, **4**:275, **4**:276, **7**:509–513, **8**:623, **8**:636, **8**:637, **9**:676, **10**:726–730, **10**:768, **10**:774, **10**:779

Tang dynasty **1**:48, **2**:158, **6**:445
Trinovantes **2**:129
Trojans **1**:24–25, **2**:98, **2**:99, **4**:246, **5**:392–393, **8**:581, **10**:758–759

Ubaidians **10**:726, **10**:727
Urnfield Culture **2**:153, **2**:155

Visigoths **2**:103–104, **4**:298, **4**:299, **4**:312, **4**:314, **4**:315, **4**:319

White Huns **5**:341, **5**:342, **9**:680

Yamato culture **1**:43, **6**:411, **6**:412, **6**:413
Yankunytjatjara **10**:766
Yoruba people **8**:568

Zapotecs **7**:534–535, **10**:788–790
Zhou dynasty **2**:157, **3**:172, **3**:173, **3**:203

# Cultural and Literary Index

Page numbers in *italic type* refer to illustrations. **Boldface** numbers preceding a colon indicate the volume number.

*Aeneid* (Virgil) **1**:22–23, **9**:649, **9**:651

Afro-Asiatic languages **6**:450

afterlife **1**:71, **2**:127–128, **3**:228, **3**:229–230, **4**:255–256, **4**:257, **4**:264, **4**:281, **4**:310, **7**:527, **8**:635, **8**:636, **9**:663, **10**:747

agora **1**:66, **2**:101, **3**:211, **5**:327

Akkadian language **1**:31–32, **2**:89, **2**:159, **3**:221, **6**:409, **6**:450, **6**:452

*Almagest* (Ptolemy) **2**:97, **8**:624, **8**:625

alphabet **10**:783, **10**:785
  Greek **10**:785
  Latin **8**:609
  Phoenician **8**:606, **8**:609

altars **10**:740, **10**:748
  fire **10**:796, **10**:*797*

American Indian languages **6**:450

Amharic language **6**:450

amphitheaters **1**:66, **1**:79, **3**:201, **3**:239, **4**:*271*, **8**:615, **9**:716

amulets **3**:200, **3**:239, **4**:257, **5**:351, **6**:424, **10**:772

*Analects* (Confucius) **1**:48–49, **3**:203, **9**:706

ancestor worship **1**:14, **1**:15, **3**:178, **3**:180, **3**:203, **4**:283, **6**:415, **7**:504

animal deities **8**:586, **8**:636

*Annals* (Tacitus) **10**:732

Apocrypha **4**:284

*Apology* (Plato) **8**:610

apostles **3**:184, **3**:187, **3**:239, **8**:597

aqueducts **1**:58–59, **2**:93, **3**:194, **4**:288, **8**:564–565, **8**:639, **10**:734
  Roman **1**:59, **1**:65, **9**:663, **9**:665

Arabic **6**:450

Aramaic language **6**:452,

**10**:765

architecture **1**:64–66
  Babylonian **2**:118
  Chinese **1**:64
  Egyptian **1**:64–65
  Etruscan **4**:280
  Greek **1**:66, **1**:74
  Mesopotamian **1**:64–65
  Moche **7**:525–526
  Olmec **8**:585
  Roman **9**:663

Ark of the Covenant **3**:224, **3**:*225*, **6**:416, **6**:417, **7**:536, **10**:739

art **1**:70–74, **7**:500
  aboriginal **1**:16
  Assyrian **2**:92
  Celtic **2**:155
  Chavín **3**:165
  Chinese **1**:74, **4**:248
  Egyptian **4**:254, **7**:556
  gender in **7**:507
  Greek **1**:70, **1**:73, **5**:330
  Indian **4**:248
  Japanese **6**:413
  and magic **1**:70–71
  Mayan **4**:244
  Melanesian **7**:504
  Mesopotamian **7**:512
  Minoan **7**:522
  Neolithic **2**:152
  Olmec **8**:585
  and religion **1**:71
  Sumerian **10**:729–730
  Visigothic **4**:*314*

*Arthashastra* (Chanakya) **7**:494

*Art of War* (Sun Tzu) **10**:775

ashram **4**:251, **4**:319

astrology **2**:96, **3**:239

athletics **2**:101, **9**:718

atman **5**:395

Austronesian language family **6**:452

avatar **5**:367, **6**:473, **6**:479, **8**:631

ball courts **1**:52
  Mayan **1**:52, **9**:717–718
  Monte Albán **7**:535
  Olmec **1**:52, **8**:583, **8**:585
  Zapotec **10**:788, **10**:*790*

baptism **6**:420

bards **2**:156, **5**:392, **5**:399

basilica **9**:665, **9**:719, **10**:799

bas-relief **2**:159, **9**:690, **9**:719

baths **5**:389, **5**:390, **5**:391, **9**:662, **9**:666

*Bhagavad Gita* **6**:473

Bible **3**:185, **3**:226–227, **5**:355, **7**:536, **8**:564, **8**:634, **9**:701
  translation into Gothic **4**:313
  Vulgate **7**:538
  *see also* New Testament; Old Testament

*Biographies of Heroic Women* (Liu Xiang) **10**:782

bishop **3**:185, **3**:186

blasphemy **8**:596, **8**:639

bodhisattvas **1**:71, **1**:79, **2**:136, **2**:137

Bon-po religion **2**:138

*Book of the Dead* **2**:127–128, **3**:228, **4**:*255*, **4**:*264*, **5**:*377*

*Book of Lao-tzu see Tao Te Ching*

boxing **9**:716, **9**:717

*brahman* **5**:366, **5**:395

Brahmans **1**:76, **1**:77, **4**:252, **5**:364, **5**:*365*, **9**:705

Brahmi script **1**:*78*

bridges, Roman **9**:646, **9**:663, **9**:665

broch **9**:698, **9**:719

bronze **1**:73, **3**:177, **3**:217, **3**:236, **3**:237, **3**:238, **4**:287, **5**:380, **10**:773

Buddhism **2**:84, **2**:131–133, **2**:134–138, **3**:178, **3**:180, **3**:182–183, **5**:342, **5**:398, **6**:412, **6**:446, **6**:447, **6**:448, **7**:497, **8**:595, **8**:638, **9**:670, **9**:672–673, **10**:773
  art **4**:247
  beliefs **2**:133, **2**:134, **2**:135
  cave temples **10**:739, **10**:*740*
  Indian **10**:739
  middle way **2**:136
  paper scrolls **6**:461
  split **2**:136
  spread of **2**:133, **2**:136, **4**:248

teaching **2**:132–133, **2**:134–135
  "three jewels" **9**:673
  women and **10**:779
  *see also* Mahayana Buddhism; Theravada Buddhism

buildings *see* architecture

bulla **3**:*171*, **6**:424, **6**:479

burial customs
  Egyptian **1**:71, **3**:229–230, **4**:256, **7**:486, **10**:744, **10**:748
  Etruscan **10**:750
  Frankish **4**:298
  Greek **3**:229, **3**:230
  Hebrew **3**:229, **3**:231
  Persian **1**:29
  prehistoric **8**:621, **8**:635
  Roman **3**:229, **3**:230, **10**:750
  Scythian **9**:689
  *see also* tombs

cairn **9**:698, **9**:719

calendars **2**:141, **2**:144–146, **8**:578, **9**:684
  Babylonian **2**:144, **2**:145, **8**:578
  Chinese **2**:144, **5**:379, **9**:684
  Egyptian **2**:144, **8**:578, **9**:684
  Mayan **2**:145, **3**:210, **7**:500, **7**:501, **8**:578, **9**:682, **10**:790
  Mesopotamian **2**:144
  Roman **2**:141, **2**:145
  Zapotec **10**:790

calligraphy **10**:782

cannibalism **4**:315, **8**:614

catacombs **3**:185, **3**:230, **5**:386, **10**:740, **10**:750

cave paintings **1**:70
  aboriginal **1**:16, **10**:767
  Indian **1**:72
  Lascaux **6**:459–460, **8**:635
  prehistoric **8**:621
  Stone Age **5**:387

Celestial Masters movement **6**:455

cella **1**:20, **3**:239, **8**:587,

**8**:639, **10**:740

Celtic languages **1**:55

cenotaph **10**:749, **10**:799

*chakra* **9**:715

Chan *see* Zen

Chandogya Upanishad **5**:365, **5**:397

chariot racing **3**:234, **8**:588, **9**:716, **9**:717

Chester Beatty Medical Papyrus **5**:*353*

children **3**:169–171
Greek **5**:328, **5**:329
legitimate **7**:484
Roman **9**:662

chorus **4**:244, **4**:245, **4**:319

Christianity **1**:41, **2**:105–106, **2**:145, **3**:184–188, **3**:200, **3**:207–208, **3**:227, **3**:230, **4**:271, **4**:312–313, **5**:355, **6**:418, **6**:419–421, **6**:427, **8**:596–597, **8**:638, **10**:740
Arian **4**:313, **4**:319
early Celtic **2**:155

*Chuang-tzu* **3**:182, **3**:183, **6**:455

churches **1**:41, **2**:106, **3**:184–185, **3**:188

Circus Maximus **4**:319, **9**:663, **9**:719

citadel **1**:20, **1**:79, **7**:528

cities **3**:191–193, **5**:388
Chinese **3**:175
health and sanitation **3**:193
Indus valley **6**:405–406
Roman **3**:193, **9**:661–662
Sumerian **10**:726–727, **10**:729

city planning **1**:65–66

clay
tablets **7**:546, **7**:*548*
for writing **10**:783, **10**:784

clothes **3**:198–200
Chinese **3**:176
Christian **3**:200
Egyptian **3**:198, **4**:259
female **10**:780
Greek **3**:200, **5**:331
Indus valley **3**:199, **6**:408
Mesopotamian **3**:198
Roman **3**:171, **3**:200
Sumerian **3**:198

*Cloud Messenger* (Kalidasa) **6**:435

Coffin Texts **2**:127

colors
of mourning **3**:229

of pottery **8**:617–618
purple **3**:200, **8**:606, **9**:703, **10**:731
yellow **9**:704, **9**:*705*

comedy **4**:245–246, **5**:*330*

Confucianism **1**:48–49, **2**:138, **3**:173, **3**:178, **3**:180, **3**:181, **3**:182, **3**:203–206
Five Classics **3**:206
in Japan **6**:412
and Taoism **6**:455

*Conversations* (Confucius) *see Analects*

copper **8**:602, **8**:623, **10**:773

cosmetics **3**:199, **3**:200, **3**:239

*Creation Epic* (Babylonian) **2**:89

creation myths **4**:264, **5**:332, **7**:550

cremation **3**:230, **5**:374, **9**:663, **10**:748–749

*Crito* (Plato) **8**:610

cults **3**:182, **5**:399, **8**:637

cuneiform **1**:32, **6**:479, **8**:577, **8**:609, **8**:623
Sumerian **9**:*696*, **10**:*783*, **10**:784
tablets **2**:89, **2**:120, **2**:159

*Curse of Akade* **1**:34, **1**:36

cymbals **3**:238, **9**:718

Cynics **5**:339

*Cyropaedia* (Xenophon) **2**:126

dams **4**:285, **6**:467, **8**:565, **10**:734

dance **7**:541–544
Egyptian **7**:541, **7**:542
Greek **7**:542–543
Roman **7**:544

*Daodejing see Tao Te Ching*

Daoism *see* Taoism

Days of the Dead **4**:292–293

Dead Sea Scrolls **3**:226–227, **6**:461

death
and burial **3**:228–231
colors of **3**:229
masks **7**:490

dharma **2**:84–85, **2**:133, **2**:134, **6**:479, **9**:673

*Divine Comedy* (Dante) **1**:23

dolls **3**:171, **4**:302

drama **4**:244–246
Egyptian **4**:244
Greek **2**:101, **4**:244–246, **5**:330
Indian **4**:244

Roman **4**:244

dreamtime **1**:15, **1**:16, **6**:433, **6**:451, **10**:766

druids **2**:156, **9**:668

drums **3**:238, **7**:541, **7**:543, **7**:544, **9**:718

dyes **9**:681, **9**:703, **9**:704, **10**:765

Ebers papyrus **5**:353

*Eclogues* (Virgil) **1**:23

education **3**:169–170, **4**:249–252
Athenian **3**:170
of boys **4**:252, **10**:731
Chinese **3**:206
Egyptian **3**:168, **3**:169, **4**:249–250
Greek **4**:251–252, **5**:328
of Greek girls **4**:251
Indian **4**:250–251
Mesopotamian **3**:169, **4**:249
music in **7**:543
Roman **3**:170, **4**:*252*, **9**:654
Spartan **3**:170, **5**:328
values and beliefs **4**:250–251

Edwin Smith papyrus **5**:353

Egyptian language **4**:259, **4**:260

embalming **3**:229, **3**:239, **4**:256, **4**:257, **7**:540, **10**:762

English language **1**:55

enlightenment **9**:673, **9**:719

entertainment *see* sports

*Enumma Elish* **6**:477

epic **1**:22, **1**:33, **1**:79, **4**:307, **4**:319, **6**:463, **8**:631–632

*Ethics* (Aristotle) **1**:68

faience **8**:618, **8**:637

fertility **7**:489, **10**:*769*
goddesses **7**:491, **7**:493, **8**:637

festivals **1**:20, **1**:21, **4**:290–293, **7**:493, **7**:543, **9**:669
Akidu **4**:290, **9**:669
Christian **1**:55, **3**:186, **4**:293
Mayan **4**:293
spring **4**:291–292, **9**:718

figurines
Cycladic marble **3**:217–219
Mesopotamian **7**:512
Neolithic female **7**:491
Nok **8**:569

fire worship **7**:519, **10**:796, **10**:*797*, **10**:798

flute **7**:541, **7**:542, **7**:543, **9**:718

forum **8**:615, **8**:639

frescoes **1**:72, **1**:79, **3**:218, **3**:239, **4**:248, **6**:*440*, **10**:750

fuchsite **10**:746, **10**:799

Gagadju language **6**:432

gambling **4**:301

games **3**:201, **4**:300–302
Asclepieia **4**:273
ball games **4**:244, **4**:*245*
blind man's buff **3**:171
board **4**:301–302, **10**:*729*, **10**:730
children's **4**:302
Chinese **4**:301
Egyptian **4**:301
gladiatorial **9**:668, **9**:702, **9**:713–714, **9**:716
hopscotch **3**:171
Mayan **3**:209, **9**:717
Olmec **1**:52, **4**:300
Olympic **3**:234, **4**:300, **5**:325, **8**:587, **8**:588, **9**:711, **9**:716
Pythian **3**:234
Roman **4**:301, **9**:663, **9**:716
of skill **4**:300–301
snake **3**:*170*, **4**:301
tic-tac-toe **3**:171

*Gallic War* (Julius Caesar) **10**:775

*Georgics* (Virgil) **1**:23

*Gilgamesh Epic* **1**:33, **2**:89, **4**:274, **4**:307–308, **6**:410, **6**:451, **6**:463, **7**:511, **10**:730

gladiators **3**:202, **3**:*202*, **3**:239, **5**:352, **5**:354, **7**:544, **9**:668, **9**:702, **9**:713–714, **9**:716

glass **8**:608, **9**:681, **10**:765

glyphs **3**:209, **3**:*210*, **7**:500, **7**:*535*, **7**:559, **10**:789, **10**:790

God **3**:187, **3**:188, **3**:214, **3**:231
earliest idea of **8**:635
*see also* Yahweh

gods and goddesses **7**:506, **7**:549, **10**:779
Babylonian **2**:119, **7**:551
and days of the week **2**:145
earth **7**:506, **8**:637, **10**:*779*
fertility **7**:491, **7**:493, **8**:637
Greek **9**:648, **10**:737,

gods and goddesses
Greek *(cont.)*
**10**:793
Olympian **5**:326, **5**:332,
**5**:333, **7**:551
Roman **9**:648, **9**:650,
**10**:793
gold **3**:164, **3**:217, **6**:422,
**6**:424, **8**:574, **10**:777
Gothic language **4**:313
graves *see* tombs
Greek language **3**:170, **6**:450
guru **4**:251, **5**:395
gymnasium **1**:66, **2**:101,
**4**:252, **4**:272, **4**:319, **5**:327,
**5**:328, **8**:588
Gymnosophists **5**:398

Hades **5**:333, **5**:*334*, **5**:393,
**5**:399, **7**:550, **7**:551, **8**:582,
**10**:793
*Harmonica* (Ptolemy) **8**:625
harp **7**:541, **7**:542, **7**:544,
**9**:718, **10**:730
heaven and hell **6**:474
Hebrew language **3**:226, **6**:450
heroes and heroines **7**:549,
**10**:761, **10**:782
hieroglyphs **3**:209, **3**:239,
**4**:249, **4**:259, **6**:449, **6**:479,
**7**:535, **8**:572, **8**:578, **8**:614,
**8**:623, **8**:639, **10**:784,
**10**:789
Hinduism **2**:132, **2**:136,
**2**:138, **5**:364–367, **6**:449,
**6**:464, **8**:635, **9**:669, **9**:670,
**9**:705, **10**:781
asceticism **5**:366, **5**:367
caste system **1**:76, **4**:252,
**5**:365, **6**:479, **9**:705
festivals **4**:291
goddess **5**:*342*
gods **5**:366–367
Laws of Manu **4**:252
reincarnation **5**:364–365
sacred texts of **8**:631–632,
**8**:638
and Sanskrit **6**:450
hippodrome **8**:588, **10**:765,
**10**:799
*Historia Naturalis* (Pliny the
Elder) **9**:685
history **2**:112, **5**:362, **5**:381,
**10**:732
Jewish **6**:425–426, **10**:773
language and **6**:452
Roman **10**:731–732

Hittite language **5**:368, **6**:450
houses **5**:375–378
Anasazi **1**:50
Assyrian **2**:95
Celtic **5**:375–376
Chinese **5**:376–377, **5**:379
Egyptian **1**:64, **4**:253, **5**:377
Greek **5**:328–329
Indus valley **1**:64
Mayan **5**:377
Mesopotamian **7**:510, **7**:512
Micronesian **7**:514
Neolithic **2**:151
Roman **5**:378
hymns **7**:544, **9**:695, **9**:696,
**10**:744
Egyptian **4**:265
Sumerian **10**:730
Vedic **4**:244
hypostyle hall **10**:738

*Iliad* (Homer) **1**:24, **1**:68,
**2**:98, **2**:99, **5**:324, **5**:325,
**5**:362, **5**:392–394, **6**:463,
**6**:472, **7**:518, **7**:545, **8**:581,
**10**:758, **10**:759
*Indica* (Megasthenes) **7**:496,
**7**:497, **8**:594
Indo-European languages
**5**:368, **6**:436, **6**:450, **6**:451,
**6**:479
Indo-Iranian languages **9**:686
inscriptions **6**:464, **7**:511
*Instruction of Ptahhotep, The*
**4**:250
Instructress, the (Chinese
writer) **1**:*74*
intaglio **6**:423, **6**:479
Islam **5**:355, **5**:399, **6**:427,
**9**:679, **9**:680, **10**:795,
**10**:798
Isthmian Games **3**:212
ivory **7**:545, **8**:574, **8**:608,
**9**:*718*, **10**:765
fossil **5**:374, **5**:399

jade **6**:424, **7**:500, **7**:518,
**8**:583, **8**:585, **10**:789
Jain religion **5**:398, **7**:496
jewelry **3**:198, **3**:200, **3**:217,
**6**:422–424, **10**:752
Chinese **6**:424
Etruscan **4**:280, **4**:281
function of **6**:422
Greek **5**:331
Mayan **7**:500
Roman **6**:423–424

Stone Age **6**:422
Sumerian **3**:*228*, **6**:422,
**6**:424, **10**:*728*,
**10**:729–730, **10**:*768*,
**10**:769
Judaism **5**:355, **5**:357,
**6**:427–431, **7**:536, **8**:638
festivals and fasts **6**:427
and Hebrew **6**:450

kaolin **8**:586, **8**:639
Koine **6**:452
kava ceremonies **7**:505
keel **9**:692, **9**:719, **10**:764,
**10**:799

labyrinth **5**:335, **6**:440
lacquer **6**:413, **6**:479, **10**:752,
**10**:799
languages **6**:449–452
American **6**:451
Babylonian **6**:436
Bantu **2**:121, **2**:123
comparisons of **6**:452
families **6**:450
and history **6**:452
international **6**:452
Mesoamerican **6**:451, **6**:*452*
Phoenician **8**:607, **8**:609
Polynesian **7**:503
and society **6**:450
lapis lazuli **6**:422, **7**:510,
**7**:541, **7**:559, **10**:*768*,
**10**:799
Latin **3**:185, **3**:189, **9**:663
alphabet **8**:609
legends **5**:379–380, **7**:549
leisure *see* sports and
entertainment
libraries **6**:461–462
Egyptian **6**:461–462
Greek **6**:461
Roman **6**:461
*Life of Julius Agricola* (Tacitus)
**10**:732
lighthouses **8**:607
lingua franca **6**:452
literature **6**:463–465
Chinese **3**:179, **6**:464
early written **6**:464
Egyptian **6**:465
entertainment and leisure
**6**:465
Greek **6**:463, **6**:464,
**9**:674–675
Indian **6**:463
Jewish **6**:461

Mayan **6**:461
Mesopotamian **1**:34,
**4**:307–308
oral **6**:463
religion and **6**:464
Roman **9**:651, **9**:663
Sumerian **4**:307, **6**:451,
**10**:730
logic, Aristotelian **1**:67, **1**:69,
**5**:338
lotus eaters **5**:393, **8**:581
*Lun Yu see Analects* (Confucius)
lyre **5**:399, **7**:*541*, **7**:542,
**9**:675, **9**:718

*Mabinogion* **7**:550
magic **5**:351, **7**:549, **8**:613
and art **1**:70–71
language and **6**:449
numbers and religion **8**:579,
**8**:636
magus **3**:222, **3**:239
*Mahabharata* **4**:251, **6**:463,
**6**:472–474, **8**:631
Mahayana Buddhism **2**:136,
**2**:137, **6**:446, **6**:448
mana **7**:504, **8**:613
mantra **6**:449
marble **3**:217–219, **10**:738
marriage **7**:484–486
Babylonian **2**:116, **9**:659
ceremonies and rituals
**7**:485–486
Chinese **3**:176, **7**:484
Egyptian **7**:485, **7**:486
India **7**:486
Roman **3**:171, **7**:486
martial arts **2**:138
masks **4**:246, **5**:*330*,
**7**:489–490
African **7**:489, **7**:490
Aztec **10**:*741*
death masks **7**:490
Egyptian **7**:489, **7**:490
Greek **7**:489
Mayan **7**:*500*, **10**:746
Melanesian **7**:504
Roman **7**:489, **7**:490
Stone Age **7**:489
theatrical **7**:489–490
mastaba tombs **4**:311, **8**:626
matriarchy **7**:491–493,
**10**:781, **10**:799
matrilineal **7**:491, **7**:514,
**7**:559
maul stone **10**:725, **10**:799
mausoleum **8**:603, **10**:749

Mayan languages 6:451, 7:500
meditation 5:396, 6:476, 6:479
*Meditations* (Marcus Aurelius) 6:476
Melanesian languages 7:503
memorizing 4:250–251, 5:328
men 7:506–508
   coming of age rituals 7:507
   Egyptian 7:506
   Greek 5:327, 7:506
   male dominance 7:506–507
   Roman 7:508
   Spartan 9:712
   and women 5:327, 7:508
   *see also* patriarchy
Meroitic language 8:576
messiah 3:184, 3:225, 3:227, 5:359, 6:421, 6:479
missionaries 7:517
*moai* statues 8:614
monogamy 7:484
monolith 10:799
monotheism 6:427, 6:429
mosaics 9:663, 10:789
mummies 2:128, 3:229, 4:257, 4:*262*, 7:539–540, 9:689, 10:762, 10:772
muses 1:*23*
music 7:541–544
   aboriginal 1:16
   Babylonian 7:541
   Chinese 7:543
   in Christianity 7:544
   Egyptian 7:541, 7:542, 9:718
   Greek 7:542–543
   instruments 7:541
   Mesopotamian 7:541, 7:543
   Neolithic 7:541
   Roman 7:544
   theory 8:625
myrrh 5:391, 5:399, 8:602, 8:639
mythology 7:549–552
   aboriginal 1:15, 6:433, 10:779
   Celtic 7:550, 7:552
   common themes 7:551
   creation myths 7:550
   Egyptian 4:254–256, 4:261–265, 4:288, 4:290–291, 4:292
   European 2:145
   explanatory myths 7:550
   Greek 2:98–99, 5:332–335, 9:648

hero myths 7:549–550
   Irish 7:550, 7:552
   lands-of-the-dead myths 7:550
   Mesopotamian 4:276
   Native Americans 7:550, 7:551
   Norse 7:550, 7:551
   Polynesian 7:551
   Roman 9:648–651
   Sumerian 7:550, 7:551
   Welsh 7:550

natron 4:257, 5:391, 5:399, 7:540, 7:559
Navajo language 1:50
necropolises 4:281, 10:744, 10:765, 10:799
   Etruscan 10:749–750
Neoplatonism 9:655
Neshite *see* Hittite language
New Testament 3:184, 3:185, 3:186, 6:420, 6:449, 6:452, 6:471, 6:479, 8:597, 8:638
   Acts of the Apostles 8:596
   Epistles of Saint Paul 8:597
   Gospels 3:185, 3:*188*, 6:419, 6:421, 8:638
   *see also* Bible
Nicene Creed 3:188
Niger-Congo languages 6:450
Nilometers 2:144, 4:258
nirvana 2:132, 2:133, 2:134, 3:183, 5:398
nomadism 4:285, 4:289, 7:492, 8:570–571
North American languages 6:451

obelisk 2:159, 5:350, 5:399
obsidian 3:192, 3:217, 4:277, 5:374, 6:458, 7:500, 7:504, 8:583, 8:585, 8:639, 10:741, 10:745, 10:799
ocher 3:229, 3:239, 6:433, 10:767
*Odyssey* (Homer) 2:98, 5:324, 5:325, 5:392–394, 6:463, 6:472, 8:581, 8:582
Old Testament 3:185, 3:214, 6:414, 6:464, 8:638, 9:690, 9:693, 9:701
   Book of Daniel 2:126, 7:*553*
   Book of Esther 10:787
   Book of Ezekiel 5:357
   Book of Judges 3:232,

3:233
   Book of Psalms 3:225
   Ecclesiasticus 3:225, 4:284
   Exodus 5:355, 5:357, 7:518, 7:537, 7:538, 8:634
   Genesis 5:355, 7:508, 8:564
   Pentateuch 6:430
   *see also* Bible
*Optics* (Ptolemy) 8:625
oracle 3:234, 5:333, 9:719, 10:799
oratory 10:731
*Oresteia* (Aeschylus) 1:25, 4:246

paganism 1:41, 3:239, 4:293, 4:298, 5:339
palaces 8:589–590
palaestra 5:327, 8:588, 8:639
pantheon 7:551, 7:559, 8:636, 8:639, 10:779
paper 3:179, 9:681, 10:785
papyrus 2:127, 2:159, 4:257, 5:353, 5:361, 5:399, 6:461, 9:681, 10:785
parchment 10:785
patriarchy 7:491–493, 10:781, 10:799
Pentateuch 6:430
percussion instruments 7:541, 9:*718*
Peripatetics 1:68
persecution 7:557–558, 8:597, 8:630, 9:678, 9:719, 10:732
*Persians* (Aeschylus) 4:245, 4:246
*Peutinger's Tabula* 4:*305*
*Phaedo* (Plato) 8:610, 8:611
philosophy 5:336, 5:395
   Chinese 3:178–179, 3:180–183, 3:203–206, 6:453–455
   Greek 1:67–69, 2:101, 2:102, 2:106, 3:180, 5:326, 5:336–339, 8:610–611, 9:652, 9:707–708, 10:782
   Indian 5:395–398
   Japanese 6:413
   Platonic 8:610–611
   Roman 9:652–655
pictograph 4:275, 4:319, 7:*512*, 7:529
pilgrims 5:367, 8:*595*
*pithoi* 6:439, 8:618
Platonism 8:610–611

plaza 8:584, 10:788
*Poetics* (Aristotle) 1:68
poetry 6:463–464
   Greek 9:674–675
   Indian 8:631–632
   Latin 2:109
   Roman 1:22–23, 2:109
*Politics* (Aristotle) 1:68, 1:69
polygamy 7:484, 7:486
pope 3:186
potter's wheel 8:618, 10:728
pottery 1:72, 3:165, 3:166, 3:169, 3:239, 8:617–619
   Anasazi 1:52, 1:53
   Anglo-Saxon 1:55
   Aryan 1:78
   Athenian 2:102, 8:619
   Babylonian 8:617–618
   Bantu 2:122–123
   black-figure 3:212, 3:239, 5:330
   Chavín 3:165, 3:166
   combware 6:441, 6:443
   Corinthian 3:212
   Cycladic 3:217
   Egyptian 8:618
   firing 8:617
   first 8:623, 9:681
   from Eridu 4:277
   Greek 3:*230*, 5:330, 8:618–619
   Harappan 6:406, 6:*408*
   Hopewell 5:*374*
   Japanese 8:617, 8:622
   Jomon 6:413
   Lapita 6:458
   La Tène style 2:*154*
   Mayan 4:249
   Melanesian 7:504
   Mesopotamian 8:617
   Mimbres style 1:52
   Moche 1:*72*, 7:524, 7:525, 7:526
   Mogollon 1:52
   Neolithic 2:152
   Nok culture 8:566, 8:568–569
   Olmec 8:586
   painted gray ware 1:78
   Peruvian 8:617
   red-figure 3:169, 5:330
   Roman 8:619
   Samian ware 8:619
   Shang 5:379, 5:380
   Spartan 9:711
   Turkey 8:617
Praktri 5:396

priests **3**:169, **7**:506, **7**:511, **7**:549, **9**:703, **10**:737, **10**:779
  Celtic **9**:668
  hygiene **5**:391
  medicine **5**:351
  and priestesses in Egypt **4**:254, **4**:261
prophets **3**:214, **3**:239, **5**:358, **6**:429
Proto-Indo-European language **6**:450
Psalm 48 **6**:418
*Psalm of Marduk* **6**:478
puppets, Indonesian **6**:*473*
pyramids **1**:45, **1**:64–65, **4**:258, **4**:309–311, **8**:626–628
  of the Americas **8**:626–628
  Babylonian **10**:737
  building **4**:309–311, **10**:733
  Egyptian **8**:626, **10**:733, **10**:748
  Mayan **7**:498, **8**:628
  Mesoamerican **1**:65
  Olmec **8**:585, **8**:627
  size of **4**:311
  stepped **10**:737
  *see also* ziggurats
pyramid texts **2**:127

rabbi **6**:431, **6**:479, **8**:596, **8**:639
*Ramayana* **4**:251, **6**:435, **6**:463, **8**:631–632
reincarnation **2**:134, **5**:364–365, **9**:705, **9**:719
religion **8**:635–638
  Achaemenid **1**:28–29, **10**:795, **10**:798
  in the Americas **10**:779
  Anasazi **1**:50
  and art **1**:71
  Aryan **1**:76–77
  Assyrian **2**:92, **2**:142
  Babylonian **4**:290, **4**:*307*, **6**:477–478, **9**:691
  Celtic **2**:155, **10**:779
  Chinese **3**:178–179, **6**:453–455, **8**:579
  earliest idea of God **8**:635
  Egyptian **1**:46–47, **2**:127–128, **8**:636
  Etruscan **4**:280
  of Germanic tribes **1**:55
  Greek **4**:288, **4**:292, **5**:326, **8**:636–637

Hebrew **4**:290, **4**:291, **4**:292, **4**:*293*
Hittite **5**:370–371
holy scriptures **8**:638
Hopewell culture **5**:374
India **5**:364–367, **10**:795
Japanese **1**:42–43, **6**:413
Jewish **6**:427–431, **10**:739
and language **6**:450
and literature **6**:464
Mayan **4**:283, **7**:502
Melanesian **7**:505
Mesopotamian **3**:228, **6**:409, **8**:564
Minoan **7**:521
Nubian **8**:575, **8**:576
numbers and magic **8**:579
Persian **1**:28–29, **4**:290, **10**:795–798
and philosophy **5**:395, **6**:413
Phoenician **4**:290, **8**:609
Roman **4**:283, **4**:290, **8**:637, **9**:650, **9**:662–663
Sasanian **9**:678, **10**:795, **10**:798
Sumerian **4**:290, **4**:295, **6**:409, **8**:636
and warfare **10**:773
Zapotec **10**:788
*Republic* (Plato) **5**:337, **8**:611
resurrection **3**:188, **3**:230–231, **4**:293, **4**:319, **6**:421
*Revolving Spheres* (Sosigenes of Alexandria) **2**:146
rhetoric **2**:105, **2**:106, **2**:159, **3**:170, **3**:239, **10**:731
*Rhind papyrus* **8**:*578*
Rig-Veda **5**:395, **8**:638
ritual **8**:639, **10**:737
roads **9**:644–647
  Chinese **3**:176, **9**:645
  construction **9**:646
  Indian **9**:646
  Mauryan **9**:644
  Roman **9**:644, **9**:645, **9**:646, **9**:647, **10**:757
  and soldiers **9**:645–646
rock art
  aboriginal **6**:432–433
  Kakadu **6**:432–433
Roman Catholic Church **3**:186

sacred **8**:587, **8**:638, **8**:639
sacred sites **1**:15, **1**:16, **10**:737
sacrifice **1**:76–77, **4**:293, **6**:428, **7**:502, **8**:588, **8**:636,

**8**:637, **9**:667–669, **10**:737
  animal **1**:78, **5**:364, **5**:365, **8**:621, **9**:662, **9**:668, **10**:737
  Babylonian **9**:667
  Christian **9**:669
  crop **9**:668–669
  Greek **9**:668
  human **1**:55, **2**:150, **2**:156, **9**:667–668, **9**:689, **10**:746
  Moche **7**:526, **9**:667
  Persian **1**:29
  Scythian **9**:689
Sanskrit **1**:77, **1**:78, **6**:435, **6**:450, **6**:479, **8**:632, **9**:673
sarcophagus **1**:38, **3**:230, **3**:*231*, **3**:239, **4**:*279*, **8**:*638*, **9**:*694*, **10**:*749*, **10**:799
scarab **1**:44, **4**:263, **10**:*744*
scribes **1**:40, **1**:44, **1**:45, **2**:159, **3**:209, **4**:249, **4**:259, **7**:511, **7**:512, **10**:785
scribe schools **4**:249
script
  Indus valley **6**:406, **6**:407
  Linear A and B **7**:548
sculpture
  Assyrian **2**:92
  of Buddha **1**:71
  Cycladic marble **3**:217–219
  Greek **1**:73
  Nok **8**:568
  Zapotec **10**:788–789
seals
  Assyrian **6**:*410*
  cylinder **7**:512, **7**:513
  glass **9**:681
  Indus valley **6**:407
  Sumerian **10**:*727*
Semitic languages **1**:31, **2**:115, **2**:159, **8**:609, **10**:785
Seven Wonders of the World **2**:159, **3**:201, **8**:587, **8**:639, **10**:749, **10**:794
  lighthouse at Alexandria **1**:40
  Mausoleum at Halicarnassus **5**:*363*
  statue of Zeus **1**:21
  Temple of Artemis **4**:270
shaman **5**:373, **7**:549, **7**:559
Shinto **1**:42–43, **2**:138, **6**:413
shrines **4**:261, **10**:*761*, **10**:779
silk **3**:178, **3**:*179*, **5**:379, **9**:681, **10**:752
Sino-Tibetan languages **6**:450
sirens **5**:394, **10**:748, **10**:799

slip **5**:330, **8**:568
smelting **8**:567, **10**:734
soapstone **8**:635, **8**:639
South American languages **6**:451
spindles **3**:198, **3**:199
sports **4**:300, **6**:465, **9**:715–718
  Chinese **9**:716
  Egyptian **9**:716, **9**:717, **9**:718
  Greek **9**:716
  hunting and fighting **9**:715
  Indus valley **9**:715
  Japanese **9**:716
  Mesopotamian **9**:716
  racing with horses **8**:570, **9**:716
  Sumerian **9**:716
  weaponless combat sports **9**:715–716
standing stones **2**:111, **9**:698, **10**:724–725
stelae **1**:32, **3**:209, **5**:370, **7**:498, **7**:500, **7**:559, **10**:746, **10**:790
stoa **1**:74, **1**:79
Stoicism **5**:338, **6**:476, **9**:652–653
stone circles *see* standing stones
stonemasons **1**:52
storytelling **6**:451
stupas **9**:672–673, **9**:719
stylus **1**:32, **2**:120, **2**:159, **3**:170, **4**:*251*, **5**:328, **5**:399, **7**:512, **7**:559, **10**:*732*
Sumerian language **1**:31, **1**:32, **2**:89, **2**:159, **7**:511
sundials **8**:625
sutras **2**:159, **4**:252, **5**:396
*Symposium, The* (Xenophon) **5**:325
synagogue **6**:431, **6**:479
syntax **10**:783, **10**:799

tablet **7**:512, **7**:546–547, **7**:*548*, **7**:559
*Tale of Sinhue* **6**:465
Talmud **6**:431
tannic acid **7**:539, **7**:559, **9**:667
Taoism **2**:138, **3**:173, **3**:178, **3**:180, **3**:181–182, **6**:453–455
  Celestial Masters movement **6**:455
  and Confucianism **6**:455

*Tao Te Ching* **3**:181, **3**:182, **6**:453–454
*tell* **6**:479, **7**:510
temples **1**:64–65, **1**:79, **4**:261, **10**:737–740
  Christian **10**:740
  Egyptian **10**:738
  the first **10**:737
  Greek **10**:738
  Indian **10**:739
  Mayan **8**:*627*, **8**:628
  Mesopotamian **10**:737
  Roman **10**:740
Ten Commandments **3**:214, **3**:224, **3**:239, **7**:536
terra-cotta **5**:329, **5**:376, **5**:399, **7**:*496*, **7**:*502*, **7**:*511*, **8**:568, **8**:619, **8**:639, **9**:*700*, **10**:*781*
Terra-cotta Army **3**:168
tombs **3**:228, **10**:747–750
  builders **10**:771
  Egyptian **10**:748
  graves of Ur **10**:747, **10**:768–769
  guards **10**:747
  inscriptions **10**:750
  Nabataean **8**:*602*
  writings inside **2**:127–128
Torah **3**:214–215, **6**:430, **6**:431, **7**:536
towns **5**:388
  plans **3**:175
  walled **1**:64
toys **3**:170–171, **4**:302
  Egyptian **3**:170–171
  Elamite **4**:*302*
  Indus valley **3**:170, **6**:408
  Roman **3**:171
tragedy **4**:244, **4**:245–246
trilithon **10**:725, **10**:799

underworld **1**:22, **1**:50, **4**:255, **4**:265, **5**:333, **6**:410, **7**:550, **7**:551
Upanishads **5**:395–397

Vedanta **5**:397
Vedas, the **1**:75, **1**:78, **4**:251, **4**:252, **5**:364, **5**:395, **5**:397, **6**:464, **9**:705
Vedic religion **4**:244, **7**:519

wall paintings **2**:152, **7**:522
weaving **3**:199, **7**:524
West African language group **2**:123

witchcraft **7**:504
women **10**:779–782
  admission to school **9**:653
  Athenian **7**:493
  authors **9**:677
  Babylonian **2**:116
  charioteers **9**:716
  Chinese **7**:492, **10**:782
  doctors in Egypt **10**:782
  Egyptian **7**:506, **7**:507, **7**:508, **10**:781–782
  Etruscan **4**:280
  goddesses **10**:779
  Greek **5**:327, **7**:492, **7**:507, **7**:508
  Jewish **7**:493
  and men **7**:508
  as mistresses of the household **10**:780
  poets **9**:674–675
  prestige **7**:493, **7**:555
  priestesses **10**:779
  role among Israelites **3**:233
  Roman **1**:26, **7**:492, **7**:508, **9**:662, **10**:781–782
  Scythian **9**:688
  Spartan **9**:712
  *see also* matriarchy
*Works and Days* (Hesiod) **6**:463
worship **8**:635
  *see also* ancestor worship; fire worship
writing **10**:783–785
  Akkadian **1**:32–33, **10**:784
  arrival of **8**:620, **8**:623
  Assyrian **10**:784
  Babylonian **2**:120, **10**:784
  Chinese **3**:179, **5**:380, **6**:412, **8**:623, **10**:784
  and civilization **10**:783, **10**:785
  cuneiform **1**:32, **6**:479, **8**:577, **8**:609, **8**:623, **9**:*696*, **10**:*783*, **10**:784
  Dorian **9**:711
  Egyptian **2**:127, **4**:249, **4**:259, **4**:260, **8**:623, **10**:784
  Etruscan **4**:280
  and Greek philosophy **5**:339
  hieratic **4**:259
  Indian **1**:75, **1**:78
  Indus valley **6**:406
  Japanese **10**:784
  Kassite **6**:438
  and male power **7**:506
  materials **10**:784–785

  Mayan **7**:500, **10**:789
  Mesoamerican **4**:249
  Mesopotamian **2**:89, **7**:511, **7**:512
  Minoan **7**:521
  Phoenician **8**:609
  proto-cuneiform **4**:274
  Roman **5**:346, **10**:*732*
  science and **9**:681
  Sumerian **8**:623, **9**:*696*, **10**:728, **10**:783
  words **10**:784
  Zapotec **10**:789
writing tablet **5**:346, **5**:399

yin and yang **3**:182, **5**:354, **6**:454
Yoga **5**:396, **5**:*397*

Zapotecan languages **6**:451
Zen **2**:138
Zend Avesta **10**:796
*Zhuangzi see Chuang-tzu*
ziggurats **1**:65, **2**:86, **2**:113, **2**:142, **2**:159, **3**:192, **4**:*269*, **4**:276, **7**:510, **7**:512, **8**:628, **10**:769
  Assyrian **8**:628, **10**:737
  Babylonian **8**:628, **9**:667
  Mesopotamian **8**:628
  Sumerian **8**:628, **8**:636
zodiac **2**:96, **2**:*97*, **2**:159
Zoroastrianism **9**:678, **10**:795–798

# Geographical Index

This index includes place-names appearing in the articles and captions. For place-names mentioned in the maps and site plans, see the Index of Maps and Site Plans.

Page numbers in *italic type* refer to illustrations. **Boldface** numbers preceding a colon indicate the volume number.

Abu Simbel **8**:*576*, **8**:633
Abydos **8**:623
Acre **8**:607
Acropolis **1**:20–21, **2**:101, **7**:498, **7**:534, **8**:598, **8**:*599*, **10**:745–746
Actium **1**:57, **2**:108
Adrianople **4**:313, **4**:314
Aegean Islands **7**:518
Aegean Sea **7**:548
Afghanistan **7**:510
Africa **2**:121–124, **7**:489, **7**:490, **8**:617
Agade *see* Akkad
Ajanta **1**:72, **10**:*738*
Akkad **1**:30, **1**:32, **1**:34, **1**:36, **3**:221, **4**:303, **9**:676, **9**:685
Akrotiri **1**:72, **3**:218, **7**:522, **7**:523
Alesia **2**:139
Alexandria **1**:38, **1**:40–41, **1**:56, **3**:196, **4**:306, **6**:*461*, **6**:*462*, **6**:470, **8**:580, **9**:680, **10**:744
Algeria **8**:622, **10**:*754*
Allahabad **9**:671
Alodia **8**:576
Altamira, Spain **5**:387
Al-Ubaid **10**:726
Amadeus Basin **10**:766
Amarna **1**:45, **4**:254, **7**:555–556, **8**:*573*, **8**:589, **10**:762
Amazon Valley **8**:622
Amber Route **9**:646
Amu Darya **8**:591
Anagni **5**:354
Anatolia **3**:215, **5**:368, **8**:608
Andes Mountains **8**:622
Anshan **1**:18, **3**:220
Antioch **9**:680
Apennines **4**:278, **4**:319
Arabia **8**:570, **9**:716
Aral Sea **8**:591
Aratta **4**:275
Armenia **9**:679
Arretium **8**:619
Artemisium **10**:786
Arzawa **5**:368

Ashur **2**:86–87, **2**:90, **2**:91, **2**:95
Asia **8**:570, **8**:617, **8**:621, **10**:732
Asia Minor **3**:239, **7**:517, **9**:679, **10**:791
Assur *see* Ashur
Assyria **1**:58, **2**:86–87, **2**:88–89, **2**:90–95, **2**:142–143, **7**:509, **7**:510, **8**:607, **9**:690–691, **10**:764
Atacama Desert **7**:539, **7**:540
Athens **1**:18, **1**:19, **1**:20–21, **1**:68, **1**:74, **2**:98, **2**:99, **2**:100–102, **5**:*325*, **5**:330, **7**:533, **7**:546, **8**:598, **8**:610, **9**:653, **9**:708, **9**:709, **9**:710, **10**:786, **10**:794
   Acropolis **1**:20–21, **1**:*20*, **2**:101, **7**:498, **7**:534, **8**:598, **8**:*599*, **10**:745–746
   Erechtheion **1**:21, **2**:99
   Parthenon **1**:20, **1**:*21*, **1**:74, **2**:99, **2**:101, **8**:598
Atlantis, site of **7**:522
Aul Ul **9**:687
Australia **1**:14–17, **6**:432–433, **6**:*451*, **7**:503, **7**:506, **10**:766–767, **10**:779
Avebury **2**:110–111
Axum **8**:573, **8**:576
Ayers Rock *see* Uluru
Ayodhya **8**:631

Babylon **1**:39, **2**:88, **2**:91, **2**:93, **2**:112–114, **2**:*119*, **3**:192, **3**:199, **3**:220, **3**:221, **3**:222, **4**:266, **4**:267, **4**:268, **5**:356, **5**:357, **5**:358, **5**:368, **5**:369, **5**:370, **6**:417, **6**:436, **6**:437, **6**:470, **6**:477, **6**:478, **7**:510, **7**:532, **7**:538, **7**:554, **8**:600, **9**:691
   Hanging Gardens **2**:113, **2**:114, **7**:553, **7**:554
Babylonia **6**:436–437
Babylonian Empire **2**:125, **7**:509, **7**:553
Bactria **1**:39, **6**:446, **6**:447, **8**:595
Badon Hill **1**:55
Baghdad **9**:676
Bakhtaran **6**:436
Balkans **7**:518

Bath (Aquae Sulis) **5**:*390*
Beijing **3**:228, **10**:747
Beirut **8**:606
Belize **7**:498
Bellona **9**:650
Benares *see* Varanasi
Benin **8**:568
Berot (Berytus) **8**:606, **8**:608
Bethlehem **3**:224, **3**:225, **6**:419
Bismarck Archipelago **6**:457, **7**:503, **7**:504, **9**:694
Black Sea **9**:686
Bodh Gaya **2**:132, **2**:135
Bosporus **3**:223
Britain **2**:129–130, **10**:724–725, **10**:732, **10**:753
   Anglo-Saxon **1**:54–55
   Celtic **7**:493, **7**:539
   Roman **1**:54, **1**:55, **2**:148, **2**:154, **2**:155, **3**:194, **5**:343, **5**:345–346, **8**:637, **9**:657
British Columbia **7**:518
Brittany **1**:55, **2**:155
Bubastic **8**:589
Burkina Faso **2**:124
Byblos **4**:265, **5**:350, **8**:606, **8**:608
Byzantium **3**:207, **3**:208, **9**:657, **9**:660
   *see also* Constantinople

Caere **4**:281
Calah **2**:86, **2**:92, **2**:95, **2**:116, **2**:142–143, **6**:*409*, **8**:565
Caledonia **7**:493
Cambodia **3**:237
Cameroon **8**:*567*
Camulodunum (Colchester) **2**:130
Canaan **5**:355, **5**:357, **7**:537
Canary Islands **8**:626
Cannae **5**:348
Capua **9**:713
Caracalla **5**:390, **9**:666
Caral **8**:626
Carchemish **7**:553
Caria **10**:749
Carthage **2**:149–150, **5**:347, **5**:399, **8**:607, **8**:608, **9**:657, **9**:658, **9**:693, **10**:764
Caspian Sea **8**:591
Çatal Hüyük **1**:66, **1**:70,

**2**:151–152, **3**:192, **5**:376, **10**:751, **10**:779
Caucasus Mountains **8**:570, **10**:794
Cayster River **4**:271
Central America **3**:209, **3**:192, **7**:498–502
Chaco Canyon **1**:51, **1**:53
Chaeronea, Battle of **5**:325, **6**:469, **8**:605
Chalcatzingo **8**:586
Chalôns **2**:104, **5**:381, **5**:382, **5**:383, **5**:384
Chang'an **2**:157–158, **3**:175, **6**:466, **9**:704
Chavín de Huantár **3**:164, **3**:165, **3**:166
Chichen Itza **7**:499
Chile **7**:540
Chillicothe, High Bank **5**:373
China **2**:157–158, **3**:167, **3**:172–179, **3**:180, **3**:183, **3**:192, **3**:204, **3**:237, **4**:247–248, **4**:291, **6**:411, **8**:617, **10**:747
Chogha Zanbil **4**:268, **4**:269
Chomsongdae Observatory **6**:*445*
Choson **6**:442
Chu Dien **10**:760
Cilicia **3**:189
Cisalpine Gaul **2**:154, **2**:155
Citium **9**:*652*
Coatzacoalcos River **8**:583
Colchester *see* Camulodunum
Colosseum **3**:201–202, **3**:*201*, **9**:716
Congo **7**:490
Constantinople **3**:208, **8**:590, **9**:660, **9**:666, **9**:680
   *see also* Byzantium
Copán **3**:209–210
Corfu **3**:211
Corinth **3**:211, **10**:*773*
Cornwall **2**:155
Corsica **7**:517
Crete **3**:218, **3**:219, **6**:439–440, **7**:520–523, **7**:547, **7**:548, **9**:693
Crimea **9**:686
Croton **8**:629, **8**:630
Ctesiphon **8**:591, **9**:680
Cumae **4**:279, **9**:650
Cyprus **8**:608

Czech Republic **8**:*622*

Dacia **4**:312, **5**:345
Dahshur **8**:*626*
Dainzu **10**:788
Danube River **5**:382, **6**:475, **9**:686
Dattassa **5**:369
Deir el-Bahri **5**:349, **5**:*350*
Deir el-Medina **10**:771
Delos **3**:217, **3**:219
Delphi **1**:74, **3**:234–235, **5**:333, **9**:707
Denderah **2**:97
Denmark **7**:539, **7**:543
Dholavira **6**:405
Diapolis **8**:629
Dodona **10**:794
Don River **9**:686
Dor **8**:607
Duma **8**:602
Dunhuang **3**:183, **4**:247–248, **4**:316, **6**:461
Dur-Kurigalzu **6**:437
Dur Sharrukin **2**:91, **2**:92, **2**:118, **2**:143
Dur Untash **4**:267

East Africa **8**:566, **8**:620, **8**:621
Easter Island **8**:612, **8**:613, **8**:614, **9**:694
Eastern Roman Empire **9**:660, **9**:680
*see also* Roman Empire
Ecbatana **8**:591, **8**:600
Edessa **9**:679
Edfu **4**:291
Egypt **1**:18, **1**:40, **1**:41, **1**:56, **1**:63, **2**:88, **2**:89, **2**:122, **2**:127, **2**:140, **3**.192, **3**:196–197, **4**:253–260, **6**:469, **8**:572, **8**:573–574, **8**:622, **8**:633–634, **9**:700, **10**:743, **10**:744, **10**:762
  Lower **4**:253, **10**:743
  Upper **4**:253, **10**:743
Elam **4**:266–267, **4**:267–268, **9**:696
El Mirador **8**:628
El Salvador **8**:628
Emesa **10**:791
England **1**:54, **2**:110–111, **2**:155, **10**:*755*

Ephesus **4**:270–271, **5**:348, **6**:462, **7**:492
Epidaurus **4**:272–273, **5**:*389*
Epirus **8**:605
Eran **9**:671
Erech **1**:30, **4**:274–275, **4**:307–308, **6**:409, **7**:510, **9**:676, **10**:726, **10**:729
Erechtheion **1**:21, **2**:99
Eridu **4**:276–277, **6**:410, **7**:510, **7**:511, **10**:726, **10**:730
Erishti-Aya **2**:117
Esagila, Babylon **2**:119
Ethiopia **8**:576
Euphrates River **2**:113, **2**:117, **7**:509, **8**:621, **9**:692, **10**:768
Eurasia **8**:570
Europe **8**:621

Fars **8**:600
Fertile Crescent **6**:477, **7**:541, **8**:621
Fiji **6**:456, **6**:457, **7**:503, **7**:504
Flavian Amphitheater *see* Colosseum
Four Corners **1**:50, **1**:51
Franconia **4**:298

Galilee **6**:425
Gandhara **6**:448
Ganges River **1**:75, **5**:341, **5**:367, **8**:594, **9**:670
Ganweriwala **6**:405
Gaul **1**:56, **2**:103–104, **2**:139, **2**:153, **2**:154, **2**:155, **4**:298, **4**:299, **5**:382, **9**:700, **9**:714
Gaza **8**:602
Gedrosian Desert **1**:39
Germany, Iron Age **3**:215
Gila River **1**:52
Gilbert Islands **7**:516
Giza **4**:258, **4**:309–311, **8**:626, **8**:627, **9**:692, **10**:748
Gordium **1**:38
Gournia **7**:520
Granicus River **1**:38
Great Wall of China **3**:168, **3**:173, **4**:247, **4**:316–318, **10**:774–775
Greece **2**:98–102, **3**:193, **3**:211, **3**:215–216, **3**:234, **7**:518, **8**:587, **8**:604
  classical **5**:324–331

Dark Ages **5**:324
  Hellenistic period **2**:159, **3**:230, **6**:470–471, **8**:565, **8**:639
  Mycenaean period **5**:324, **7**:545–548, **10**:748
Guam **7**:515
Guatemala **7**:498, **8**:627, **8**:628, **10**:745
Gupta Empire **5**:340–342, **5**:365, **5**:367, **6**:434, **6**:447, **8**:594, **8**:595

Hacilar **10**:779
Hadrian's Wall **5**:343, **5**:345–346, **9**:646, **9**:657
Hadrumetum **5**:386
Hagar Qim, Malta **10**:737
Halicarnassus **5**:362, **5**:*363*, **10**:749
Hamadan **6**:436, **8**:591
Hanging Gardens of Babylon **2**:113, **2**:114, **7**:553, **7**:554
Harappa **1**:64, **1**:65, **3**:199, **6**:405, **6**:406, **7**:519, **7**:528
Harran **2**:91
Hasholme **10**:*755*
Hastings **1**:55
Hat Giang River **10**:761
Hatti **5**:368, **5**:369
Hattusha (Hattusas) **5**:368, **5**:369
Hawaii **7**:517, **8**:612, **8**:613
Hegra **8**:602
Heliopolis **10**:787
Hellespont **10**:786
Herculaneum **5**:360–361
Himalayas **6**:405
Hippo **2**:105, **2**:106
Hissarlik **10**:758–759
Hittite Empire **5**:*368*, **7**:548
Honduras **7**:498
Honshu **1**:42, **6**:411
Hopeton **5**:373
Huaca de la Luna **7**:526
Huaca del Sol **7**:526

India **2**:84, **2**:131–133, **3**:182, **3**:192, **5**:340–342, **7**:494–497, **8**:594–595, **9**:670–671, **9**:672–673
Indonesia **3**:237, **7**:514
Indus plain **6**:404
Indus River **7**:528, **7**:529

Iolkos **7**:548
Ionia **3**:239
Ipsus, Battle of **6**:470, **6**:471, **7**:494
Iran **3**:213, **3**:222, **8**:591, **9**:678
Iraq **10**:736
Ireland **2**:153, **7**:523, **7**:550
Israel **5**:356, **5**:357, **8**:606
Italy **2**:104, **2**:154, **2**:155, **7**:540
Ithaca **5**:393, **8**:581
Itjtawy **10**:743

Japan **1**:43, **4**:294, **6**:411–413
Jericho **1**:64, **3**:191, **3**:*191*, **5**:386, **6**:414–415, **10**:773, **10**:779
Jerusalem **2**:125, **3**:224, **3**:225, **3**:226, **5**:356, **5**:*356*, **5**:357, **5**:358, **5**:359, **6**:416–418, **6**:428, **6**:430–431, **7**:487, **7**:536, **7**:553–554, **8**:596, **9**:680, **9**:690, **10**:739
Jerwan **8**:565
Joppa **8**:607
Jordan **8**:602
Jotapata **6**:425
Judaea **5**:344, **5**:357, **5**:359, **6**:425
Judah **3**:220, **5**:356, **5**:357, **6**:416–417, **7**:553, **9**:688, **9**:690

Kadesh **5**:368, **5**:369
Kakadu region **6**:432–433
Kalhu *see* Calah
Kalinga **2**:84
Karduniash (Babylon) **6**:437
Karnak **1**:46, **4**:*261*, **5**:369, **8**:*634*, **10**:738, **10**:743
Kashi **5**:367
Kastri **3**:219
Kefala Hill **6**:440
Kerma, kingdom of **8**:573, **8**:575
Keros **3**:219
Khafra **4**:309, **4**:311
Khania **7**:520, **7**:548
Khorasmia **10**:797
Khorsabad **8**:590
Kish **4**:274, **4**:275, **8**:580, **9**:677
Knossos **3**:218, **6**:439–440,

Knossos (cont.)
7:520–522, 7:547, 7:548,
8:619
Koguryo 6:444, 6:445
Korea 6:411, 6:441–445
Kostromskaya 8:570
Krisa 3:234
Kroton 9:718
Kuei-shuang see Kushan
Kush 8:566, 8:567, 8:573,
8:575, 8:576
Kushan Empire 6:446–448
Kusinagara 2:133
Kutau 6:458
Kyrgyzstan 8:571
Kyushu 6:411

Lachish 9:690
Laconia 9:711
Lagash 4:275
Lake Turkana 8:620
Lang Bac 10:761
Lanka 8:631, 9:670
see also Sri Lanka
Larsa 2:119
Lascaux 6:459–460, 8:635
La Venta 8:583, 8:584, 8:585
Lebanon 8:606, 10:764
Lefkandi 7:548
Lesbos 9:674
Leuktra 5:325, 9:712
Levant 8:606, 8:607, 8:639,
10:743
Levkas 9:674
Lhasa 2:138
Libya 3:218, 8:622, 9:699
Londinium (London) 2:130
London see Londinium
Lumbini, Nepal 2:131
Luoyang 2:158, 6:466, 6:467
Luristan 1:28
Luxor see Thebes
Lydia 3:220, 3:235, 3:239
Lysimachus 4:271

Macedon 1:37, 3:223, 6:468
Macedonia 5:325, 6:471,
8:604–605, 8:608, 9:713
see also Macedon
Madhya Pradesh 9:672
Maes Howe, Orkney 9:698
Maghada 7:494, 7:497, 8:595
Maiden Castle, southwest
England 2:156
Makuria 8:576
Malatya, Gate of 1:70
Malkata 8:589, 8:590

Malta 8:637, 10:737
Marathon 1:18, 1:19, 2:100,
3:223, 4:245, 4:246, 5:325,
9:712, 10:787
Mari 2:119
Marianas 7:514, 7:515
Marlborough Downs 10:725
Marquesas Islands 8:613
Marshall Islands 7:516
Masada 7:487–488
Mathura 6:446, 6:448
Media 8:591, 9:690
Medinet Habu 5:389, 7:517,
8:589
Mediterranean Sea 7:517,
9:694, 10:752, 10:755,
10:757
Melanesia 6:456, 7:486, 7:504,
7:514
Me Linh 10:760, 10:761
Melos 3:217
Memphis 8:589, 10:743
Meroe 8:566, 8:573, 8:575,
8:576
Mesa Verde 1:50, 1:51, 1:53
Mesoamerica 8:627, 10:741
Mesopotamia 1:30, 2:90,
2:96, 2:115, 2:119, 3:192,
4:266, 4:268, 4:274, 4:286,
5:356, 6:436, 7:509–513,
9:676–677, 9:679, 9:688,
9:695, 9:714, 10:733,
10:756, 10:768
Lower 8:623
Metapontum 8:630
Mexico 7:534–535,
8:583–585, 8:622, 9:703,
10:741–742, 10:788–790
Micronesia 6:456
Middle East 7:531
Miletus 8:629
Milvian Bridge 3:207
Mississippi River valley 5:372
Mitla 10:788–789
Mittani 1:44
Moche River 7:524
Mogao Ku caves 4:247, 4:248
Mohenjo Daro 1:64, 1:65,
1:71, 3:192, 3:199, 5:388,
6:405, 6:406, 7:528–529,
8:635, 10:777
Monte Albán 1:65, 6:451,
7:534–535, 10:788, 10:789,
10:790
Moravia 7:541
Morelos 8:583, 8:586
Mosul 8:565

Mount Olympus 8:587, 8:636
Mount Sinai 7:536
Mount Vesuvius 5:360, 8:615,
9:657, 9:685, 9:713
Mumbai (Bombay) 10:739
Musa River 8:603
Mutina 1:56
Myanmar (Burma) 2:137,
3:237
Mycenae 1:24, 7:545, 7:546,
7:547, 7:548, 8:619

Nan Madol, islets of 7:515,
7:516
Napata 8:573, 8:576
Naples 10:750
Naqsh-e Rustam 10:797,
10:798
Nazareth 6:419
Neapolis 5:360
Nefud Desert 8:602
Newark, Ohio 5:373
New Caledonia 6:458, 7:503,
7:504
New Guinea 6:456, 7:503,
7:504
New Ireland 7:504
New Zealand 8:612
Nicaea 3:186, 3:188
Nigeria 8:566–568
Nile River 2:144, 4:253,
4:254, 4:258, 4:261, 4:262,
4:290, 4:304, 4:310, 8:572,
8:574, 8:575, 8:633, 10:738,
10:751, 10:778
delta area 3:239, 4:262
Nile valley 3:192
Nimrud see Calah
Nineveh 1:33, 1:58, 2:88,
2:89, 2:91, 2:92, 2:95,
2:114, 6:409, 6:461,
8:564–565, 9:690, 9:691,
9:702
Ninua see Nineveh
Nisa 8:591
Nobatia 8:576
North Africa 5:348, 8:566,
8:570, 8:608
Nubia 8:572, 8:573–574,
8:575, 8:626, 8:627
Lower 8:572, 8:575, 8:576
Upper 8:575

Oaxaca 4:249, 7:534, 8:583,
10:741, 10:788
Olympia 8:587–588, 10:794
Orkney 9:697–698

Ostia 3:195, 4:315
Ostia Antica 9:647
Oxus River 8:591

Pacific Ocean 6:456, 8:612
Paekche 6:444
Palatine Hill, Rome 8:589,
9:665
Palau 7:514, 7:515
Palenque 7:498, 7:499
Palestine 3:184, 5:355–356,
5:357, 5:359, 5:369, 9:690
Palmyra 10:791
Pannonia 4:313, 5:383, 5:384
Pantheon (Rome) 1:65, 9:665,
9:666
Papua New Guinea 7:504
Paris 4:299
Paros 3:217
Parsa see Persepolis
Parsa region 1:18
Parthava 8:591
Parthenon (Athens) 1:20, 1:21,
1:74, 2:99, 2:101, 8:598
Parthia 1:56, 6:475
Pasargadae 3:220, 3:221,
8:600, 10:796
Pataliputra 5:341, 5:342,
7:494, 7:495, 7:496,
8:594–595
Patna 8:594–595
Peloponnese 5:324, 5:325,
7:545, 9:711, 9:712
Persepolis 1:29, 1:66, 3:222,
3:223, 4:290, 8:590,
8:600–601, 10:787, 10:796
Persia 9:678
Persian Empire 1:18–19,
3:220–223, 4:268, 5:324,
6:417, 6:470, 8:600, 10:764,
10:786
Persian Gulf 1:18, 7:509
Peru 1:71, 1:72, 3:164,
7:524–527, 7:540, 8:577,
8:626, 9:703
Perugia 4:315
Petra 8:602–603
Phaistos 7:520, 7:521
Pharsalus 2:140
Philippi 1:56, 2:107
Philippines 7:514
Phoenicia 7:533, 8:574
Phrygia 9:65
Piramesse 8:633
Plataea 1:18, 1:19, 3:223,
5:325, 10:786
Pnyx, Athens 2:100

Pohnpei 7:515, 7:516
Polynesia 6:456, 7:518
Pompeii 3:169, 5:360, 5:*378*,
    7:*544*, 8:*611*, 8:615–616,
    9:657
Pons Aemilius 9:*646*
Propylaia 1:21
Pueblo Bonito 1:50, 1:53
Punjab 1:75, 1:77, 7:494
Punt 5:350, 5:399
Purushapura 6:446
Pylos 7:546, 7:*547*, 7:548
Pythagoria 5:389

Qin 3:167
Qufu, Shandong Province
    3:*204*
Quin (Ireland) 5:*375*
Quirigua 3:210, 7:500
Qumran 3:226, 3:*227*, 6:*430*
Qurna 10:744

Rakhigari 6:405
Rano Raraku 8:614
Ravenna 9:660
Red Sea 6:*427*, 7:*519*, 7:536,
    7:*537*, 8:634
Resina 5:361
Rhodes 9:*684*
Ring of Brodgar 9:698
Roman Empire 1:41, 1:47,
    2:103, 2:107, 2:147, 2:154,
    3:194, 3:196–197, 3:207,
    4:288, 5:343, 5:381,
    5:382–383, 8:597, 8:603,
    8:606, 8:637, 9:656–663,
    9:665–666, 10:791, 10:792
    frontier in Britain
        5:345–346
    see also Eastern Roman
        Empire; Western Roman
        Empire
Roman Republic 2:139, 4:278,
    4:279
Rome 1:22, 1:56, 2:104,
    2:109, 2:139, 2:149, 3:186,
    3:*187*, 3:*208*, 4:313, 4:314,
    4:315, 5:388, 7:557, 9:654,
    9:657, 9:664–666,
    Colosseum 3:201–202,
        3:*201*, 9:666, 9:716
    Forum 3:*193*, 9:664, 9:665
    Palatine Hill 8:589, 9:665
    Pantheon 1:*65*, 9:665,
        9:666
    seven hills 9:656
Rubicon 2:140

Russia 7:519

Saguntum 5:347
Sahara Desert 2:122, 8:566,
    8:571
Saint Albans see Verulamium
Salamis 1:18, 1:19, 2:100,
    4:245, 4:246, 5:325, 10:786
Salisbury Plain 10:724–725
Samoa 6:456, 6:457, 8:612,
    9:694
Samos 1:66, 6:461, 8:629
Sanchi 7:*497*, 9:672–673
San Lorenzo 8:583, 8:585
Santorini see Thera
Saqqara 4:258, 9:*717*
Sardis 3:220
Sarnath 2:132, 2:133
Sasan 9:678
Scioto River 5:372, 5:373
Scotland 2:155, 5:345, 7:493
Scythia 8:591, 9:686
Sea of Galilee 6:419
Seip 5:373
Seleucia 2:120
Shandong Province 3:205
Shanxi 10:*740*
Shaolin Monastery (near
    Zhengzhou) 2:138
Shortugai 6:404
Siberia 7:539
Sicily 2:102, 2:149, 3:211,
    5:347, 7:517, 8:580, 9:674,
    9:714
Sidon 1:38, 8:606, 8:607,
    8:608
Silk Road 2:138, 2:158, 3:172,
    3:178, 3:183, 4:247–248,
    6:447, 8:591, 10:752
Silla 6:444, 6:445
Sinai 5:350, 5:399
Sinai Desert 7:536, 8:602
Sind 7:528
Sipan 7:525, 7:527
Sippar 3:214
Skara Brae, Orkney 1:64,
    9:697–698
Skipshelleren, Norway 5:386
Snaketown 1:52
Society Islands 8:612
Solomon Islands 7:503, 7:504
Son River 8:594
South Africa 7:543
South America 7:518, 10:734
Southeast Asia 2:137, 3:183,
    3:237
Spain 2:153, 4:314, 5:347

Sparta 2:102, 5:324, 5:325,
    5:392, 7:508, 9:711–712,
    10:758
Sphinx 4:309, 4:*311*
Sri Lanka 2:136, 2:137, 3:183,
    8:595
    see also Lanka
Stanegate 5:345
Stenness, Stones of 9:698
Stonehenge 2:110,
    10:724–725
stone-money island see Yap
Styx, River 3:230, 3:*231*
Sudan 8:566, 8:572
Sumer 3:192, 3:221, 3:228,
    4:266, 4:274, 4:275, 4:276,
    8:623, 8:636, 8:637,
    10:726–730, 10:768,
    10:774, 10:779
Susa 2:88, 2:91, 4:266, 4:267,
    4:268, 6:478, 8:600, 8:601,
    8:617, 10:787, 10:*795*
Syracuse 2:102, 2:149, 8:580,
    9:674, 9:683
Syria 3:215, 5:343, 5:369,
    7:553, 8:602, 8:606, 8:608,
    9:676, 9:679, 9:688, 9:690,
    10:735, 10:791
Syros 3:217

Tabasco 8:627
Tahiti 8:612, 8:613
Taklamakan Desert 7:539
Tarpeian Rock 3:216
Tarsus 8:596
Taruga 8:567
Ta-Seti see Nubia
Tassili caves, Sahara 1:72
Taxila 6:446, 8:591
Tayma 2:125
Tebtunis 5:391
Teotihuacán 1:65, 7:534,
    8:628, 10:741–742, 10:790
Teotitlan del Valle 10:788
Thailand 2:137, 3:237, 8:622
Thanh Haa 3:238
Thebes (Egypt) 1:44, 1:46,
    1:71, 2:88, 7:556, 8:589,
    8:590, 10:743–744, 10:770,
    10:772
Thebes (Greece) 7:546, 8:604
Thera (Santorini) 1:72, 3:218,
    3:219, 7:518, 7:522, 7:523,
    9:*693*
Thermopylae 1:18, 5:325,
    9:*711*, 9:712, 10:786
Thessalonika 4:312, 6:468

Thessaly 3:215
Thrace 3:223, 9:713
Thuria 5:362
Tiber River 5:388, 5:390,
    9:664
Tibet 2:138, 3:183
Tibur 5:344
Ticinus 5:348
Tigris River 2:90, 2:93, 2:142,
    7:509, 8:565, 8:591, 8:621,
    9:692
Tikal 7:498, 8:*627*,
    10:745–746
Tiryns 7:546, 7:548
Tonalà River 8:583
Tonga 6:456, 6:457, 8:612,
    9:694
Transalpine Gaul 2:154
Trasimene 5:348
Trebia 5:348
Tres Zapotes 8:583
Troy 1:22, 1:*61*, 5:325, 7:518,
    10:758–759
Trujillo 7:524
Tuna-el-Gebel 10:*735*
Tunisia 8:607
Tunnel of Eupalinos (Samos)
    1:66, 5:389
Turkey 2:151–152, 2:153,
    8:617, 9:676, 10:758–759
Tyre 8:606, 8:607, 8:608,
    8:609, 10:764–765
Tyrolean Alps 7:540

Uaxactun 10:745
Ugarit 8:607
Ujjain 8:595
Ukraine 5:385, 7:541, 8:571,
    9:685, 9:686
Ulster 7:550
Uluru 10:766–767
Upper Zab River 2:142
Ur 1:30, 1:64, 3:228, 4:266,
    4:267, 4:275, 4:301, 5:355,
    6:409, 6:422, 7:510, 7:511,
    7:*513*, 7:541, 9:677,
    9:695–696, 10:726, 10:727,
    10:728, 10:729, 10:730,
    10:747, 10:768–769
Urarta 9:690
Uruk see Erech
Utica 8:607, 9:*661*
Uxmal 7:499

Valley of the Kings 4:256,
    4:259, 5:350, 10:743,
    10:744, 10:748, 10:762,

Valley of the Kings (cont.)
  **10**:763, **10**:770–772
Valley of the Queens **4**:256,
  **10**:744, **10**:770
Vanuatu **7**:503, **7**:504
Varanasi (Benares) **5**:367
Vasio **10**:731
Veracruz **8**:585
Vergina **6**:469
Verulamium (Saint Albans)
  **2**:130
Vesuvius, Mount **5**:360,
  **8**:615–616, **9**:657, **9**:685,
  **9**:713
Vidisha **9**:673
Vietnam **3**:236–237,
  **10**:760–761
Vindolanda **5**:346
Vouillé **4**:314

Wales **2**:155, **7**:550, **10**:724
Warka *see* Erech
West Africa **7**:543, **8**:566–568
Western Roman Empire **9**:660
  *see also* Roman Empire

Xi'an **2**:157
Xianyang **2**:157, **3**:167, **3**:175

Yagul **10**:788, **10**:789
Yam, kingdom of **8**:573, **8**:575
Yap (the stone-money island)
  **7**:515
Yazd **10**:797, **10**:*798*
Yellow River (Huang He)
  **3**:172, **5**:380

Zagros Mountains **6**:436
Zama **5**:348, **10**:*774*
Zambia **2**:122
Zengzhou **3**:175
Zion **6**:416

# Comprehensive Index

Page numbers in *italic type* refer to illustrations. **Boldface** numbers preceding a colon indicate the volume number.

Aaron **7**:536
abacus **5**:328, **8**:577, **8**:639
*abaton* **4**:272
aboriginal culture **1**:14–17,
  **6**:432–433, **6**:*451*, **7**:506,
  **10**:766–767, **10**:779
  art and music **1**:16
  dreamtime **1**:15, **1**:16,
    **6**:433, **6**:451, **10**:766
  hunting **1**:16, **1**:17
  mythology **6**:433, **10**:779
  rock art **6**:432–433
  six seasons **6**:432
Abraham **5**:355, **6**:427, **8**:638
Absalom **3**:225
Abu Simbel (Temple of
  Ramses II) **8**:*576*, **8**:633
Abydos **8**:623
Academy, Plato's **1**:67
Achaemenes **1**:18
Achaemenids **1**:18–19, **3**:220
  kings **8**:600, **10**:786–787
  map of empire **1**:*18*
  religion **1**:28–29, **10**:795,
    **10**:798
Achilles **1**:25, **5**:393, **8**:581,
  **8**:605, **10**:759
Acre **8**:607
Acropolis **1**:20–21, **1**:*20*,
  **2**:101, **7**:498, **7**:534, **8**:598,
  **8**:*599*, **10**:745–746
Actaeon **5**:334
Actium, Battle of **1**:57, **2**:108
Acts of the Apostles **8**:596
acupuncture **3**:179, **5**:354,
  **9**:682
Adad-nirari II **2**:90
Adapa **4**:277
Adena culture **5**:372, **5**:373
*Admonition for Girls* (Ban
  Zhao) **10**: 782
adobe bricks **7**:525
Adrianople, Battle of **4**:313,
  **4**:314
adze **4**:287, **4**:319
Aegean Islands **7**:518
Aegean Sea **7**:548
Aegeus **5**:334
Aegisthus **1**:25, **4**:246
Aelia Capitolina (Jerusalem)

**5**:359
Aeneas **1**:22, **9**:664
*Aeneid* (Virgil) **1**:22–23, **9**:649,
  **9**:651
aeolipile ("windball") **10**:736
Aeolus **8**:581
Aeschylus **5**:330
  *Oresteia* **1**:25, **4**:246
  *The Persians* **4**:245, **4**:246
Aesop **9**:700
Aetius **2**:103–104, **5**:383,
  **5**:384
Afghanistan **7**:510
Africa **2**:121–124, **7**:489,
  **7**:490, **8**:617
Afro-Asiatic languages **6**:450
afterlife **1**:71, **2**:127–128,
  **3**:228, **3**:229–230,
  **4**:255–256, **4**:257, **4**:264,
  **4**:281, **4**:310, **7**:527, **8**:635,
  **8**:636, **9**:663, **10**:747
Agade *see* Akkad
Agamemnon **1**:24–25, **4**:246,
  **5**:393, **10**:758
Agesilaus II **9**:716
Agni **1**:76, **1**:*77*, **5**:364, **5**:*364*
Agnodice **10**:782
agora **1**:66, **2**:101, **3**:211,
  **5**:327
Agricola, Gnaeus Julius **10**:731
agriculture **2**:122, **3**:175, **5**:386
  early **6**:415
  first farmers **8**:621–622
  iron making and **10**:734
  *see also* farming
Agrippa, Marcus **2**:108, **2**:*109*
Agrippina, Julia (the Younger)
  **1**:26–27, **3**:195, **7**:493,
  **7**:557, **9**:653, **10**:782
Agrippina, Vipsania (the Elder)
  **1**:26, **1**:27
A-Group culture (Nubia)
  **8**:572, **8**:573
Ahab **10**:765
Ahasuerus **10**:787
*ahau* **3**:209, **7**:498, **7**:499,
  **7**:502, **7**:559, **10**:746
Ahenobarbus, Lucius Domitius
  *see* Nero
Ahenobarbus, Cnaeus
  Domitius **9**:669
Ahmose I **1**:46
Ahriman **1**:28, **10**:795
Ahura Mazda **1**:28–29, **3**:222,
  **8**:600, **10**:787, **10**:795,

**10**:797
Ajashatru **8**:594
Ajax **8**:581
*akh* **4**:257
Akhenaten **4**:254, **6**:437,
  **7**:555, **7**:556, **8**:589, **10**:762
  *see also* Amenhotep IV
Akidu festival **9**:669
Akitu **4**:290
Akkad **1**:30, **1**:32, **1**:34, **1**:36,
  **3**:221, **9**:676, **9**:685
  map of **4**:*303*
Akkadian language **1**:31–32,
  **2**:89, **2**:159, **6**:409, **6**:450,
  **6**:452
  Assyrian dialect **1**:31
  Babylonian dialect **1**:31
  inscription **3**:221
Akkadians **1**:30–36, **4**:275,
  **7**:509–513, **8**:577, **9**:677,
  **10**:727
  kingship **1**:33
  military power **1**:35
  monuments **1**:33, **1**:35
  writing **1**:32–33, **10**:784
Akrotiri **1**:72, **3**:218, **7**:522,
  **7**:523
Aksapadama Gautama **5**:396
alabaster **7**:511, **7**:513, **10**:749
Alans **5**:383
Alaric **3**:212, **4**:313, **4**:314,
  **4**:315
Alcibiades **5**:*337*
Alcyoneus **5**:*332*
Alesia, siege of **2**:139
Alexander (twin son of
  Cleopatra) **3**:197
Alexander the Great **1**:19,
  **1**:37–39, **1**:47, **1**:68, **2**:113,
  **2**:117, **2**:120, **3**:221, **4**:271,
  **5**:325, **5**:*339*, **5**:358, **5**:398,
  **6**:417, **6**:469, **6**:470, **8**:601,
  **8**:607, **8**:608, **9**:687, **9**:688,
  **10**:758, **10**:764, **10**:773,
  **10**:775
  Alexander Hoard **7**:*533*
  Alexander Mosaic **6**:*470*
  empire **6**:*468*, **6**:469, **6**:470
  invasion of India **7**:494,
    **7**:495
  royal mint **7**:532
  sarcophagus **1**:*38*
  statue **1**:*37*
Alexandria **1**:38, **1**:40–41,
  **1**:56, **3**:196, **6**:470, **8**:580,

**9**:680, **10**:744
  Bruchium **6**:462
  Christianity in **1**:41
  city plan **1**:*40*
  library **1**:40, **1**:*41*, **4**:306,
    **6**:*461*, **6**:462
  lighthouse **1**:40
  Mouseion **1**:40, **1**:*41*,
    **6**:*461*, **6**:462
  patriarch of **3**:186
  Serapeum **6**:462
  Temple of Serapis **1**:41
Algeria **8**:622, **10**:*754*
Algonquins **7**:531
Allahabad **9**:671
All Saints Day **4**:293
Almudj **6**:433
Alodia **8**:576
alphabet **10**:783, **10**:785
  Greek **10**:785
  Latin **8**:609
  Phoenician **8**:606, **8**:609
Altamira, Spain **5**:387
altars **10**:740, **10**:748
  fire **10**:796, **10**:*797*
Al-Ubaid **10**:726
Alvaro de Mendaña y Neyra,
  Don **7**:504
Amarna **1**:45, **4**:254,
  **7**:555–556, **8**:*573*, **10**:762
  palace of Akhenaten **8**:589
Amaterasu **1**:42–43, **6**:412,
  **6**:413
Amazons **7**:491, **7**:492
Amazon Valley **8**:622
amber **7**:545, **9**:719
Amber Route **9**:646
Ambrose **2**:105
*amelu* **2**:115, **9**:706
Amenemhat I **10**:743
Amenemhat III **8**:589
Amenhotep III **1**:44–45, **1**:46,
  **6**:461, **8**:589, **10**:*743*
Amenhotep IV **1**:45, **1**:46
Amenhotep (son of Hapu)
  **1**:45
Amenpanufer **10**:772
American Indian languages
  **6**:450
Americas
  languages **6**:451
  religion **10**:779
Amharic language **6**:450
Amitrochates *see* Bindusara
Ammianus Marcellinus **5**:381

Ammut 2:127, 3:230, 4:255
Amorites 1:36, 2:86, 10:728
amphitheaters 1:66, 1:79,
    3:201, 3:239, 4:271, 8:615,
    9:716
amphorae 7:551, 8:588, 8:619,
    10:748
Amu Darya 8:591
amulets 3:200, 3:239, 4:257,
    5:351, 6:424, 10:772
Amulius 9:648, 9:649
Amun 1:45, 1:46–47, 3:229,
    4:261, 4:263–264, 4:290,
    5:349, 5:350, 10:743
    statue 1:47
Amun Kematef 1:46
Amun Ra 1:46, 4:263
Amun, Temple of 4:261
Amyitis 7:554
Amyntas II 8:604
Amyntas III 1:67
Anagni, church of 5:354
Anahita 1:29
Analects (Confucius) 1:48–49,
    3:203
Anangu 10:766
Anasazi 1:50–53
    houses 1:50
    pottery 1:52, 1:53
    religion 1:50
Anatolia 3:215, 5:368, 8:608
Anaxagoras 5:326, 5:336,
    8:598
Anaximander 2:96, 4:304,
    8:629
Anaximenes 5:336
ancestor worship 1:14, 1:15,
    3:178, 3:180, 3:203, 4:283,
    6:415, 7:504
ancestry 7:484
Andes Mountains 8:622
Andromeda 5:335
anesthetic 5:352, 5:399
Angles 1:54–55
Anglo-Saxons 2:155
animals
    as deities 8:586, 8:636
    domestication of 4:285,
        4:289, 8:622, 9:716
    for transportation 10:754
Ankhesenpaaten
    (Ankhesenamen) 3:198,
    7:485, 7:555, 10:762
Anshan 1:18, 3:220
Anshanite dynasty 4:267–268
antakaeos 9:688
Anthesteries 4:292

Antioch 9:680
    patriarch of 3:186
Antiochus IV 5:358, 5:359
Antiochus of Syria 6:417
antiquarian 1:60, 1:79
antler pick 10:725, 10:799
Antoninus Pius 5:344, 6:475
Antony, Mark 1:56–57, 2:107,
    2:108, 3:196–197
Anubis 2:127, 3:229, 4:255,
    4:265, 7:489
Anu 2:119, 4:307
apatheia 5:338
Apennines 4:278, 4:319
Aphrodite 1:24, 5:333, 5:334,
    8:637, 9:675
Apocrypha 4:284
Apollo 1:25, 3:211, 3:219,
    3:234, 4:273, 4:292, 5:333,
    7:543, 9:668
Apollonius 8:630
apostles 3:184, 3:187, 3:239,
    8:597
Apostolic Churches 3:184–185
Appenine Mountains 4:278
aqueducts 1:58–59, 2:93,
    3:194, 4:288, 8:564–565,
    8:639, 10:734
    Roman 1:59, 1:65, 9:663,
        9:665
    Sennacherib's 1:58
Aquila, Tiberius Julius 6:462
Arabia 8:570, 9:716
Arabs 6:418, 9:680
    geographers 4:306
Arachne 2:99
Aral Sea 8:591
Aramaeans 2:90
Aramaic language 6:452,
    10:765
Aratta 4:275
Arcadius 4:271
archaeology 1:60–63, 1:78,
    2:121
    evidence of prehistory 8:620
    modern techniques 1:62–63
    the Three Age System 1:62
    see also environmental
        archaeology; experimental
        archaeology
archery 8:573, 9:715, 9:717
Archimedes 8:580, 9:682,
    9:683
    principle 8:580, 9:683
    screw 1:40, 4:288, 4:319,
        8:580, 9:683
architecture 1:64–66

Babylonian 2:118
    Egyptian 1:64–65
    Etruscan 4:280
    Moche 7:525–526
    Roman 9:663
architraves 9:672
archons 9:709, 9:710
Ardashir (Artaxerxes) 9:678,
    9:679
Ardavan 9:679
ardu 2:115
Areopagus 8:598, 9:710
Ares 2:98, 5:333, 7:492
Aretium 8:619
Argonauts 5:335
Ariadne 5:335
Arian 4:313, 4:319
Arinna 5:370
Arinnitti see Arinna
Aristarchos of Samos 2:97,
    8:624
aristocracy 5:325, 9:709
Aristophanes 2:101, 5:330,
    9:707
Aristotle 1:37, 1:67–69, 2:96,
    5:336, 5:338, 5:339, 5:398,
    6:461, 7:532, 8:579, 9:652,
    9:654, 9:707
    Ethics 1:68
    Poetics 1:68
    Politics 1:68, 1:69
    round-earth theory 4:304
    sculpture 1:67
arithmetic 5:328
Arius 4:312–313
Arjuna 6:473, 8:631
Ark of the Covenant 3:224,
    3:225, 6:416, 6:417, 7:536,
    10:739
Armenia 9:679
armies 7:506
    Sargon of Akkad's 9:676
armor 10:774
Arrian 3:221, 5:398
arrows, quivers for 9:689
Arsaces 8:591
Arsacid kingdom 8:591
arsenal 8:564
art 1:70–74
    gender in 7:507
    and leisure 1:72–74
    and magic 1:70–71
    as a public record 1:72
    and religion 1:71
Arta 1:28
Artabanus 3:223
Artaxerxes I 1:19, 8:601

Artaxerxes II 1:19
Artaxerxes III 1:19
Artemis 3:219, 5:333, 5:334,
    7:492, 9:668
    Temple of 4:270
Artemisia 10:749
Artemisium 10:786
artifacts 1:60, 1:79, 2:159
    dating 1:62–63
Art of War, The (Sun Tzu)
    10:775
Aryabhata 5:341
Aryans 1:75–78, 5:364, 7:519,
    9:705, 10:798
    archaeology 1:78
    kingdoms 1:77–78
    pottery 1:78
    religion 1:76–77
    society 1:76
    warfare 1:76
Arzawa 5:368
asceticism 5:366, 5:367, 5:399
Asclepieia games 4:273
Asclepius 4:272, 4:273, 5:352
    sanctuary at Epidaurus
        4:272, 4:273
Ashoka 2:84–85, 2:136, 7:495,
    7:497, 7:517, 8:595, 9:672
    Great Stupa at Sanchi 2:85,
        7:497, 9:672–673
    pillars of stone 4:251
ashram 4:251, 4:319
Ashur 2:86–87, 2:90, 2:91,
    2:95
Ashurbanipal 2:88–89, 2:91,
    2:95, 4:266, 4:268, 4:307,
    6:461, 8:565
Ashurnasirpal 1:72
Ashurnasirpal II 2:86, 2:87,
    2:92, 2:116, 2:142
Ashur-uballit I 2:91
Asia 8:570, 8:617, 8:621,
    10:732
Asia Minor 3:239, 7:517,
    9:679, 10:791
Asklepios 6:468
Asoka see Ashoka
asphalt 7:528, 7:559
Assur see Ashur
Assyria 1:58, 2:86–87,
    2:88–89, 2:90–95,
    2:142–143, 8:607,
    9:690–691, 10:764
Assyrian Empire 7:509, 7:510
    map 2:90
Assyrians 2:90–95, 2:117,
    4:266, 4:267, 4:268, 5:356,

5:357, 5:369, 5:371, 6:438,
7:553, 8:564, 8:565, 10:764,
10:774, 10:775
  army 2:94
  art and sculpture 2:92
  beliefs 2:92
  food and farming 2:93–95
  houses 2:95
  religion 2:142
  stepped pyramids 10:737
  wheeled vehicles 10:756
  writing 10:784
  ziggurats 8:628
Astarte 8:609
astrolabe 8:625
astrology 2:96, 3:239
astronomy 2:96–97, 2:120,
  2:144, 2:146, 3:179, 9:684
  Egyptian 2:96
  Greek 1:67
  Handy Tables 8:624
  Hopewell 5:373
  Mayan 3:210
  Ptolemaic 8:624–625
  Sumerian 10:728
Astyages 3:220
Atacama Desert 7:539, 7:540
Aten 1:45, 1:46, 4:254,
  10:762
*ateshperest* 10:798
Athanasius, bishop of
  Alexandria 3:186
Athena 1:20, 1:21, 1:79,
  2:98–99, 5:*332*, 5:333,
  5:393, 7:551, 8:581, 8:*582*,
  8:637, 9:*704*, 10:779
Athene Nike, temple of 1:21
Athenians 2:100–102, 3:223,
  8:598
  democracy 1:68, 2:100,
    5:325, 5:326, 6:468,
    8:598–599, 9:708,
    9:709–710
  pottery 2:102, 8:619
  rank among 9:706
  slaves 9:699, 9:701, 9:702,
    9:709
  war with Sparta 2:102
Athens 1:20–21, 2:98, 2:99,
  2:100–102, 5:330, 7:546,
  8:610, 9:653, 9:709, 10:786
  the Academy 8:610
  Acropolis 1:20–21, 1:*20*,
    2:101, 7:498, 7:534,
    8:598, 8:*599*, 10:745–746
  Areopagus 8:598, 9:710
  city plan 2:*100*

commerce 7:533
Constitution of 1:68, 1:69
  education 3:170
  Erechtheion 1:21, 2:99
  Lyceum 1:68
  Olympic Games 8:588
  Painted Stoa 1:74
  Parthenon 1:20, 1:*21*, 1:74,
    2:99, 2:101, 8:598
  Pnyx 5:*325*
  sacked by Persians 1:18,
    1:19, 1:20
  Temple of Nike 2:*99*
  Temple of Zeus 10:794
  Theater of Dionysus 2:*101*
  Thirty Tyrants 9:708
  women of 7:493
athletics 2:101, 9:718
Atlantis, site of 7:522
atman 5:395
atoll 7:514, 7:559
Atossa 10:786
Atreus 1:24
Attila the Hun 2:103–104,
  4:314, 5:382–384
Atum 4:263
Atwater, Caleb 5:374
Augustan Age 2:108
Augustine of Hippo
  2:105–106, 3:185
Augustus 1:22, 1:23, 1:56,
  2:107–109, 3:190, 4:284,
  4:306, 7:485, 8:608, 9:652,
  9:657, 9:659, 9:665, 9:666
aulos 7:543
Aul Ul 9:687
Aurelian 4:312, 10:791
aureus 7:532
auroch 5:387, 5:399
Ausonius 4:251
Australia
  aborigines 1:14–17,
    6:432–433, 6:*451*, 7:503,
    7:506, 10:766–767,
    10:779
  European settlement 1:15,
    1:16
  Northern Territory
    6:432–433, 10:766–767
*Australopithecus Africanus*
  8:620
Austronesian language family
  6:452
auxiliaries 9:657, 9:719
avatar 5:367, 6:473, 6:479,
  8:631
Avebury 2:110–111

map of 2:*110*
awls 5:385
ax 5:385
axle 10:735
Axum 8:573, 8:576
Ay 10:762, 10:763
Ayers Rock *see* Uluru
Ayodhya 8:631
Aztecs 10:741, 10:789

*ba* 4:257
Baal Hamon 2:150, 8:609
Babylon 1:39, 2:88, 2:91,
  2:93, 2:112–114, 3:192,
  3:199, 3:221, 3:222, 4:266,
  5:356, 5:357, 5:358, 6:417,
  6:436, 6:437, 6:470, 6:478,
  7:510, 7:538, 8:600, 9:691
  capture of 3:220, 3:222
  Hanging Gardens 2:113,
    2:114, 7:553, 7:554
  Hittite conquest of 5:368,
    5:369, 5:370
  Holy Way 7:554
  Ishtar Gate 2:112, 2:*113*,
    2:*119*
  plan of 2:*112*
  royal mint 7:532
  sack of 4:267, 4:268, 7:554
  Temple of Marduk 3:220,
    6:477
Babylonia 6:436–437
Babylonian Empire 2:*115*,
  2:125, 7:509, 7:553
Babylonians 1:58, 2:90, 2:91,
  2:95, 2:115–120, 5:356,
  5:357, 6:430, 7:553–554,
  8:577, 10:764
  architecture 2:118
  astronomy 2:96, 2:144,
    9:684
  calendar 2:144, 2:145,
    8:578
  canals 2:117
  food 2:116
  gods and goddesses 2:119,
    7:551
  language 6:436
  law 2:119, 3:213–214,
    3:222
  legends 4:*307*
  mapmaking 4:303, 9:685
  mathematics 8:577, 8:579,
    8:580, 9:682, 9:685
  measures 10:776, 10:777
  medicine 3:213
  music 7:541

pottery 8:617–618
religion 4:290, 6:477–478,
  9:691
  sacrifice 9:667
  slavery 2:115
  social rank 9:706
  society 2:115
  stepped pyramids 10:737
  trade 2:117
  transport 2:118
  wheeled vehicles 10:756
  women 2:116
  writing 2:120, 10:784
  ziggurats 8:628
Bacchus 4:*297*, 8:637
Bactria 1:39, 6:446, 6:447,
  8:595
Badon Hill, Battle of 1:55
Baghdad 9:676
Bakhtaran 6:436
Bakuba tribe 7:*490*
*balche* 7:499
Balder 7:551
Balkans 7:518
ball courts 1:52
  Mayan 9:717–718
  Monte Albán 7:535
  Olmecs 8:583, 8:585
  Zapotec 10:788, 10:*790*
bamboo 3:237, 9:681
Bantu culture 2:121–124,
  8:566
  agriculture 2:122
  languages 2:121, 2:123
  pottery 2:122–123
  spread of 2:*121*, 2:123,
    2:124
baptism 6:420
Barak 3:233
barbarians 3:239, 4:312,
  4:315, 6:450
bards 5:392, 5:399
  Celtic 2:156
barter 7:530
basilica 9:665, 9:719, 10:799
Basket Maker culture 1:50–53
bas-relief 2:159, 9:690, 9:719
Bassus, Junius 8:*638*
Bath, Aquae Sulis 5:390
bathing 5:390
baths, Roman 9:662, 9:666
Batiatus, Lentulus 9:713
battering rams 7:487, 9:693,
  10:757, 10:775
beer 4:295, 4:297, 9:698
Beijing 3:228, 10:747
Beirut 8:606

Bel **6**:478
  *see also* Marduk
Belize **7**:498
Bellona **9**:650
Belshazzar **2**:125–126
bema **3**:211
Benares *see* Varanasi
Benin **8**:568
Berot (Berytus) **8**:606, **8**:608
Bes **4**:261, **4**:*263*, **7**:489
Bethlehem **3**:224, **3**:225,
  **6**:419
*Bhagavad Gita* **6**:473
Bible **3**:185, **3**:226–227,
  **5**:355, **7**:536, **8**:564, **9**:701
  Ramses II and the **8**:634
  translation into Gothic
    **4**:313
  Vulgate **7**:538
  *see also* New Testament; Old
    Testament
Bindusara **7**:495, **7**:496
*Biographies of Heroic Women*
  (Lu Xiang) **10**:782
bireme **9**:692, **10**:757
birth **3**:169
bishop **3**:185, **3**:186
Bismarck Archipelago **6**:457,
  **7**:503, **7**:504, **9**:694
bitumen **7**:511, **7**:513, **7**:541,
  **8**:602, **9**:646, **10**:769
Black Sea **9**:686
blasphemy **8**:596, **8**:639
Bleda **2**:103
Blegen, Carl **10**:*758*, **10**:759
Blom, Frans **8**:585
bloodletting **7**:559, **10**:746
bluestone **10**:724, **10**:799
boat chambers **5**:361
boats *see* ships
Bodh Gaya (near Bihar) **2**:132,
  **2**:135
Bodhidharma **2**:138
bodhisattvas **1**:71, **1**:79, **2**:136,
  **2**:137
Bolon Tzaicat **7**:502
Bon-po religion **2**:138
*Book of the Dead* **2**:127–128,
  **3**:228, **4**:*255*, **4**:*264*, **5**:*377*
*Book of Lao-tzu see Tao Te*
  *Ching*
boomerang **1**:17
Bosporus **3**:223
Boudicca **2**:129–130, **7**:493
boule **4**:271
boundary stones **6**:438
boxing **9**:716, **9**:717

boys **3**:169, **3**:171
  education **4**:252, **10**:731
  Greek **4**:252, **5**:328
  Roman **9**:662
  Spartan **5**:328, **9**:711
Brahma **5**:366–367, **5**:*395*
*brahman* **5**:366, **5**:395
Brahmans **1**:76, **1**:77, **4**:252,
  **5**:364, **5**:*365*, **9**:705
Brahmi script **1**:78
bread **4**:294–295
Brhadratha **7**:495, **7**:497
bricks **5**:376, **6**:405, **10**:738,
  **10**:769
bride price **4**:283
bridges, Roman **9**:646, **9**:663,
  **9**:665
Brigantes **7**:493
Briseis **5**:393
Britain **2**:129–130,
  **10**:724–725, **10**:753
  Anglo-Saxon **1**:54–55
  Celts **7**:493, **7**:539
  festivals **4**:292
  history of **10**:732
  map of **1**:*54*
  Roman **1**:54, **1**:55, **2**:154,
    **2**:155, **5**:343, **5**:345–346,
    **8**:637
  Roman expeditions to
    **2**:139, **2**:148
  Roman invasion **3**:194,
    **9**:657
  stone circles **2**:111
  tribes of **2**:129
Britannicus **1**:27, **3**:195,
  **7**:557, **10**:*780*
British Columbia **7**:518
Britons **1**:54, **5**:346, **10**:775
Brittany **1**:55, **2**:155
broch **9**:698, **9**:719
bronze **3**:177, **3**:217, **3**:236,
  **3**:237, **4**:287, **5**:380, **10**:773
  drums **3**:238
  Greek sculpture **1**:73
Bronze Age **3**:217, **3**:218,
  **3**:219, **3**:236, **8**:587
  horn music **7**:543
  tools **1**:62
  weapons **10**:774
Brutus **2**:107, **2**:141
Bubastic **8**:589
Bucephalus **1**:37
Buddha **2**:131–133, **2**:134,
  **3**:182–183, **3**:*183*, **3**:222,
  **4**:248, **4**:251, **5**:342, **6**:447,
  **6**:448, **8**:638, **9**:673

  representations of **9**:672
  sculptures of **1**:71
Buddhism **2**:84, **2**:131–133,
  **2**:134–138, **3**:178, **3**:180,
  **3**:182–183, **5**:342, **5**:398,
  **6**:412, **6**:446, **6**:447, **6**:448,
  **7**:497, **8**:595, **8**:638, **9**:670,
  **9**:672–673, **10**:773
  art **4**:247
  beliefs **2**:133, **2**:134, **2**:135
  cave temples **10**:739,
    **10**:*740*
  Indian **10**:739
  middle way **2**:136
  paper scrolls **6**:461
  split **2**:136
  spread of **2**:133, **2**:136,
    **4**:248
  teaching **2**:132–133,
    **2**:134–135
  "three jewels" of **9**:673
  women and **10**:779
  *see also* Mahayana
    Buddhism; Theravada
    Buddhism
Budha Gupta **5**:341
buildings *see* architecture
bulla **3**:*171*, **6**:424, **6**:479
bull leaping **9**:715
bull worship **6**:440
Buluk Chaptan **7**:502
Burgundians **4**:298, **4**:299
burial customs
  Egyptian **1**:71, **3**:229–230,
    **4**:256, **10**:744, **10**:748
  Hebrew customs **3**:229,
    **3**:231
  Persian **1**:29
  prehistoric **8**:621, **8**:635
  Roman **10**:750
  Scythian **9**:689
  *see also* tombs
Burnaburiash II **6**:437
Burrus, Africanus **1**:27, **7**:557
Byblos **4**:265, **5**:350, **8**:606,
  **8**:608
Byrsa, Hill of, Carthage **2**:*149*
Byzantium **3**:207, **3**:208,
  **9**:657, **9**:660
  *see also* Constantinople

Caere **4**:281
Caesarion **2**:141, **3**:196, **3**:197
Caesar, Julius **1**:22, **1**:56,
  **2**:107, **2**:139–141, **2**:146,
  **2**:154, **2**:155, **3**:189, **3**:190,
  **3**:196, **3**:212, **5**:361, **9**:652,

  **9**:653, **9**:657, **9**:659, **9**:700,
    **9**:714, **10**:753, **10**:758
  bust of **2**:*139*
  calendar **2**:141, **2**:146
  *Gallic War* **10**:775
cairn **9**:698, **9**:719
  chambered **9**:698, **9**:719
Calah **2**:86, **2**:92, **2**:95, **2**:116,
  **2**:142–143, **6**:*409*, **8**:565
  Black Obelisk **2**:143
  city plan **2**:*142*
  Fort Shalmaneser **2**:143
  Northwest Palace **2**:143
*caldarium* **5**:390
Caledonia **7**:493
calendars **2**:141, **2**:144–146,
  **8**:578, **9**:684
  Chinese **5**:379, **9**:684
  Egyptian **2**:144, **8**:578,
    **9**:684
  Mayan **3**:210, **9**:682,
    **10**:790
Caligula **1**:26, **1**:27,
  **2**:147–148, **3**:194
  bust of **2**:*147*
Calixtus, catacombs of **3**:*185*
calligraphy **10**:782
Calypso **5**:393, **8**:582
Cambodia **3**:237
Cambyses **1**:18
camels **3**:220, **8**:*570*, **10**:754
cameo **6**:*423*, **6**:424, **6**:479
Cameroon **8**:*567*
Camulodunum (Colchester)
  **2**:130
Canaan **5**:355, **5**:357, **7**:537
Canaanites **3**:233, **6**:416
canals **2**:117, **3**:178, **3**:223,
  **4**:287, **6**:467, **7**:509, **7**:524,
  **8**:565, **10**:734
Canary Islands **8**:626
Cang Jie **5**:379, **5**:380
Cannae, Battle of **5**:348
cannibalism **4**:315, **8**:614
canoes **3**:237, **8**:585, **9**:692
  dugout **6**:456, **7**:504, **7**:516,
    **10**:755
  with outriggers **6**:456,
    **7**:516, **9**:694
canopic jars **3**:229, **3**:239
Capella (star) **7**:535
Capua **9**:713
Caracalla **9**:666
  baths at **5**:390
Caral **8**:626
caravan **8**:602, **8**:639, **10**:752,
  **10**:*754*, **10**:799

carbon dating **6**:415
Carchemish **7**:553
Caria **10**:749
Carnarvon, Lord **10**:763
carnelian **6**:422
Carter, Howard **10**:763
Carthage **2**:149–150, **5**:347,
  **8**:607, **8**:608, **9**:657, **9**:658,
  **10**:764
Carthaginians **5**:347, **6**:471
  culture **2**:150
  wars **2**:149
Cartimandua **7**:493
caryatids **1**:21
Caspian Sea **8**:591
Cassandra **1**:25
Cassius **2**:107, **2**:141
caste system **1**:76, **4**:252,
  **5**:365, **6**:479, **9**:705
catacombs **3**:185, **3**:230,
  **5**:386, **10**:740, **10**:750
  of Calixtus **3**:*185*
  of Saint Januarius **10**:*750*
Çatal Hüyük **1**:66, **1**:70,
  **2**:151–152, **3**:192, **10**:751,
  **10**:779
  houses **5**:376
  map of **2**:*151*
cataphracts **8**:592
catapults **8**:580, **9**:694, **10**:775
Catherwood, Frederick **7**:499
Catiline **3**:189, **3**:190, **3**:*190*,
  **9**:*659*
Cato the Elder **9**:669
Cato the Younger **9**:653,
  **9**:*654*
Catullus **9**:663
Caucasus Mountains **8**:570,
  **10**:794
cavalry **8**:604, **9**:657, **10**:774
cave dwellers **5**:375, **5**:385
cave murals, Ajanta **1**:72,
  **10**:738
cave paintings **1**:70
  aboriginal **1**:16, **10**:767
  Indian **1**:72
  Lascaux **6**:459–460, **8**:635
  prehistoric **8**:621
  Stone Age **5**:387
cave temple, Shanxi **10**:740
Cayster River **4**:271
Celestial Masters movement
  **6**:455
cella **1**:20, **3**:239, **8**:587,
  **8**:639, **10**:740
Celts **2**:129, **2**:153–156,
  **4**:278, **4**:279, **4**:292–293,

**7**:531, **7**:539, **9**:658, **9**:667,
  **9**:687, **9**:688
  arts and crafts **2**:155
  boats **10**:756
  early history **2**:153–154
  homes **5**:375–376
  in Ireland **2**:155, **7**:493
  language **1**:55
  map of movements **2**:*153*
  mythology **7**:550, **7**:552
  priests **9**:668
  religion **2**:155, **10**:779
  society **2**:156
  wheeled vehicles **10**:756
cenotaph **10**:749, **10**:799
Centaur **9**:687
Central America **3**:209,
  **7**:498–502
  cities **3**:192
ceramic clay figures **8**:583,
  **8**:586
Cerberus **3**:230
Ceres **9**:668
C-Group culture (Nubia)
  **8**:572, **8**:573
Chaco Canyon **1**:51, **1**:53
Chadwick, John **7**:548
Chaeronea, Battle of **5**:325,
  **6**:469, **8**:605
chain mail **10**:774
*chakra* **9**:715
Chalandriani, Syros **3**:217,
  **3**:219
Chalcatzingo **8**:586
Chalcedon, Council of **3**:186
chalcedony **6**:422
Chalôns, Battle of **2**:104,
  **5**:*381*, **5**:382, **5**:383, **5**:384
chamberlain **10**:787
Chanakya **7**:494
  *Arthashastra* **7**:494
Chandogya Upanishad **5**:365,
  **5**:397
Chandra Gupta I **5**:341,
  **8**:595, **10**:775
Chandra Gupta II **5**:341,
  **6**:434, **8**:595, **9**:670
Chandragupta Maurya **5**:341,
  **7**:494–496
*chang* **10**:778
Chang'an **2**:157–158, **3**:175,
  **6**:466, **9**:704
  plan of **2**:*157*
Chang Heng **9**:685
Changsu **6**:445
Chang Taoling *see* Zhang
  Daoling

channels **4**:285
Chaos **5**:332
characters, Chinese **10**:784
charcoal **5**:387, **10**:767
chariot racing **3**:234, **8**:588,
  **9**:716, **9**:717
chariots **2**:88, **5**:368, **5**:380,
  **10**:774
charms **5**:351
Charon **3**:230, **3**:*231*
Charvaka **5**:397
Charybdis **5**:393, **8**:582
Chavín **3**:164–166, **10**:734
  art **3**:165
  pottery **3**:165, **3**:166
Chavín de Huantár **3**:164,
  **3**:165, **3**:166
  map of **3**:*164*
  Old Temple **3**:166
Cheng **2**:157, **3**:167–168,
  **3**:173, **3**:174, **3**:175,
  **3**:204–205, **4**:316, **4**:318,
  **10**:775, **10**:778
Chester Beatty Medical
  Papyrus **5**:*353*
Chichen Itza **7**:499
chieftains **2**:156
childbirth **3**:169, **4**:284
Childeric **4**:298, **4**:299
children **3**:169–171
  legitimate **7**:484
  Roman **9**:662
Chillicothe, High Bank **5**:373
Ch'in *see* Qin dynasty
China **2**:157–158, **3**:167,
  **3**:172–179, **3**:183, **3**:237,
  **4**:247–248, **4**:291, **6**:411,
  **8**:617
  ancestor worship **4**:283
  ancient tombs **10**:747
  Buddhism in **2**:138
  cities **3**:175, **3**:192
  extended family **4**:283
  farming **4**:286, **4**:287,
    **4**:288
  food and farming
    **3**:174–175
  games **4**:301
  Great Wall **3**:168, **3**:173,
    **4**:247, **4**:316–318,
    **10**:774–775
  heroic women **10**:782
  map of **3**:*172*
  mapmaking **4**:304
  marriage **7**:484
  period of disunity **3**:173,
    **3**:174, **4**:247, **4**:248

philosophy and religion
    **3**:178–179
  prehistoric **3**:172
  rebellion **6**:467
  roads in **9**:645
  slaves **9**:700
  trade and transport
    **3**:176–178
  war and weapons **3**:178
  writing system **8**:623
  *see also* Han dynasty; Qin
    dynasty; Shang dynasty;
    Tang dynasty
Chinchorro **5**:386
  mummies **7**:540
Chinese **7**:518
  architecture **1**:64
  art **1**:74, **4**:248
  astronomy **2**:96
  boating house **5**:*376*
  bowing **9**:704
  calendars **2**:144, **9**:684
  civil servants **1**:47
  color yellow for rank **9**:704,
    **9**:*705*
  education **3**:206
  geography **9**:685
  houses **5**:376–377, **5**:379
  influence on Dong Son
    culture **3**:237
  inventions **3**:177
  iron making **10**:734
  jewelry **6**:424
  legends **5**:379–380
  literature **3**:179, **6**:464
  mathematics **9**:684
  medicine **5**:354, **9**:682
  mourning colors **3**:229
  music **7**:543
  navigation **10**:755, **10**:756
  numbers **8**:577, **8**:578,
    **8**:580
  occupation of Vietnam
    **10**:760–761
  papermaking **9**:681
  philosophy **3**:180–183,
    **3**:203, **6**:453–455
  religion **6**:453–455, **8**:579
  society **3**:176
  "son of heaven" legend
    **5**:379–380
  sports **9**:716
  standard weights **10**:778
  tribute **10**:751
  walled towns **1**:64
  wheeled vehicles
    **10**:756,**10**:*757*, **10**:774

Chinese *(cont.)*
  writing 10:784
Chinese Empire 1:47, 3:172,
  3:173, 3:174, 3:181
Chin-han tribal league 6:442
Chiron 4:273
chiton 3:200, 5:331, 9:703
Chlodwig *see* Clovis I
Chogha Zanbil 4:268, 4:269
Chomsongdae Observatory
  6:*445*
chorus 4:244, 4:245, 4:319
Choson 6:442
Chosroes I 9:679, 9:680
Chosroes II 9:679
Christ *see* Jesus Christ
Christian festivals 4:293
Christianity 2:105–106, 2:145,
  3:184–188, 3:200, 3:227,
  3:230, 5:355, 6:418–421,
  6:427, 8:596–597, 8:638
  in Alexandria 1:41
  Arian 4:313, 4:319
  at Ephesus 4:271
  beliefs and practices
    3:187–188
  catacombs 10:750
  Catholic Church 2:106
  clothes 3:200
  Constantine and 3:207–208
  early Celtic 2:155
  Goths converted to
    4:312–313
  in Jerusalem 6:418
  legalized in Rome 3:186
  money and morality 7:533
  in the Roman Empire
    10:740
  sacred music 7:544
Christians 7:436
  persecution by Nero
    7:557–558, 8:597, 10:732
  sacrifice 9:669
  temples 10:740
Christmas 4:293
*Chuang-tzu* 3:182, 3:183,
  6:455
churches 3:185, 3:188
Cicero 2:105, 2:141, 9:654,
  9:*659*
  villa of 7:*544*
Ciconians 5:393, 8:581
Cimon 1:74, 8:598
Circe 5:393, 8:582
circle 9:685
circumcision 5:359, 6:427,
  7:506, 8:596, 8:597, 8:639

Circus Maximus 4:319, 9:663,
  9:719
Cisalpine Gaul 2:154, 2:155
cisterns 7:559, 8:603
citadel 1:20, 1:79, 7:528
cities 3:191–193, 5:388
  Chinese 3:175
  government 3:193
  health and sanitation 3:193
  Indus valley 6:405–406
  Roman 9:661
  Sumerian 10:726–727,
    10:729
citizenship 9:657, 9:706
  Roman 3:171
  Spartan 9:711
city planning 1:65–66
city-states 1:20, 2:159
  Etruscan 4:279, 4:280
  Greek 3:193, 3:234, 3:235,
    5:324, 6:469, 9:711
  Hittite 5:371
  Mesopotamian 6:436
  Phoenician 10:764
civil servants 1:47
civil service, Chinese 3:167,
  3:174, 3:205–206
*clabularium* 10:757
clans 4:282
clappers 9:718
class system, Moche 7:526
Claudius 1:26–27, 2:148,
  3:194–195, 7:493, 7:557,
  9:657, 10:780, 10:782
clay (for writing) 10:783,
  10:784
clay firing 8:568, 8:569
clay tablets 7:546, 7:*548*
Cleis 9:674
Cleisthenes 2:100
Cleitus 1:38
Clement of Alexandria 3:185
Cleopatra 1:41, 1:56–57,
  2:108, 2:140–141, 2:146,
  3:196–197, 6:469, 6:470,
  8:605, 9:*663*, 10:781
climate change 7:518
Cloaca Maxima 5:388
clothes 3:198–200
  Chinese 3:176
  Egyptian 3:198, 4:259
  female 10:780
  Indus valley 6:408
Clotilda, Saint 4:299
Clovis I 4:298, 4:299, 4:314
clowns 4:244
Clytemnestra 1:25, 4:246

Coatzacoalcos River 8:583
Code of Hammurabi 2:119,
  3:213–214, 5:370, 9:701,
  10:753
codes, law 3:213–214
Coffin Texts 2:127
cohorts 9:657
coins 3:207, 7:530,
  7:531–532, 7:533
  Chandra Gupta's 9:670
  Chinese 3:167, 7:532
  clipping 7:532
  first 7:531
  and fraud 7:532
  in Greek graves 3:230,
    3:231
  Gupta 5:341
  Jewish 5:*359*
  Kushan 6:447
  Lydian 7:531
  Roman 1:*26*, 1:*56*, 3:*197*,
    3:207, 4:*313*, 5:383,
    6:423
  Samudra Gupta's 9:670
  sweating 7:532
  tetradrachm 7:*532*
  Zenobia's 10:*791*
Colchester *see* Camulodunum
colonization 7:517
colors
  of mourning 3:229
  of pottery 8:617–618
  purple 3:200, 8:606, 9:703,
    10:731
  yellow 9:704, 9:*705*
Colosseum 3:201–202, 3:*201*,
  9:716
Colossi of Memnon 1:*44*
columns 9:663
combware peoples 6:441,
  6:443
comedy 4:245–246, 5:*330*
comets 2:96, 9:684
Commodus 6:476
compensation *see* restitution
Conchobor 7:550, 7:552
concrete 9:663, 9:681
concubine 1:79
Confucianism 1:48–49, 2:138,
  3:173, 3:178, 3:180, 3:181,
  3:182, 3:203–206
  Five Classics 3:206
  in Japan 6:412
  spread of 1:49
  and Taoism 6:455
Confucius 1:48–49, 3:173,
  3:181, 3:203, 3:205, 3:*205*,

4:250, 6:455
  *Analects* 1:48–49, 9:706
  and the civil service
    3:205–206
Congo 7:490
Constantine 1:41, 2:145,
  3:184, 3:186, 3:202,
  3:207–208, 6:418, 9:657,
  9:660, 9:666, 10:740,
  10:794
  and Christianity 3:207–208
Constantine III 1:54
Constantinople 3:208, 9:660,
  9:666, 9:680
  Council of 3:186
  patriarch of 3:186
  Sacred Palace of 8:590
  *see also* Byzantium
Constantinus II 9:679
consuls 1:56, 1:79, 2:139,
  2:159, 9:658, 9:659, 10:731
*Conversations see Analects*
converts 8:596–597
*convivium* 4:296
Cook, Captain James 1:15
Copán 3:209–210
  plan of 3:*209*
  Stairway of Hieroglyphs
    3:209
Copernicus 2:97
copper 8:602, 8:623, 10:773
Coptic church 1:41
coracles 10:756
Corfu 3:211
Corinth
  bronze helmet 10:*773*
  Fountain of Peirene 3:211
  plan 3:*211*
  Sacred Spring 3:211
  Temple of Apollo 3:211
Corinthians
  black-figure pottery 3:212
  Paul's Epistles to the 3:212
corn dolls 4:292
Cornwall 2:155
Coronis 4:273
corroboree 1:16
Corsica 7:517
cosmetics, Egyptian 3:199
cotton 3:199–200, 4:287,
  8:565
Council of Nicaea 3:186,
  3:188
Crassus, Marcus 2:139, 2:141,
  3:189, 9:714
*Creation Epic* (Babylonian)
  2:89

creation myths 7:550
  Egyptian 4:264
  Greek 5:332
cremation 3:230, 5:374, 9:663
  Greek 10:748–749
Crete 3:218, 3:219,
  6:439–440, 7:547, 7:548,
  9:693
  Minoan 7:520–523, 7:547
crime, and punishment
  3:213–216
Crimea 9:686
Criton 8:610
Croesus 3:235, 4:270
Cronus 5:332, 10:793
crop mark 1:62, 1:79
crops
  cultivation 4:285
  Greek 5:330
  rotation 4:288
Croton 8:629, 8:630
Crow Indians 7:491
crucifixion 3:188, 3:216,
  6:421, 6:479, 8:596
Ctesiphon 8:591, 9:680
cubit 10:776, 10:778
Cuchulainn 7:550, 7:552
Culann the Smith 7:552
Cult of the Immortals 3:182
cults 5:399, 8:637
Cumae, Battle of 4:279
Cumae, Sibyl of 9:650
cuneiform 1:32, 6:479, 8:577,
  8:609, 8:623
  Sumerian 9:696, 10:783,
    10:784
  tablets 2:89, 2:120, 2:159
cupbearer 9:719
currency, animals as 7:531
Curse of Akade 1:34, 1:36
Cyaxares 2:87
Cybele 7:544, 9:650
Cyclades, map of 3:217
Cycladic culture 3:217–219
  marble figurines 3:217–219
  tools and artifacts 3:217
Cyclops 8:581
Cyclops, Polyphemus the
  5:393, 5:394
cylinder seals 7:512, 7:513
cymbals 3:238, 9:718
Cynics 5:339
Cynisca 9:716
Cyprus 8:608
Cyrus the Great 1:18, 1:19,
  2:120, 2:125, 2:126,
  3:220–221, 3:235, 6:417,

6:478, 7:554, 9:687, 9:688,
  10:786
  tomb at Pasargadae 8:600

Dacia 4:312, 5:345
Dahshur (bent pyramid) 8:626
Dainzu 10:788
dams 4:285, 6:467, 8:565,
  10:734
Danae 10:794
dance 7:541–544
  Egyptian 7:542
  Greek 7:542–543
  Roman 7:544
Dang Thi Sach 10:760
Daniel 3:231
  Book of 2:126, 7:553
Danta Pyramid, El Mirador
  8:628
Danube River 5:382, 6:475,
  9:686
Daoism see Taoism
Darius I 1:18, 1:19, 1:38,
  3:222–223, 9:687, 9:688,
  10:786, 10:797
Darius III 1:19, 10:787
darshanas 5:396
Daryavahvsh see Darius I
Dattassa 5:369
David 3:224–225, 5:356,
  5:357, 6:416, 6:428
days 2:144
  names of 2:145
Days of the Dead 4:292–293
Dead Sea Scrolls 3:226–227,
  6:461
death
  and burial 3:228–231
  colors of 3:229
  masks 7:490
  penalty 3:213, 3:216
debasement 7:532
deben 7:531
Deborah 3:232–233, 3:232,
  10:782
decimal system 8:577, 9:682,
  9:684
Deir el-Bahri (funerary temple
  of Hatshepsut) 5:349, 5:350
Deir el-Medina 10:771
Delian League 2:100–101
Delos 3:217, 3:219
Delphi 3:234–235, 9:707
  Apollo's oracle at 3:234,
    5:333
  murals 1:74
  plan of 3:234

Sanctuary of Athena
  Pronoas 3:235
  Temple of Apollo 3:235
delta 8:633, 8:639, 10:743
Demeter 4:292, 5:333, 7:493,
  9:668
democracy, Athenian 1:68,
  2:100, 5:325, 5:326, 6:468,
  8:598–599, 9:708,
  9:709–710
Democritus 5:336
denarius 7:532
Denderah 2:97
dendrochronology 1:63, 1:79
Denmark 7:539, 7:543
desiccation 7:539, 7:559
Devanampiya Piyadasi, edicts
  of 2:84–85
dharma 2:84–85, 2:133,
  2:134, 6:479, 9:673
Dholavira 6:405
dialogue, Socratic 8:610, 9:707
Diana 4:270, 7:492
Diapolis 8:629
diaspora, Jewish 5:359
dice 4:301
didgeridoo 1:16, 1:79
Dido of Carthage 1:22, 2:149,
  2:150
digits 10:776
dikes 4:285
dilly bag 1:16
Dimpimekug 3:228
dingo 1:15
Dio Cassius 2:129, 2:130,
  3:202, 5:359
Diocletian 9:657, 9:659
Diogenes 3:171, 5:339
Diomedes 2:98, 2:99
Dionysus 4:244, 4:246, 4:282,
  4:297, 5:333, 7:489, 7:492,
  7:543, 8:605, 8:637
dioptra 10:736
disease 5:351–354, 5:390–391
displaced peoples 7:518
distillation 2:95
Divine Comedy, The (Dante
  Alighieri) 1:23
diviners 8:637
division of labor 10:751
  family 10:780
Diwali 8:632
Djoser 4:258, 8:626, 10:748
dolls 3:171, 4:302
Domitian 9:666
domus 5:378
Dong Son culture 3:236–238

map of 3:236
Don River 9:686
Dorians 7:518, 7:548, 9:711
dowry 2:116, 2:159, 3:169,
  7:486, 7:559
Draco 3:215, 9:709
draconian penalties 3:215
drainage 5:388–389
drama 4:244–246
  Egyptian 4:244
  Greek 2:101, 4:244–246,
    5:330
dreamtime 1:15, 6:433, 6:451,
  10:766
drink 4:258, 4:286, 4:294–297
druids 2:156, 9:668
drums 7:541, 7:543, 7:544,
  9:718
  bronze 3:238
Drusilla 1:27
Duat (underworld) 3:230
Duma 8:602
Dumuzi 6:410
Dumuzi-Amaushumgalana
  4:275
Dunhuang 3:183, 4:247–248,
  4:316, 6:461
Dur-Kurigalzu 6:437
Dur Sharrukin 2:91, 2:92,
  2:118, 2:143
Dur Untash 4:267
duty work 4:310, 4:319
dyes 9:681, 9:703, 9:704
  purple 10:765
dykes 7:509

Ea 2:119, 4:276, 4:277, 6:477
Early Harappan period 6:405
Early Horizon see Chavín
earth 5:336, 5:341
  circumference 4:304
  round-earth theory 4:304
  shape and position 2:96–97
  study of the 4:303–306
earthquakes 3:179, 5:360,
  7:520–523, 8:603, 8:615,
  9:685
earthwork 2:159
East Africa 8:566, 8:620,
  8:621
Easter 4:293
  dating of 3:186
  origin of name 1:55
Easter Island 8:612, 8:613,
  8:614, 9:694
  moai statues 8:613, 8:614
Eastern Roman Empire 9:660,

Eastern Roman Empire (cont.)
9:680
see also Roman Empire
Ebers, George Maurice 5:353
Ebers papyrus 5:353
ebony 8:574
Ecbatana 8:591, 8:600
Ecclesiasticus, Book of 3:225,
4:284
Echo 9:651
eclipses of the moon see lunar
eclipses
Eclogues (Virgil) 1:23
Edessa, Battle of 9:679
Edfu 4:291
Edict of Milan 3:207
education 3:169–170,
4:249–252
boys 4:252, 10:731
Chinese 3:206
Egyptian 3:168, 4:249–250
of Greek girls 4:251
music in 7:543
Roman 9:654
values and beliefs
4:250–251
Edwin Smith papyrus 5:353
Egypt 1:18, 1:40, 1:56, 2:88,
2:89, 2:122, 2:127, 2:140,
4:253–260, 6:469, 8:622,
8:633–634, 10:743, 10:762
cities 3:192
Eleventh Dynasty 10:743
empire 8:572
escape of Israelites from
5:355
excavations 1:63
Fifth Dynasty 8:618
intermediate periods 4:254,
4:255, 10:743
Lower 4:253, 10:743
Middle Kingdom 4:255
Moses and 7:536
New Kingdom 4:253,
4:255, 4:256, 8:589,
10:770
and Nubia 8:573–574
Old Kingdom 4:255,
10:743
pharaohs of 3:196
plagues 6:427, 7:536, 8:634
Ptolemaic (Greek) period
4:255, 9:700, 10:744
and the Roman Empire
1:41, 3:196–197, 4:255
slaves 9:700
Twelfth Dynasty 10:743

Upper 4:253, 10:743
women rulers 10:781–782
Egyptians 1:44–47, 2:88,
5:369
architecture 1:64–65
art 4:254, 7:556
astronomy 2:96
beliefs 2:127–128
boats 9:692, 10:756
burial customs 1:71,
3:229–230, 4:256,
10:744, 10:748
calendars 2:144, 8:578,
9:684
clothes 3:198, 4:259
cosmetics 3:199
dance 7:541, 7:542
drama 4:244
education 3:169, 4:249–250
farming and food 4:258,
4:287, 4:288, 4:294,
4:295, 4:297
games 4:301
houses 1:64, 4:253, 5:377
hygiene 5:391
irrigation 10:734
language 4:259, 4:260
libraries 6:461–462
literature 6:465
mapmaking 2:128, 4:303,
4:304
marriage rituals 7:485,
7:486
masks 7:489, 7:490
mathematics 8:578, 9:682
measures 10:776
medicine 4:265, 5:351,
5:353, 9:682, 10:782
men and women 7:506
money 7:531
mummies 7:540
music 7:541, 7:542, 9:718
mythology 4:254–256,
4:261–265, 4:288,
4:290–291, 4:292
numbers 8:577, 8:578
palaces 8:589
papermaking 9:681
and Phoenicia 8:606
pottery 8:618
pyramid building 10:733
pyramids 8:626, 10:748
religion 1:46–47, 8:636
royal family 7:556
sports 9:716, 9:717
temples 10:738
toys 3:170–171

trade 4:258–259, 5:350,
10:751
war 4:260, 10:775
wheeled vehicles 10:756
writing 2:127, 4:259,
4:260, 8:623, 10:784
Egyptology 5:399, 8:627
Ekur Temple, Ashur 2:91
Elam 9:696
map of 4:266
Middle and Late Elam
4:267–268
Old Elam 4:266–267
Elamites 1:30, 1:32, 2:88,
4:266–269, 6:437, 6:438,
6:478, 8:565, 9:676, 9:695,
10:727
culture 4:268
toys 4:302
elders, Spartan council of
9:712
Eleazer ben Yair 7:487, 7:488
electrum 5:399
Elements (Euclid) 1:40–41
elephants 5:347, 10:774
El 8:609
Elijah 10:765
Ellil 1:34, 2:119, 4:307
El Salvador 8:628
embalming 3:229, 3:239,
4:256, 4:257, 7:540
resins 10:762
Emesa, Battle of 10:791
Empedocles 5:339
empire 7:495
emu 1:17
England 1:54, 10:755
English language 1:55
Enheduanna 9:677, 10:730
Enki 6:409, 6:410
Enkidu 4:307
Enlightened One see Buddha
enlightenment 9:673, 9:719
Enlil see Ellil
entertainment see sports
entrepreneurs, merchants as
10:752–753
Enumma Elish 6:477
environmental archaeology
1:63
Eostre 1:55
Epari dynasty 4:266
Ephesus 4:270–271, 5:348,
7:492
city plan 4:270
earthquake 4:271
the library of Celsus 6:462

new city 4:271
Temple of Artemis 4:270
ephors 9:712
epic 1:22, 1:33, 1:79, 4:307,
4:319, 6:463
Epicureanism 9:653–654
Epicureans 5:338
Epicurus 5:338, 9:653
Epidaurus 4:272–273, 5:389
Asclepius's Sanctuary at
4:272, 4:273
theater 4:272, 4:273
Epirus 8:605
Epistles of Saint Paul 8:597
equites 9:660
Eran 9:671
Eratosthenes of Alexandria
1:41, 4:304, 4:305
Erech 1:30, 4:274–275,
4:307–308, 7:510, 9:676,
10:726, 10:729
plan of 4:274
Temple of Ishtar 6:409
Erechtheion 1:21, 2:99
Erechtheus 1:21
Ereshkigal 7:550
Eridu 4:276–277, 6:410,
7:510, 7:511, 10:726,
10:730
artifacts 4:276–277
plan of 4:276
temples and palaces 4:276
Erishti-Aya 2:117
Eros 5:332, 5:334
Esarhaddon 2:88
Eshmunazar 8:609
Essenes 3:226, 6:425, 6:430,
6:431, 6:479
Etemenanki (Tower of Babel)
2:113
Ethiopia 8:576
Etruscan Empire, map 4:278
Etruscans 2:154, 4:278–281,
5:388
archaeology 4:280–281
architecture 4:280
culture 4:279, 4:280
food 4:296
kings 9:665
navigation 10:755
necropolises 10:749–750
religion 4:280
writing 4:280
Eucharist 3:184, 3:188, 9:669
Euclid 9:682
Elements 1:40–41
Euphrates River 2:113, 2:117,

7:509, **8**:621, **9**:692, **10**:768
Eupolis **9**:707
Eurasia **8**:570
Euripides **2**:101, **4**:245, **5**:330, **6**:461
Europa **10**:793
Europe **8**:621
Eusebius **3**:208
Evans, Arthur **6**:440, 7:521
excavation **1**:61
exile, Jewish **2**:125, **5**:358–359
Exodus **5**:355, **5**:357, 7:518, 7:537, 7:538, **8**:634
experimental archaeology **1**:63
exploration **4**:304, **10**:753
Ezekiel **5**:357, 7:554

Fabiola **10**:782
fables, animal **6**:465
Fabulus (Famulus) 7:*558*
Fagg, Bernard **8**:566
Fa Hsien **5**:342, **8**:595
faience **8**:618, **8**:637
fallow **4**:288
families **3**:169, **4**:249, **4**:282–284
   division of labor **10**:780
   education and **4**:249, **4**:250
   extended **4**:283
   heads **4**:282–283
   names **4**:284
   and the state **4**:284
farming **4**:258, **4**:285–289
   goddesses of **4**:288
   prehistoric **3**:191
   tools and machinery **4**:287
Fars **8**:600
fasting **5**:366
fate **9**:652
fathers **4**:282
   Roman and Hebrew 7:492
Faunus **9**:650
Faustina **6**:476
fermentation **4**:295, **4**:297, **4**:319
Fertile Crescent **6**:477, 7:541, **8**:621
fertility **10**:*769*
   ceremonies 7:489
   goddesses 7:491, 7:493, **8**:637
festivals **4**:290–293
fibula **6**:423, **6**:479
Field of Reeds **4**:255, **4**:*259*
fieldwork **1**:62
figurines
   Cycladic marble **3**:217–219

Mesopotamian 7:512
   Neolithic female 7:491
   Nok **8**:569
Fiji **6**:456, **6**:457, 7:503, 7:504
*fines* **5**:375
Fiorelli, Giuseppe **8**:616
fire serpent **10**:742
fire worship 7:519, **10**:796, **10**:*797*, **10**:798
First Triumvirate **2**:139
fishhooks **5**:386
fishing **5**:385–387
   Vietnamese **10**:*760*
flax **3**:198, **4**:259, **4**:319
Flood, the **2**:159
flute 7:541, 7:542, 7:543, **9**:718
food **4**:258, **4**:286, **4**:294–297
   Egyptian **4**:258, **4**:287, **4**:288, **4**:294, **4**:295, **4**:297
   fruit and vegetables **4**:286–287
   Roman **9**:663
   trade in **10**:752
forge **10**:*734*
*foricae* **5**:390
forum **8**:615, **8**:639
fossil ivory **5**:374, **5**:399
Four Corners **1**:50, **1**:51
fractions, decimal **9**:684
*francisca* **4**:298
Franconia **4**:298
Franks **4**:298–299, **4**:313
   burial customs **4**:298
   Christianization **4**:299
   map of kingdom **4**:*298*
   social rank **9**:704
fraud, coins and 7:532
freemen **9**:703, **9**:704
frescoes **1**:72, **1**:79, **3**:218, **3**:239, **4**:248, **6**:*440*, **10**:750
Frigg **2**:145
*frigidarium* **5**:390
Frisians **1**:54, **1**:55
fuchsite **10**:746, **10**:799
fulcrum **9**:683
funeral pyre 7:486
funerals, Etruscan **10**:750
funerary temple **5**:349, **5**:*350*, **5**:399
furnaces **8**:567, **8**:569
future, foretelling the **9**:662

Gadatas **2**:126
Gaea **4**:288
Gagadju **6**:432

Gaia **5**:332, 7:551
Gaius Octavius *see* Augustus
Galba, Servius Sulpicus 7:558
Galen, Claudius **5**:354
Galilee **6**:425
galleys **1**:79, **9**:692, **9**:693, **9**:719
Gallic War **2**:139
gambling **4**:301
games **4**:300–302
   at the Colosseum **3**:201
   blind man's buff **3**:171
   board **4**:301–302, **10**:*729*, **10**:730
   children's **4**:302
   Egyptian **4**:301
   gladiatorial **9**:668, **9**:702, **9**:713–714, **9**:716
   hopscotch **3**:171
   Mayan **3**:209, **9**:717
   Olympic **3**:234, **4**:300, **5**:325, **8**:587, **8**:588, **9**:711, **9**:716
   Pythian **3**:234
   Roman **9**:663, **9**:716
   of skill **4**:300–301
   snake **3**:*170*
   tic-tac-toe **3**:171
Gandhara **6**:448
Ganesha **5**:367
Ganges River **1**:75, **5**:341, **5**:367, **8**:594, **9**:670
Ganweriwala **6**:405
Gaozu **2**:157, **2**:158, **3**:168, **6**:467
Garuda **9**:670
*garum* sauce **4**:296
Gaul **1**:56, **2**:153, **2**:154, **5**:382, **9**:700, **9**:714
   conquest of **2**:139, **2**:155, **4**:298, **4**:299
   invasion by Huns **2**:103–104
Gautama Buddha *see* Buddha
Gaza **8**:602
Geb **4**:264
Gedrosian Desert **1**:39
Genesis **5**:355, 7:508, **8**:564
*gens* **4**:282
Gentiles, and Jews **8**:596–597
geography **4**:303–306, **8**:625, **9**:685
geometry **4**:304, **4**:319, **8**:577, **9**:682
geophysical survey **1**:62
*Georgics* (Virgil) **1**:23
ger **8**:571

Germanic tribes **1**:54, **4**:298, **10**:732
   religion **1**:55
Germanicus **1**:27
Germanicus, Gaius Caesar Augustus *see* Caligula
Germany, Iron Age **3**:215
Gessius Florus 7:487
Gifford, Edward **6**:458
Gila River **1**:52
Gilbert Islands 7:516
gild 7:559, **8**:639
Gildas **1**:54
*Gilgamesh* epic **1**:33, **2**:89, **4**:274, **4**:307–308, **6**:410, **6**:451, **6**:463, 7:511, **10**:730
ginseng root **5**:354
girls **3**:169, **3**:171
   in ancient China 7:492
   education of Greek **4**:251
   Greek **4**:251, **5**:328
   Roman **9**:662
   Spartan **5**:328
Giza
   Great Pyramid of Khufu **4**:258, **4**:309, **4**:*309*, **4**:311, **8**:626, **9**:692, **10**:748
   pyramids of **4**:258, **4**:309–311, **8**:627
gladiators **3**:202, **3**:239, 7:544, **9**:668, **9**:702, **9**:713–714, **9**:716
   helmet **9**:*714*
   schools **5**:352, **5**:354
glass **8**:608, **9**:681, **10**:765
glaze **8**:618, **8**:639
glyphs **3**:209, **3**:*210*, 7:500, 7:*535*, 7:559, **10**:789, **10**:790
*go* **4**:301
Gobryas **2**:126
God **3**:187, **3**:188, **3**:214, **3**:231
   earliest idea of **8**:635
   *see also* Jehovah; Yahweh
goddesses
   earth 7:506, **10**:*779*
   fertility 7:491, 7:493, **8**:637
   women as **10**:779
gods
   and days of the week **2**:145
   Greek **9**:648, **10**:737, **10**:793
   male 7:506, **10**:779
   myths 7:549
   Olympian **5**:326, **5**:332,

gods
  Olympian *(cont.)*
    **5**:333, **7**:551
  Roman **9**:648, **9**:650,
    **10**:793
gold **3**:217, **6**:422, **6**:424,
  **8**:574
  weighing **10**:777
Golden Fleece **5**:335
goldsmiths **3**:164
Goliath **3**:224
goosefoot grass **5**:372–373
Gordian III **9**:679
Gordium, knot **1**:38
Gospels **3**:185, **3**:*188*, **6**:419,
  **6**:421, **8**:638
Goths **3**:212, **3**:235,
  **4**:312–315, **5**:383
  language **4**:313
  social rank **9**:706
Gournia **7**:520
government
  Athenian democracy **1**:68,
    **1**:69, **2**:100, **5**:325, **5**:326,
    **6**:468, **8**:598–599, **9**:708,
    **9**:709–710
  by pharaohs **4**:254
  city **4**:271
  Confucian **1**:47
  early form **8**:623
  Greek city-states **3**:193,
    **3**:234, **3**:235, **5**:324–326,
    **6**:469, **9**:711
  Hittite **5**:370
  imperial **9**:659, **9**:660
  kingship as **1**:33, **1**:36
  Mauryan **7**:496
  Parthian **8**:591
  Spartan **9**:712
governors, Roman **9**:660
grain **4**:286, **10**:751
grammar **10**:783
*grammatistes* **4**:252
granaries **4**:286, **6**:406, **7**:528,
  **7**:559
Granicus, Battle of River **1**:38
granulation **6**:424
grave goods **8**:574
graves *see* tombs
Great Stupa, Sanchi **2**:*85*,
  **7**:*497*, **9**:672–673
Great Wall of China **3**:168,
  **3**:173, **4**:247, **4**:316–318,
  **10**:774–775
  map of **4**:*316*
Greece **2**:98–102, **3**:193,
  **3**:211, **3**:215–216, **3**:234,

**5**:324–331, **7**:518, **8**:587,
  **8**:604
  children **5**:328, **5**:329
  city-states **5**:324–325
  classical **5**:324–331
  Dark Ages **5**:324
  food and farming **5**:329
  Hellenistic period **2**:159,
    **3**:230, **6**:470–471, **8**:565,
    **8**:639
  men and women **5**:327
  Mycenaean period **5**:324,
    **7**:545–548, **10**:748
  slaves **9**:701
Greek art **1**:70, **1**:73, **5**:330
Greek civilization, map **5**:*324*
Greek education **4**:251–252,
  **5**:328
Greek homes **5**:328–329
Greek language **3**:170, **6**:450
Greek medicine **5**:326, **5**:352
Greek mythology **2**:98–99,
  **5**:332–335
  creation myths **5**:332
  gods and mortals **5**:334
  heroes **5**:334–335
  Olympian gods **5**:333
  and the Romans **9**:648
Greek philosophy **1**:67–69,
  **2**:101, **2**:102, **2**:106, **5**:326,
  **5**:336–339, **8**:610–611,
  **9**:652, **9**:707–708, **10**:782
  Hellenistic **5**:338
  and writing **5**:339
Greek poetry **9**:674–675
Greek religion **4**:288, **4**:292,
  **5**:326, **8**:636–637
Greeks **2**:102, **2**:104, **2**:109,
  **2**:139, **2**:149, **8**:595
  alphabet **10**:785
  architecture **1**:66, **1**:74
  astronomy **2**:96, **9**:684
  birth **3**:169
  burial customs **3**:229, **3**:230
  clothes **3**:200, **5**:331
  colonies **7**:517
  cremation **10**:748–749
  culture **2**:101
  defeat of Celts **2**:154, **2**:155
  drama **4**:244–246, **5**:330
  fathers **4**:283
  food **4**:295
  geographers **4**:303,
    **4**:304–305, **4**:306, **9**:685
  government **5**:324, **5**:325
  hairstyles **3**:199
  Ionic **3**:219

jewelry **5**:331
law **3**:215–216
libraries **6**:461
literature **6**:463, **6**:464,
  **9**:674–675
and Macedonians
  **6**:470–471
male coming-of-age
  ceremonies **7**:506
masks **7**:489
mathematics **8**:579, **8**:580,
  **8**:629–630, **9**:682
measures **10**:776, **10**:777
men and women **7**:507
music and dance **7**:542–543
pottery **8**:618
public bathhouses **5**:391
sacrifice **9**:668
schools **4**:251–252
sculpture **1**:73
ships **9**:693
slavery **5**:331
sports **9**:716
temples **10**:738
and Trojans **8**:581
war with Persians **3**:223
Greek science **5**:326, **5**:336
Guam **7**:515
Guatemala **7**:498, **8**:627,
  **8**:628, **10**:745
*gufas* **9**:692
guilds **5**:342
Gujewg **6**:*432*
Gu Kaizhi **1**:74
Gupta dynasty **9**:670–671
Gupta Empire **5**:340–342,
  **5**:365, **5**:367, **6**:434, **6**:447,
  **8**:594, **8**:595
  map of **5**:*340*
  science and the arts **5**:341,
    **5**:341–342
  society **5**:342
guru **4**:251, **5**:395
Gutians **1**:36, **10**:727, **10**:728
gymnasium **1**:66, **2**:101,
  **4**:252, **4**:272, **4**:319, **5**:327,
  **5**:328, **8**:588
Gymnosophists **5**:398
*gynaeceum* **5**:328
gynecology **10**:782

Hacilar **10**:779
Hades **5**:333, **5**:*334*, **5**:393,
  **5**:399, **7**:550, **7**:551, **8**:582,
  **10**:793
Hadrian **1**:65, **3**:212,
  **5**:343–344, **5**:345–346,

**5**:359, **6**:475, **9**:666
  villa **5**:*344*
Hadrian's Wall **5**:343,
  **5**:345–346, **9**:646, **9**:657
  map of **5**:*345*
  Stanegate **5**:*345*
Hadrumetum, catacombs of
  **5**:386
Hagar Qim, Malta **10**:737
Hagia Triadha **7**:521
Hahca **8**:*585*
Hai Ba Trung day **10**:761
Hakhamanish **1**:18
Hakhamanishiya *see*
  Achaemenids
Halicarnassus **5**:362
  Mausoleum at **5**:*363*,
    **10**:749
Halloween **4**:293
Halstatt Culture **2**:154, **2**:155
Hamadan **6**:436, **8**:591
Hamilcar Barca **5**:347
Hammurabi **2**:115, **2**:117,
  **2**:119, **3**:213, **3**:214, **4**:266,
  **4**:267, **7**:509
  Code of **2**:119, **3**:213–214,
    **5**:370, **9**:701, **10**:753
Hammurabi dynasty **6**:436
Han dynasty **1**:47, **2**:157,
  **3**:173, **3**:174, **3**:175, **3**:176,
  **3**:178, **3**:181, **3**:205, **3**:237,
  **4**:247, **4**:304, **4**:316, **4**:318,
  **5**:376, **5**:381, **6**:442,
  **6**:466–467, **10**:761
Hanging Gardens of Babylon
  **2**:113, **2**:114, **7**:553, **7**:554
*haniwa* **6**:*413*
Hannibal **5**:347–348, **6**:471,
  **9**:657, **10**:774, **10**:775
  crossing the Alps **5**:347,
    **5**:348
  map of route **5**:*348*
Hanuman **8**:631
Hapi **4**:254, **4**:263
Hapu **1**:45
Harappa **1**:64, **1**:65, **3**:199,
  **6**:405, **6**:406, **7**:519, **7**:528
Harappan civilization **7**:528,
  **8**:*635*
harem **7**:559
Harishena **9**:670, **9**:671
harmony **3**:182
harnesses **10**:756
harp **7**:541, **7**:542, **7**:544,
  **9**:718, **10**:730
Harran **2**:91
haruspices **4**:280

harvest festivals **4**:292
Hasdrubal **5**:347
Hasholme, log boat **10**:*755*
Hasmoneans *see* Maccabees
Hastings, Battle of **1**:55
Hat Giang River **10**:761
Hathor **4**:264, **8**:636, **8**:637
    Temple of **2**:97
Hatshepsut **5**:349–350, **7**:486,
    **7**:493, **10**:781, **10**:*782*
Hatti **5**:368, **5**:369
Hattusha (Hattusas) **5**:368,
    **5**:369
Hattusilis III **5**:369
Hawaii **7**:517, **8**:612, **8**:613
*hazarapat* **1**:19
health **5**:351–354
    and sanitation **3**:193
heaven **6**:474
Hebrew language **3**:226
    and Judaism **6**:450
Hebrews **3**:214, **5**:355–359,
    **6**:416–417, **7**:536–538,
    **7**:543, **7**:553, **8**:565, **9**:690,
    **9**:691
    burial customs **3**:229, **3**:231
    as the "chosen people"
        **7**:537
    families **4**:283, **4**:284
    kings **5**:356
    map of territories **5**:*355*
    religion **4**:290, **4**:291,
        **4**:292, **4**:*293*
    *see also* Jews
Hector **5**:393, **10**:759
Hegra **8**:602
heifer **1**:71, **1**:79
Helena (mother of
    Constantine) **6**:418
Helen of Troy **1**:24, **5**:392,
    **10**:758
Heliopolis **10**:787
Helios **8**:582, **9**:668
hell **6**:474
Hellenistic period **2**:159,
    **3**:230, **5**:338, **6**:470–471,
    **8**:565, **8**:639
Hellespont **10**:786
Helots **9**:711, **9**:712
hemlock **9**:708, **9**:719
hemp **9**:681, **9**:719
Henutmehyt **2**:128
Hephaestion **1**:39
Hephaestos **1**:70–71, **5**:333
Heraclitus **4**:271
Heraclius **9**:679, **9**:680
Hera **3**:215, **5**:326, **5**:333,

**5**:335, **8**:588, **9**:651, **10**:793
Herakles *see* Hercules
herbal medicine **3**:179, **5**:354
Herculaneum **5**:360–361
    Villa of the Papyri **5**:361
Hercules **5**:335, **6**:447, **6**:468,
    **7**:492, **7**:537, **8**:587, **10**:793
Hermes **5**:328, **5**:333
Hermod **7**:551
Hero of Alexandria **10**:736
Herod the Great **5**:359, **6**:418
Herodotus **1**:18, **1**:19, **3**:200,
    **3**:220, **3**:223, **5**:353,
    **5**:362–363, **5**:389, **5**:391,
    **8**:571, **8**:606, **9**:686, **9**:689,
    **10**:786, **10**:787
    *The Histories* **2**:112
    travels **5**:362
    writings **5**:362
heroes **7**:549
heroines **10**:761, **10**:782
Hesiod **10**:794
    *Works and Days* **6**:463
Hesperus **9**:675
Hestia **3**:169, **5**:333
*hetaireia* **9**:674
Hetepheres **8**:627
Heyerdahl, Thor **7**:518
hierarchy **3**:176, **3**:205, **3**:239,
    **9**:699, **9**:703
hieratic writing **4**:259
hieroglyphs **3**:209, **3**:239,
    **4**:249, **4**:259, **6**:449, **6**:479,
    **7**:535, **8**:572, **8**:578, **8**:614,
    **8**:623, **8**:639, **10**:784,
    **10**:789
Hieron **4**:279, **8**:580
Hillel **6**:431
Himalayas **6**:405
himation **5**:331
Hinduism **2**:132, **2**:136,
    **2**:138, **5**:364–367, **6**:449,
    **6**:464, **8**:635, **9**:669, **9**:670,
    **9**:705, **10**:781
    asceticism **5**:366, **5**:367
    caste system **1**:76, **4**:252,
        **5**:365, **6**:479, **9**:705
    festivals **4**:291
    goddess **5**:*342*
    gods **5**:366–367
    Laws of Manu **4**:252
    reincarnation **5**:364–365
    sacred texts of **8**:631–632,
        **8**:638
    and Sanskrit **6**:450
Hipparchus **4**:305, **8**:625,
    **9**:684

Hippo **2**:105, **2**:106
Hippocrates **5**:326, **5**:352,
    **5**:*354*, **9**:*682*
Hippocratic oath **5**:326
hippodrome **8**:588, **10**:765,
    **10**:799
Hiram **9**:693, **10**:764
Hissarlik **10**:758–759
historians **5**:362, **5**:381
history **5**:362
    language and **6**:452
    Roman **10**:731–732
Hittite Empire **7**:548
Hittites **5**:368–371, **6**:436,
    **6**:437, **8**:633, **8**:639, **9**:*691*
    culture and law **5**:370
    government **5**:370
    iron making **10**:734
    language **5**:368, **6**:450
    law **3**:215
    map of empire **5**:*368*
    New Kingdom **5**:368, **5**:369
    Old Kingdom **5**:368, **5**:369
    religion **5**:370–371
    wars **5**:368–369
Hohokam people **1**:50, **1**:51,
    **1**:52
Holi festival **4**:291
Holy Communion *see*
    Eucharist
Holy Spirit **3**:187
Holy Week **6**:420
Homer **3**:170, **4**:288, **5**:324,
    **5**:325, **5**:328, **5**:332,
    **5**:392–394, **6**:451, **8**:629
    *see also Iliad*; *Odyssey*
homes *see* houses
*homo habilis* **8**:620–621
*homo sapiens sapiens* **8**:621
Honduras **7**:498
Honorius **3**:202, **4**:315
Honshu **1**:42, **6**:411
Hopeton **5**:373
Hopewell culture **5**:372–374
    arts and crafts **5**:374
    astronomy **5**:373
    buildings **5**:373
    food and farming
        **5**:372–373
    map of sites **5**:*372*
    rituals **5**:374
Hopi **1**:50
    origin myth **1**:50
Horace **2**:109, **9**:663
Horemheb **7**:556, **10**:762
horoscopes **8**:625
horsemanship **10**:774

Scythian **9**:687
horse racing **8**:588, **9**:716
horse riding **8**:570, **9**:716
horses **10**:754
    domestication of **7**:519
Horus **2**:127, **4**:263, **4**:264,
    **4**:265, **5**:351, **5**:399
Hostilian **5**:391
houses **5**:375–378
    Mesopotamian **7**:510, **7**:512
    rich and poor **5**:376–377
    stone and brick **5**:376
Hsiung-Nu **6**:446, **6**:447
Huaca de la Luna **7**:526
Huaca del Sol **7**:526
Huangdi (Huang-ti)
    **5**:379–380
Huari people **7**:527
hull **9**:692, **9**:719
Hulla **5**:371
Humbaba **4**:307
Hunefer **2**:127
Huns **2**:103–104, **4**:313,
    **4**:314, **5**:381–384
    map of kingdom **5**:*381*
    reflex bow **8**:571
hunter-gatherers **2**:122, **3**:191,
    **5**:385–387, **6**:414, **6**:479
    art **5**:387
    Nok **8**:566–569
hunting **5**:385–387, **9**:667,
    **9**:715
Hwanung, Prince **6**:442, **6**:443
hydraulics **10**:736
hygiene **5**:388–391
    personal **5**:390, **5**:391
Hyksos people **10**:743
hymns **7**:544
    Egyptian **4**:265
    Sumerian **10**:730
    to Shulgi **9**:695
    to Thebes **10**:744
    Vedic **4**:244
Hypatia **1**:41, **10**:782
hypocaust **5**:378, **5**:390, **9**:*658*
hypostyle hall **10**:738
Hystaspes **10**:797

Ibbi-Sin **9**:696
ibis **4**:262, **4**:319
Ice Age **6**:459–460, **8**:621
Iceni **2**:129
*ientaclum* **4**:296
Ife kingdom **8**:568
*Iliad* (Homer) **1**:24, **1**:68,
    **2**:98, **2**:99, **5**:324, **5**:325,
    **5**:362, **5**:392–394, **6**:463,

*Iliad* (Homer) *(cont.)*
6:472, 7:518, 7:545, 8:581, 10:758, 10:759
Imhotep 1:45, 4:258, 8:626, 10:748
Immortals 1:19
impalement 9:706, 10:772
Inanna 4:275, 4:307, 6:409, 7:550, 7:551, 8:637
Incas, mathematics 8:577
incense 5:350, 8:602
inclined plane 10:733
India 2:84, 2:131–133, 3:182, 3:192, 5:340–342, 7:494–497, 8:594–595, 9:670–671, 9:672–673
  Alexander the Great in 1:38–39
  art 4:248
  Aryans 1:75–78, 7:519
  caste system 1:76, 4:252, 5:365, 6:479, 9:705
  drama 4:244
  education 4:250–251
  epic poetry 8:631–632
  farming 4:287
  irrigation 10:734
  marriage 7:486
  numbers 8:577
  religion 5:364–367
  roads 9:646
  slaves 9:700
  temples 10:739
  Vedic period 1:75, 1:77
  Zoroastrianism 10:795
Indian literature 6:463
Indian philosophy 5:395–398
  six schools of 5:396–397
*Indica* (Megasthenes) 7:496, 7:497, 8:594
Indo-European languages 5:368, 6:436, 6:450, 6:451, 6:479
Indo-Europeans 8:638
Indo-Iranian languages 9:686
Indonesia 3:237, 7:514
Indra 1:76, 1:77, 1:78, 5:364
Indus Plain 6:404
Indus River 7:528, 7:529
Indus valley 1:75–77, 3:192, 5:364, 5:388–389, 6:404–408, 7:519, 7:528–529
  cities 6:405–406
  city planning 1:65
  clothes 3:199, 6:408
  houses 1:64

mud bricks 6:405
script 6:406, 6:407
seals 6:407
society 6:406
sports 9:715
terra-cotta figure 7:496
toys 3:170, 6:408
trade and crafts 6:406
water management 6:406
writing 6:406
infantry 8:604, 10:774
*inma* 10:767
inscriptions 6:464
  Mesopotamian 7:511
Inshushinak 4:268, 4:269
*Instruction of Ptahhotep, The* 4:250
Instructress, the (Chinese writer) 1:74
*insulae* 5:378
intaglio 6:423, 6:479
international languages 6:452
Inuits 7:506
Iolkos 7:548
Ionia 3:239
Ionian 4:319
Ionic Greeks 3:219, 3:223
Iphigenia 1:25, 4:246
Ipsus, Battle of 6:470, 6:471, 7:494
Iran 8:591, 9:678
Iranians 1:75
Iraq 10:736
Ireland 2:153, 7:523
  Celts 2:155, 7:493
  myths 7:550, 7:552
Irish 1:54
iron 3:236, 4:287, 5:368
Iron Age 2:122–123, 2:153, 2:156, 3:236
  in Germany 3:215
  in Korea 6:442
  Later 2:122
  Nok culture 8:566–569
  tools 1:62
  weapons 10:774
iron making 2:122–123, 8:566, 10:734
iron oxide 5:387, 6:460
Iroquois 7:491, 7:531
irrigation 1:52, 3:175, 3:191, 3:192, 4:285–286, 4:287–288, 7:509, 8:564–565, 8:623, 8:639, 10:778
  Moche 7:524
  technology 10:734

waterwheels 10:735
Isaac 8:*638*
Isaiah 3:231
Ishtar 1:33, 1:36, 2:87, 2:120, 2:142, 4:275, 4:307, 6:409–410, 8:564, 9:696, 10:730
Isis 4:264, 4:265, 8:636, 8:637, 9:650
Islam 5:355, 5:399, 6:427, 9:680, 10:795, 10:798
  and the Sasanians 9:679, 9:680
Islamic Empire 9:680
Israelites 2:91, 3:224, 3:232, 7:554, 8:634
  role of women 3:233
  twelve tribes 5:355
  *see also* Hebrews; Jews
Israel (name for Jacob) 5:355
Israel (place) 5:356, 5:357, 8:606
Isthmian Games 3:212
Italy 7:540
  invasion by Celts 2:154, 2:155
  invasion by Huns 2:104
Ithaca 5:393, 8:581
Itjtawy 10:743
ivory 7:545, 8:574, 8:608, 9:*718*, 10:765
  fossil 5:374, 5:399
Ixion 3:215
Izanagi 1:42

Jacob 5:355
jade 6:424, 7:500, 7:518, 8:583, 8:585, 10:789
Jade Emperor *see* Yu Huang Shang Di
Jael 3:233
jaguar 7:502, 8:586, 8:*627*, 10:741, 10:746
Jaimini 5:396
Jain religion 5:398, 7:496
James, Saint 8:597
*janas* 1:76
Janus 9:669
Japan 6:411–413
  arts and crafts 6:413
  Buddism in 2:138
  emperors 6:412
  empire of the rising sun 1:43
  food and farming 6:412–413
  Kofun period 6:412

mourning colors 3:229
Neolithic 4:294
pottery 8:617, 8:622
sports 9:716
Yayoi period 6:411
Japanese philosophy 6:413
Japanese religion 1:42–43, 6:413
Japanese writing 10:784
Jason 5:335
javelin throwing 9:715
Jebusites 3:224, 6:416
Jehoiachin 7:553
Jehovah 7:506
Jeremiah 7:554
Jericho 3:191, 3:*191*, 5:386, 6:414–415, 10:779
  farming and hunting 6:414–415
  walls of 1:64, 6:414, 10:773
Jerome, Saint 2:105, 3:185
Jerusalem 2:125, 3:224, 3:225, 3:226, 5:356, 5:*356*, 5:357, 5:358, 6:416–418, 6:428, 7:536, 8:596, 9:680, 9:690
  Christianity in 6:418
  destruction of (70 CE) 7:487
  Dome of the Rock 6:*416*
  Greek rule 6:417
  patriarch of 3:186
  Roman rule 6:418
  sack of 7:553–554
  Solomon's temple 6:416, 6:*417*, 6:428, 6:430–431, 10:739
  temple 5:359
  Wailing (Western) Wall 10:739
Jerwan, aqueduct 8:565
Jesus Christ 2:105, 3:184–185, 3:186–187, 3:188, 3:207, 3:227, 3:230–231, 6:421, 8:596, 8:638, 10:740
  sacrifice 9:669
Jesus of Nazareth 4:250, 4:293, 6:419–421
  as preacher 6:420
  as rebel 6:420–421
  resurrection 6:421
  *see also* Jesus Christ
jewelry 3:198, 3:200, 3:217, 6:422–424, 10:752
  Chinese 6:424
  Etruscan 4:280, 4:281
  Greek 5:331
  Mayan 7:500
  Roman 6:423–424

Sumerian **3**:*228*, **6**:422,
  **6**:424, **10**:*728*,
  **10**:729–730, **10**:*768*,
  **10**:769
Jewish uprising (588–587 BCE)
  **6**:430, **7**:553, **7**:*554*
Jewish War (66–73 CE) **6**:425,
  **7**:487–488
Jews **2**:126, **2**:144, **3**:184,
  **3**:185, **3**:220, **3**:225, **3**:226,
  **5**:356, **7**:536–538, **7**:*554*
  diaspora **5**:359
  in exile **2**:125, **5**:358–359
  festivals **9**:669
  first Jewish revolt (66–70
    CE) **5**:357, **5**:359
  and Gentiles **8**:596–597
  history **6**:425–426, **10**:773
  in Jerusalem **6**:416–417
  and Judaism **6**:427–431
  law **5**:358
  literature **6**:461
  religion **6**:427–431, **10**:739
  second Jewish revolt
    (132–135 CE) **5**:357,
    **5**:359
  women **7**:493
  *see also* Hebrews; Israelites
Jezebel **10**:765
Jimmu Tenno **1**:43
John the Baptist **6**:420
John, Saint **8**:597
Jokhang Temple, Lhasa **2**:138
Jomon culture **6**:411, **6**:412,
  **6**:413
Joppa **8**:607
Jordan **8**:602
Jordanes **4**:312
Joseph **6**:419
Josephus, Flavius **6**:425–426,
  **6**:430, **7**:487–488
  *The Jewish Antiquities* **6**:426
  *The Jewish War* **6**:426
Joshua **6**:414
Jotapata **6**:425
joust **9**:717, **9**:719
Judaea **5**:344, **5**:357, **5**:359,
  **6**:425
Judah **3**:220, **5**:356, **5**:357,
  **6**:416–417, **7**:553, **9**:688,
  **9**:690
  tribe of **3**:224
Judaism **5**:355, **5**:357,
  **6**:427–431, **7**:536, **8**:638
  festivals and fasts **6**:427
  and Hebrew **6**:450
  the Law **6**:431

Judas Iscariot **6**:420
judges, Hebrew **5**:355, **5**:357
Judges, Book of **3**:232, **3**:233
Julia (Caesar's daughter) **2**:109,
  **2**:141
Julian **4**:299, **9**:679
Julian calendar **2**:141, **2**:146
Jupiter **1**:47, **2**:146, **8**:637,
  **9**:648, **9**:668, **9**:*683*, **10**:793
Jupiter (planet) **8**:625
jurors **2**:101, **8**:598, **9**:*710*
Justinian **5**:339, **8**:576, **9**:655
Jutes **1**:54, **1**:55
Juvenal **3**:193

*ka* **4**:257, **8**:636
Kadesh, Battle of **5**:368, **5**:369
Kajula Kadphises **6**:447
Kakadu region **6**:432–433
  rock art **6**:432–433
Kalhu *see* Calah
Kalidasa **5**:342, **6**:434–435
  *The Cloud Messenger* **6**:435
Kali Ma **10**:781
Kalinga **2**:84
Kalokairinos, Minos **6**:440
Kanada **5**:396
Kanishka **6**:446, **6**:447, **6**:448
kaolin **8**:586, **8**:639
Kapila **5**:396
Karduniash (Babylon) **6**:437
karma **2**:137, **5**:365, **5**:398
Karnak **4**:*261*
  Temple of Amun **1**:*46*,
    **4**:*261*, **5**:369, **8**:*634*,
    **10**:738, **10**:743
  Temple of Mut **4**:*261*
Kashi **5**:367
Kassites **6**:436–438
  kings **6**:437
  land ownership **6**:438
  writing **6**:438
Kastri **3**:219
Kato Zakro **7**:521
Kautilya *see* Chanakya
kava ceremonies **7**:505
keel **9**:692, **9**:719, **10**:764,
  **10**:799
Kefala Hill **6**:440
Kenyon, Kathleen **6**:414–415
Kerma **8**:573, **8**:575
Keros **3**:219
Khafra, pyramid of **4**:309,
  **4**:311
Khania **7**:520, **7**:548
khene **3**:238
Khepri **4**:263

Khonsu **4**:291
Khorasmia **10**:797
Khorsabad (Assyrian palace)
  **8**:590
Khshayarsa *see* Xerxes
Khufu **8**:626
  Great Pyramid of **4**:258,
    **4**:309, **4**:311, **9**:*692*,
    **10**:748
Khumbannumena **4**:267
Kidin-Khutran **4**:267
kingship, Sumerian **10**:727
Kish **4**:274, **4**:275, **8**:580,
  **9**:677
kithara **7**:*542*, **7**:543
*kitharistes* **4**:252
*kivas* **1**:50, **1**:51, **1**:*53*
Kiya **10**:762
*kleroterion* **9**:*710*
Klio **1**:*23*
Knossos **3**:218, **6**:439–440,
  **7**:520–522, **7**:547, **7**:548
  Bull Portico **6**:*439*
  late Minoan period **8**:*619*
  Painted Palace **6**:439
  Shrine of the Double Axes
    **7**:521
knucklebones **4**:300
Koguryo **6**:444, **6**:445
kohl **3**:199, **3**:239
Koine **6**:452
Koldewey, Robert **2**:112
Kong Fuzi *see* Confucius
Kong Qiu *see* Confucius
Korea **6**:411, **6**:441–445
  Bronze Age **6**:442, **6**:443
  Chinese influence **6**:445
  combware peoples
    **6**:441–442, **6**:443
  Iron Age **6**:442, **6**:443
  Koryo dynasty **6**:443
  legend of Tan'gun **6**:442
  rice **6**:442, **6**:443
  sumo wrestling **9**:716
  Three Hans **6**:443
  Three Kingdoms **6**:443,
    **6**:444–445
  tribal clans and leagues
    **6**:442
  Unified Silla dynasty **6**:443,
    **6**:445
Kostromskaya **8**:570
koumiss **9**:688
Krisa **3**:234
Krishna **4**:291, **5**:367, **6**:473,
  **8**:631
Kronos **8**:587

Kroton **9**:718
Kshatriyas **1**:76, **4**:252, **9**:705
*kudurrus* **6**:438
Kuei-shuang *see* Kushan
Kumara Gupta **5**:341
Kumuradevi **5**:341
Kungnae-song **6**:445
Kunti **6**:*474*
Kurgan culture **6**:450
kurgans **9**:689
Kurigalzu I **6**:437
Kurigalzu II **6**:438
Kush **8**:566, **8**:567, **8**:573,
  **8**:575, **8**:576
Kushan Empire **6**:446–448
  art **6**:448
  coins **9**:*670*
Kusinagara **2**:133
Kutau **6**:458
Kutir-Nahhunte I **4**:267
Kwanggaet'o-wang **6**:445
Kyrgyzstan **8**:*571*
Kyushu **6**:411

labyrinth **5**:335, **6**:440
Lachish **9**:690
Laconia **9**:711
Laconians **9**:711
lacquer **6**:413, **6**:479, **10**:752,
  **10**:799
Laertes **5**:394
Lagash **4**:275
Lake Turkana **8**:*620*
Lakshmana **8**:*632*
Lakshmi **5**:367, **9**:670
land, measuring **10**:778
Lang Bac **10**:761
languages **6**:449–452
  American **6**:451
  comparisons **6**:452
  families **6**:450
  and history **6**:452
  international **6**:452
  and society **6**:450
Lanka **8**:631, **9**:670
  *see also* Sri Lanka
Lao-tzu (Laozi) **3**:*180*, **3**:181,
  **6**:453–455
lapis lazuli **6**:422, **7**:510,
  **7**:541, **7**:559, **10**:*768*,
  **10**:799
Lapita culture **6**:456–458,
  **7**:504, **8**:612, **8**:613
  mysteries **6**:457
  navigation **9**:694
  pottery **6**:458
  travels **6**:456–457

Lapiths **3**:215
Larthia Seinti **4**:279
Lascaux (cave paintings) **6**:459–460, **8**:635
Last Judgment **6**:420
Last Supper **6**:420, **6**:421
La Tène culture **2**:*154*, **2**:155
Latin **3**:185, **9**:663
　alphabet **8**:609
　Cicero's prose **3**:189
latitude **4**:303, **4**:305, **8**:625, **8**:639, **9**:685
latte stones **7**:514
La Venta **8**:583, **8**:584, **8**:585
law **3**:213–214
　Babylonian **2**:119
　codes **3**:213–214
　courts **2**:101
　Greek **9**:709–710
　Sumerian codes **10**:729
　trade **10**:753
Laws of Manu **4**:252
leap years **2**:146
leather **3**:198
Lebanon **8**:606, **10**:764
Lechares **4**:292
Leda **10**:793
Lefkandi **7**:548
legends **7**:549
legionaries **5**:345, **5**:399, **9**:657, **9**:719
legions, Roman **2**:159, **10**:774
leisure *see* sports and entertainment
Lei Zu **5**:379
*lekythos* **3**:230
Leo I, Pope **2**:104, **5**:384
Leonidas **8**:*587*, **9**:*711*
Lepidus, Marcus Aemilius **1**:56, **2**:107, **2**:108
Lesbos **9**:674
Leuktra, Battle of **5**:325, **9**:712
Levant **8**:606, **8**:607, **8**:639, **10**:743
lever **8**:580, **9**:683, **10**:733
Levkas **9**:674
*lex talionis* **3**:213
Libby, William **6**:415
libraries **6**:461–462
Libya **3**:218, **8**:622, **9**:*699*
Libyans **7**:517
Licinius **3**:208
life after death *see* afterlife
lighthouses **8**:607
Lightning Man **6**:433
limpet hammers **5**:386
Lindow Man **7**:539

Linear A and B **7**:548
linen **3**:198–199, **3**:229, **4**:257, **4**:259, **8**:608, **9**:692
lingua franca **6**:452
lintel **10**:725, **10**:*746*, **10**:799
literature **6**:463–465
　early written **6**:464
　oral **6**:463
　religion and **6**:464
　Roman **9**:663
　Sumerian **10**:730
Liu Bang *see* Gaozu
Liu Hsin **9**:684
Liu Hsiu **6**:466–467
Livia **1**:27, **7**:*484*
Livia Drusilla **2**:*108*, **2**:109
Livy **5**:348
llamas **10**:754
Lleu Llaw Gyffes **7**:550
logic, Aristotelian **1**:67, **1**:69, **5**:338
*logos* **6**:449
Lokayota **5**:397
Londinium (London) **2**:130
longitude **4**:303, **4**:305, **8**:625, **8**:639, **9**:685
Lord of Sipan **7**:525, **7**:527
lotus eaters **5**:393, **8**:581
lotus position **5**:*396*, **5**:*397*
Luckenbill, D. D. **9**:691
Lucretia **4**:279
Lucretius **7**:544
Lugalbanda **4**:275
lulav **5**:*359*
Lumbini, Nepal **2**:131
lunar eclipses **2**:96, **9**:684, **9**:695–696
lunar month **3**:210, **7**:502
Luoyang **2**:158, **6**:*466*, **6**:467
Luristan **1**:28
*lurs* **7**:543
lute **7**:*542*
lutrophoros **10**:*749*
Luxor *see* Thebes
luxuries, trade in **10**:751–752
Lydia **3**:220, **3**:235, **3**:239
　first coins **7**:531
Lydians **3**:220
Lygdamis **5**:362
lyre **5**:399, **7**:542, **9**:675, **9**:718
　bull-headed **7**:*541*
Lysimachus **4**:271
Lysippus **9**:*707*

*Mabinogion* **7**:550
macana **7**:502, **7**:559

Maccabees **5**:*358*, **5**:359, **6**:417
　priest-kings **5**:357, **5**:359
Macedon **1**:37, **3**:223, **6**:468
Macedonia **5**:325, **8**:604–605, **9**:713
　and Rome **6**:471
Macedonian Empire **8**:608
Macedonians **6**:468–471, **9**:688
machines **10**:733
Madhya Pradesh **9**:672
Maecenas **1**:23
Maes Howe **9**:698
Maghada **7**:494, **7**:497, **8**:595
magic **5**:351, **7**:549
　and art **1**:70–71
　language and **6**:449
　numbers and religion **8**:579, **8**:636
　Polynesian **8**:613
*magister ludi* **3**:170
Magi, the **10**:796, **10**:798
Magna Mater **9**:650
Magnentius **4**:298, **4**:299
magnet **5**:336
magnetic compass **3**:177, **10**:755
magnitude of stars **8**:624, **9**:684
magus **3**:222, **3**:239
*Mahabharata* **4**:251, **6**:463, **6**:472–474, **8**:631
Ma-han tribal league **6**:442
Maharajadhirajah **5**:341
Mahavira **5**:398
Mahayana Buddhism **2**:136, **2**:137, **6**:446, **6**:448
Maiden Castle, southwest England **2**:156
Maimonides, Moses **3**:214
maize **8**:585, **10**:788
Makuria **8**:576
Malatya, Gate of **1**:70
Malkata (Palace of Amenhotep III) **8**:589, **8**:590
Malta **8**:637, **10**:737
mana **7**:504, **8**:613
*mancala* **4**:302
*manes* **4**:283
Manichaeus (Mani) **9**:678
manioc **8**:622, **8**:639
manslaughter **3**:213
mantra **6**:449
Manu, Laws of **4**:252
mapmaking **4**:303–306, **8**:625, **9**:*684*, **9**:685
　Egyptian **2**:128

Sumerian **10**:728
map projection **4**:306, **4**:319
Marathon, Battle of **1**:18, **1**:19, **2**:100, **3**:223, **4**:245, **4**:246, **5**:325, **9**:712, **10**:787
marble **3**:217–219, **10**:738
marbles **4**:300–301
Marcellinus, Ammianus **5**:381
Marcellus **2**:108
Marcus Aurelius **3**:216, **5**:354, **6**:475–476, **9**:653
　*The Meditations* **6**:476
Marduk **2**:113, **2**:119, **2**:125, **2**:146, **4**:290, **5**:368, **6**:477–478, **7**:551, **7**:553, **7**:554, **9**:669, **9**:691, **10**:727, **10**:787
Mari **2**:119
Marianas **7**:514, **7**:515
Marinatos, Spyridon **3**:218
Marius **9**:659
markets **3**:192
Mark, Saint **1**:41
Marlborough Downs **10**:725
Maro, Publius Vergilius *see* Virgil
Marquesas Islands **8**:613
marriage **7**:484–486
　Babylonian **2**:116
　ceremonies and rituals **7**:485–486
　Chinese **3**:176
　and the law **7**:484
　and politics **7**:484–485
　Roman **3**:171
Mars **7**:492, **7**:549, **9**:648
Mars (planet) **8**:625
Marshall Islands **7**:516
Marshall, Sir John **7**:528, **7**:529
Martial **9**:663
martial arts **2**:138
martyr **3**:186, **8**:596
Mary Magdalene **6**:421
Mary (mother of Jesus) **6**:419
Masada **7**:487–488
　myth of **7**:488
　siege of (72 CE) **7**:487–488
masculinity **7**:507
masks **4**:246, **5**:*330*, **7**:489–490
　African **7**:489, **7**:490
　Aztec **10**:*741*
　death masks **7**:490
　Mayan **7**:*500*, **10**:*746*
　Melanesian **7**:504
　theatrical **7**:489–490

Massagetes **9**:687, **9**:688
mast **10**:756
mastaba tombs **4**:311, **8**:626
mathematics **9**:682–684
　Egyptian **8**:578, **9**:682
　Greek **8**:579, **8**:629–630
　Mayan **3**:210
　pure **9**:683
Mathura **6**:446, **6**:448
matriarchy **7**:491–493,
　**10**:781, **10**:799
　theories of **7**:491
matrilineal **7**:491, **7**:514,
　**7**:559
maul stone **10**:725, **10**:799
Mauryan Empire **2**:84, **5**:340,
　**7**:494–497, **8**:594–595,
　**9**:672
　road system **9**:644
mausoleum **8**:603, **10**:749
Mausoleum at Halicarnassus
　**5**:*363*, **10**:749
Mausolus of Caria **5**:363,
　**10**:749
Maxentius **3**:207
Maya **2**:131, **7**:498–502,
　**8**:585, **10**:745–746, **10**:754
　arts and crafts **7**:500
　ball courts **1**:52, **9**:717–718
　calendars **2**:145, **7**:500,
　　**7**:501, **8**:578, **9**:682,
　　**10**:790
　culture **3**:209–210
　families **4**:283, **4**:284
　festivals **4**:293
　food and farming
　　**7**:498–500
　games **3**:209
　huts **5**:377
　language **7**:500
　literature **6**:461
　mathematics **7**:502, **9**:682
　number system **8**:577,
　　**8**:578, **8**:579, **8**:580
　paintings **4**:244
　pottery **4**:249
　rank **9**:703
　religion **4**:283
　ritual and war **7**:502
　scientists **7**:500
　temple pyramids **8**:*627*,
　　**8**:628
　writing **7**:500, **10**:789
Mayan languages **6**:451
Ma Yuan **10**:761
measures **10**:776–778
　first units **10**:776

metric system **10**:778
Medea **5**:335, **10**:798
Medes **1**:18, **1**:19, **1**:58, **2**:87,
　**2**:91, **2**:95, **2**:125, **2**:143,
　**3**:220, **3**:239, **8**:564, **8**:565
Media **8**:591, **9**:690
medical schools, Egyptian
　**5**:351
medical texts, Egyptian **5**:353
medicine **5**:351–354, **9**:682
　Babylonian **3**:213
　Chinese **3**:179
　Egyptian **4**:265, **5**:351,
　　**5**:353, **9**:682, **10**:782
　Greek **4**:272
Medinet Habu **7**:517
　palace of Ramses III **8**:589
　temple of **5**:389
meditation **5**:396, **6**:476,
　**6**:479
Mediterranean Sea **7**:517,
　**9**:694, **10**:755, **10**:757
　trade **10**:752
Medusa **2**:98, **5**:335
Megabazus **3**:223
megalith **2**:159
Melanesia **6**:456, **7**:486, **7**:504,
　**7**:514
Melanesian culture **7**:503–505
　arts and crafts **7**:504
　beliefs **7**:505
　farmers and gatherers **7**:503
　languages **7**:503
　trading resources **7**:504
Me Linh **10**:760, **10**:761
Melos **3**:217
Melpomene **1**:*23*
Melqart **8**:609, **10**:764–765
memorizing **4**:250–251, **5**:328
Memphis **10**:743
　palace of Merneptah **8**:589
men **7**:506–508
　coming of age rituals **7**:507
　male dominance **7**:506–507
　Spartan **9**:712
　and women **7**:508
　*see also* patriarchy
Menander **8**:595
Menas **1**:37
Mencius **1**:47, **3**:181, **3**:*181*,
　**3**:204
Menelaus **5**:392, **10**:758
Menes **4**:253
Meng-tzu (Mengzi) *see*
　Mencius
menial **9**:705, **9**:706, **9**:719
Menkaura, pyramid of **4**:309,

　**4**:311
Menna **9**:*701*
Mentuhotep II **1**:46
Menvra **4**:280
mercenaries **1**:54, **1**:79, **4**:314
　Nubian **8**:*573*
merchant enterprise
　**10**:751–753
Mercury **2**:146
Mercury (planet) **8**:625
meridians **4**:305
Merneptah **8**:589
Meroe **8**:566, **8**:573, **8**:576
　pyramid **8**:*575*
Meroitic language **8**:576
Merovingians **4**:299
Meryt **7**:*508*
Mesa Verde **1**:50, **1**:51, **1**:53
Mesehti **4**:260
Mesoamerica **8**:627, **10**:741
　ball games **4**:244
　pyramid temples **1**:65
　writing **4**:249
Mesoamerican languages
　**6**:451, **6**:*452*
Mesolithic era (Middle Stone
　Age) **5**:385, **5**:386, **8**:621
Mesopotamia **2**:90, **2**:96,
　**2**:115, **2**:119, **3**:192, **4**:266,
　**4**:268, **4**:274, **4**:286, **5**:356,
　**6**:436, **7**:509–513,
　**9**:676–677, **9**:679, **9**:688,
　**9**:695, **9**:714, **10**:733,
　**10**:756, **10**:768
　early cities **7**:510
　great floods **7**:511
　Lower **8**:*623*
　map of **1**:*30*
Mesopotamians **1**:30–36
　architecture **1**:64–65
　art and writing **7**:512
　boats **9**:692, **10**:756
　calendars **2**:144
　clothes **3**:198
　education **4**:249
　food **4**:286–287, **4**:297
　literature **1**:34, **4**:307–308
　music **7**:541, **7**:543
　mythology **4**:276
　numbers **7**:513, **8**:577
　pottery **8**:617
　religion **3**:228, **6**:409, **8**:564
　schooling **3**:169
　scribes **7**:511
　sports **9**:716
　texts **2**:89
　ziggurats **8**:628

Messalina **10**:*780*, **10**:782
Messenians **9**:711
messiah **3**:184, **3**:225, **3**:227,
　**5**:359, **6**:421, **6**:479
metallurgy **3**:239
metals, trade in **10**:752
metalworking **3**:164, **9**:681
　Moche **7**:524
*Metamorphoses* (Apuleius)
　**6**:465
*Metamorphoses* (Ovid) **5**:335,
　**9**:651
Metapontum **8**:630
metic **9**:719
Metis **2**:98, **10**:793
metric system **10**:778
*metronomoi* **10**:777
Mexico **7**:534–535,
　**8**:583–585, **8**:622, **9**:703,
　**10**:741–742, **10**:788–790
Mezzulla **5**:371
Micah **3**:225
*miccaotli* **10**:741
Micronesia **6**:456
Micronesian culture
　**7**:514–516, **10**:755
　clans and families **7**:514
　food and drink **7**:514
　houses **7**:514
　water transport **7**:516
middens **5**:386
Middle East **7**:531
migration **7**:517–519
　evidence for **7**:518–519
Milan, Edict of **3**:207
miles **10**:778
Miletus **8**:629
milk **4**:297
millet **9**:719
Milo of Kroton **9**:718
milpa **7**:499, **7**:559
Milvian Bridge, Battle of **3**:207
Mimamsa **5**:396–397
Mimbres pottery **1**:52
Min **4**:292
*mina* **10**:777
Minerva *see* Athena
Ming dynasty **1**:47, **4**:316
Ming Ti **9**:*705*
Minoans **3**:218, **3**:219,
　**7**:520–523**
　art **7**:522
　bull leaping **9**:715
　culture **6**:439–440
　Linear A script **7**:548
　palaces **7**:520, **7**:521, **7**:*523*
　religion **7**:521

Minoans *(cont.)*
  second palace period
    7:520–521
Minos **6**:439
Minotaur **5**:335, **6**:440
Mishnah **6**:431
Mishneh Torah **3**:*214*
missionaries **7**:517
Mississippi River valley **5**:372
mistletoe **2**:156
Mitanni people **2**:90
Mithra **1**:29, **6**:447
Mithras **8**:*636*, **8**:637, **9**:650
Mithridates **2**:141
Mithridates II **8**:593
Mitla **10**:788–789
Mitra **1**:76
Mittani **1**:44
Mixtecs **7**:*534*, **10**:788, **10**:789
*moai* statues **8**:614
*mobad* **9**:678
Moche culture **7**:524–527
  building **7**:525–526
  class system and sacrifice
    **7**:526
  pottery **1**:*72*, **7**:524, **7**:525,
    **7**:526
  rank **9**:*703*
  sacrifice **9**:667
Moche River **7**:524
Modestinus **7**:485
Mogao Ku caves **4**:247, **4**:248
Mogollon people **1**:*50*, **1**:51,
  **1**:52
  pottery **1**:52
Mohenjo Daro **1**:64, **1**:65,
  **1**:71, **3**:*192*, **3**:199, **5**:388,
  **6**:405, **6**:406, **7**:528–529,
  **10**:*777*
  Great Bath **5**:388
  soapstone seal **8**:635
  water management **7**:528
*moksha* **5**:366, **5**:367, **5**:399
monarchy **1**:33, **1**:36, **5**:325
money **7**:515, **7**:530–533,
  **10**:753
  metal **7**:531–532, **7**:533
  paper **7**:530, **7**:532
  stone **7**:515
monogamy **7**:484
monolith **10**:799
monotheism **6**:427, **6**:429
Monte Albán **6**:451,
  **7**:534–535, **10**:788, **10**:789
  Building P **10**:790
  plaza **10**:788
  Temple of the Danzantes

**1**:65, **7**:535
months **2**:144, **3**:210, **7**:502
moon **2**:97, **2**:144, **3**:210,
  **5**:326, **5**:373, **7**:501
  *see also* lunar eclipse
morality **3**:181
Moravia **7**:541
Morelos **8**:583, **8**:586
Morgan, Lewis Henry **7**:491
mortality rate **3**:169
mortar **5**:378, **5**:399
mortuary temple **1**:79
Mosaic law **3**:214–215
mosaics **9**:663, **10**:789
Moses **3**:214, **5**:355, **5**:357,
  **6**:429, **7**:*519*, **7**:536–538,
  **8**:634, **9**:677
  biblical story **7**:536
  Covenant **7**:537
  in history **7**:537–538
  and the Promised Land
    **7**:536–537
Mosul **8**:565
Mother Goddess **8**:637
Mount Olympus **8**:587, **8**:636
Mount Sinai **7**:536
Mount Vesuvius **5**:360, **8**:615,
  **9**:657, **9**:685, **9**:713
mourning, colors of **3**:229
Muhammad edh-Dhib **3**:226
Mumbai (Bombay) **10**:739
mummies **3**:229, **4**:257, **4**:*262*,
  **10**:762
  Egyptian **2**:128, **7**:540
  made by people **7**:540
  natural bog **7**:539
  natural desert **7**:539
  natural ice **7**:539
  reburied **10**:772
mummification **7**:539–540,
  **9**:689
mural **1**:72, **1**:79
murder **3**:213
murex shellfish **8**:606
Mursilis I **5**:368
Mursilis II **5**:369
Musa River **8**:603
muses **1**:23
museums **1**:60
Mushhushshu **6**:477
music **7**:541–544
  Chinese **7**:543
  Egyptian **7**:542, **9**:718
  Greek **7**:542–543
  instruments **7**:541
  Roman **7**:544
  theory **8**:625

*muskinu* **2**:115
Mut **4**:290
  Temple of **4**:261
Mutemwia **1**:44
mutilation **3**:215
Mutina, Battle of **1**:56
Muwatallis **5**:368, **5**:369
Myanmar (Burma) **2**:137,
  **3**:237
Mycenae **1**:24, **7**:546, **7**:548,
  **8**:619
  graves **7**:545, **7**:547
Mycenaean civilization **3**:219,
  **5**:324, **7**:522, **7**:545–548
  Linear B script **7**:548
  palace period **7**:546, **7**:547
  shaft graves **10**:748
  stone tablets **10**:793
  trade **7**:545
Myron **1**:71
myrrh **5**:391, **5**:399, **8**:602,
  **8**:639
mythology **7**:549–552
  aboriginal **1**:15
  common themes **7**:551
  creation myths **7**:550
  European **2**:145
  explanatory myths **7**:550
  hero myths **7**:549–550
  lands-of-the-dead myths
    **7**:550
  in Roman literature **9**:651

Nabataeans **8**:602
Nabodinus **2**:125, **7**:554
Nabopolassar **2**:113, **2**:117,
  **7**:553
Nabu **2**:142, **7**:553
nails **10**:756
Nakht **5**:*377*
Namarrgon **6**:433
Namarrkun **6**:433
Nanda dynasty **7**:494
Nan Madol, islets of **7**:515,
  **7**:516
Nanna **6**:409
Nanna-Suen **9**:677
*naos* **10**:739
Napata **8**:573, **8**:576
Napirasu, Queen **4**:*267*
Naqsh-e Rustam **10**:*797*,
  **10**:798
Naram-Sin **1**:31, **1**:32, **1**:34
Narcissus **9**:651
Narmer **4**:253
Nasca people **1**:71
*nassesalars* **10**:797

Native Americans **7**:491
  myths **7**:550, **7**:551
natron **4**:257, **5**:391, **5**:399,
  **7**:540, **7**:559
natural disasters **7**:518, **7**:527
Navajo language **1**:50
nave **10**:740, **10**:799
navigation **3**:177, **8**:607,
  **9**:685, **10**:755
  Etruscan **10**:755
  Lapita **9**:694
  Phoenician **9**:692
  Polynesian **8**:613
Nazarenes **8**:597
Nazareth **6**:419
Neanderthal **3**:198, **3**:228,
  **3**:229, **3**:239
  food **4**:294
Neapolis **5**:*360*
Nebuchadrezzar I **6**:478
Nebuchadrezzar II **2**:113,
  **2**:114, **2**:117, **2**:125, **5**:356,
  **6**:417, **7**:509, **7**:510,
  **7**:553–554
  buildings **7**:554
necropolises **4**:281, **10**:744,
  **10**:765, **10**:799
  Etruscan **10**:749–750
Neferronpet **4**:255
Nefertari **8**:633
  tomb **4**:*256*, **4**:*265*, **4**:*301*
Nefertiti **4**:*254*, **7**:555–556,
  **10**:762, **10**:781
Neferure **5**:349
Nefud Desert **8**:602
Nemesis **8**:637
Neolithic era (New Stone Age)
  **2**:10, **2**:151, **2**:156, **2**:159,
  **3**:191, **3**:198, **3**:237, **5**:387,
  **8**:622
  art **2**:152
  artifacts **2**:152
  cave temples **10**:737
  farming **2**:151, **4**:285,
    **4**:287
  female figurines **7**:491
  houses **2**:151
  Japan **4**:294
  logs as boats **9**:692
  migration patterns **6**:452
  music **7**:541
  Orkney settlement
    **9**:697–698
  patriarchies **7**:492
  trade **2**:151
Neoplatonism **9**:655
Neoptolemus **7**:*518*

Nephthys **4**:264
Neptune **10**:793
Nerik **5**:370–371
Nero **1**:26–27, **2**:129, **3**:186,
    **3**:195, **3**:201, **6**:425, **7**:493,
    **7**:532, **7**:557–558, **8**:597,
    **9**:653, **10**:782
    Golden House **7**:557, **7**:558
    persecution of Christians
    **7**:557–558, **8**:597, **10**:732
Nervii **2**:153
Neshite *see* Hittite language
Nesilim, Code of the **5**:371
Nespanetjerenpere **3**:*229*
Nespawershepi **4**:262
Newark, Ohio **5**:373
New Caledonia **6**:458, **7**:503,
    **7**:504
New Guinea **6**:456, **7**:503,
    **7**:504
New Ireland **7**:*504*
New Stone Age *see* Neolithic
    era
New Testament **3**:184, **3**:185,
    **3**:186, **6**:420, **6**:449, **6**:452,
    **6**:471, **6**:479, **8**:597, **8**:638
    Acts of the Apostles **8**:596
    Epistles of Saint Paul **8**:597
    Gospels **3**:185, **3**:*188*,
    **6**:419, **6**:421, **8**:638
New Year festivals **4**:290–291
New Zealand **8**:612
Ngalyod **6**:433
Ngoc Lu drum **3**:238
Nicaea, Council of **3**:186,
    **3**:188
Nicene Creed **3**:188
Nicomachus **1**:67
Niger-Congo languages **6**:450
Nigeria **8**:566–568
Night (goddess) **5**:332
Nike **8**:587
Nile River **2**:144, **4**:253,
    **4**:258, **4**:*261*, **4**:262, **4**:304,
    **8**:572, **8**:574, **8**:575, **8**:633,
    **10**:738, **10**:751
    delta area **3**:239, **4**:262
    floods **4**:253, **4**:254, **4**:258,
    **4**:290, **4**:310, **10**:778
Nile valley **3**:192
Nilometers **2**:144, **4**:258
Nimrod **8**:564, **8**:565
Nimrud *see* Calah
Nineveh **2**:88, **2**:89, **2**:91,
    **2**:92, **2**:95, **2**:114,
    **8**:564–565, **9**:691
    bas reliefs **9**:690

defenses **8**:564
irrigation and aqueducts
    **8**:564–565
library of Ashurbanipal
    **6**:461
sack of **1**:58, **8**:564, **8**:565
Sennacherib's palace **8**:565,
    **9**:*702*
Temple of Ishtar **1**:33,
    **6**:409
Ninigi **1**:43
Ninkasi **4**:295
Ninua *see* Nineveh
Ninurta **2**:142
nirvana **2**:132, **2**:133, **2**:134,
    **3**:183, **5**:398
Nisa **8**:591
Nitocris **2**:125
Noah **7**:511, **8**:565
Nobatia **8**:576
Nok culture **8**:566–569
    figurines **8**:568–569
    iron making **8**:566–567
    sculptures **8**:568
nomadism **4**:285, **4**:289,
    **7**:492, **8**:570–571
    shelter **8**:571
nomads **5**:355, **5**:375, **5**:381,
    **5**:399, **8**:591, **8**:622, **9**:686,
    **9**:705, **9**:719
    Steppe nomads **8**:570–571
Norse mythology **7**:550, **7**:551
North Africa **5**:348, **8**:566,
    **8**:570, **8**:608
North Americans
    languages **6**:451
    wampum **7**:531
North Star **8**:607
Nowniz ceremony **8**:600
Nubia **8**:572, **8**:626, **8**:627
    and Egypt **8**:573–574
    Lower **8**:572, **8**:575, **8**:576
    Meroitic period **8**:*575*
    Upper **8**:575
Nubians **8**:572–576
    A-Group **8**:572, **8**:573
    archery **8**:573
    C-Group **8**:572, **8**:573
    colonial period **8**:575
    Kingdom of Kush **8**:576
    religion **8**:575, **8**:576
    royal burial **8**:574–575,
    **8**:627
    trade **8**:574
numbers **8**:577–580
    and the annual calendar
    **8**:578

base systems **8**:577
decimal system **8**:577,
    **9**:682, **9**:684
magic and religion **8**:578,
    **8**:579
negative **9**:684
representing **8**:578
weights and measures **8**:579
*numina* **9**:650
Nut **4**:263, **4**:264, **10**:*772*
Nyaya **5**:396
nymph **5**:399, **10**:799
*nymphaeum* **8**:603

Oaxaca **4**:249, **7**:534, **8**:583,
    **10**:741, **10**:788
obelisk **2**:159, **5**:350, **5**:399
obsidian **3**:192, **3**:217, **4**:277,
    **5**:374, **6**:458, **7**:500, **7**:504,
    **8**:583, **8**:585, **8**:639, **10**:741,
    **10**:745, **10**:799
ocher **3**:229, **3**:239, **6**:433,
    **10**:767
Octavian **3**:196–197
    *see also* Augustus
oculus **9**:665
Odaenathus **10**:791, **10**:792
odeon **3**:211
Odin **2**:145, **7**:550, **7**:551
Odoacer **4**:313
Odysseus **2**:98, **5**:392,
    **5**:393–394, **7**:550,
    **8**:581–582
*Odyssey* (Homer) **2**:98, **5**:324,
    **5**:325, **5**:392–394, **6**:463,
    **6**:472, **8**:581, **8**:582
oil **10**:751
Oisin **7**:550
Old Stone Age *see* Paleolithic
    era
Old Testament **3**:185, **3**:214,
    **6**:414, **6**:464, **8**:638, **9**:690,
    **9**:693, **9**:701
    Book of Daniel **7**:*553*
    Book of Ecclesiasticus
    **3**:225, **4**:284
    Book of Esther **10**:787
    Book of Ezekiel **5**:357
    Book of Judges **3**:232,
    **3**:233
    Book of Psalms **3**:225
    Exodus **7**:518, **7**:537,
    **7**:538, **8**:634
    Genesis **5**:355, **7**:508, **8**:564
    Pentateuch **6**:430
oligarchy **5**:325
olive oil **10**:733

Olmecs **6**:451, **7**:518,
    **8**:583–586
    art and architecture **8**:585
    ball courts **1**:52
    food and farming
    **8**:584–585
    games **1**:52, **4**:300
    La Venta **8**:583, **8**:584,
    **8**:585
    pyramids **8**:627
    stone heads **8**:584, **8**:*585*
Olympia **8**:587–588
    sacred sanctuary **8**:587
    Temple of Hera **8**:588
    Temple of Zeus **8**:587,
    **10**:794
Olympian gods **5**:326, **5**:332,
    **5**:333, **7**:551
Olympias **1**:37, **8**:605
Olympic games **3**:234, **4**:300,
    **5**:325, **8**:587, **8**:588, **9**:711,
    **9**:716
*omphalos* **3**:234
Opet, festival of **4**:290
oracle **9**:719, **10**:799
    Delphic **3**:234, **5**:333
    of Zeus (Dodona) **10**:794
oratory **10**:731
Orestes (Agamemnon's son)
    **1**:25
Orestes (of Alexandria) **1**:41
Origen **3**:185
Orkney **9**:697–698
    Maes Howe **9**:698
    Ring of Brodgar **9**:698
    Stones of Stenness **9**:698
ornaments **3**:198
Orpheus **7**:551
Osiris **2**:127, **3**:229–230,
    **4**:264, **4**:265, **4**:288, **4**:301,
    **7**:550
ossuary **10**:797, **10**:799
Ostia **3**:*195*, **4**:315
Ostia Antica **9**:*647*
ostracism **2**:100, **3**:216, **3**:239
*ostraka* **1**:41
ostrich eggs **7**:545
Ostrogoths **1**:59, **4**:270, **4**:313,
    **4**:314, **4**:315, **4**:319, **5**:384,
    **9**:*706*
    map of kingdom **4**:*312*
Ouranos **5**:332, **7**:551
outriggers **6**:456, **7**:516, **9**:694
Ovid **5**:332
    *Metamorphoses* **5**:335, **9**:651
oxen **4**:287, **10**:754
Oxus River **8**:591

Pacific Ocean **6**:456, **8**:612
paddy fields **1**:43, **3**:*174*,
  **3**:236, **4**:286, **6**:412
Paekche **6**:444
paganism **1**:41, **3**:239, **4**:293,
  **4**:298, **5**:339
*paidotribes* **4**:252
palaces **8**:589–590
  first **8**:589
  as little cities **8**:590
  symbols of power **8**:589
palaestra **5**:327, **8**:588, **8**:639
Palatine Hill, Rome **8**:589,
  **9**:665
Palau **7**:514, **7**:515
Palenque **7**:498, **7**:*499*
Paleolithic era (Old Stone Age)
  **2**:152, **2**:159, **5**:385, **8**:621
  patriarchies **7**:492
  Upper **9**:667
Palestine **3**:184, **5**:355–356,
  **5**:357, **5**:359, **5**:369, **9**:690
*palla* **3**:209
Pallas Athene *see* Athena
pallium **9**:703, **9**:*704*
Palmyra **10**:791
Panathenaic festival **1**:20, **1**:21
*pankration* **8**:588
Pannonia **4**:313, **5**:383, **5**:384
pantheon **7**:551, **7**:559, **8**:636,
  **8**:639, **10**:779
Pantheon (Rome) **1**:*65*, **9**:665,
  **9**:666
pantomime **7**:544
paper **3**:179, **9**:681, **10**:785
paper money **7**:532
Papua New Guinea **7**:*504*
Papuan people **7**:504
papyrus **2**:127, **2**:159, **4**:257,
  **5**:353, **5**:361, **5**:399, **6**:461,
  **9**:681, **10**:785
parallels **4**:305
Paravati **5**:342
parchment **10**:785
Paris (place) **4**:299
Paris (Trojan prince) **1**:24,
  **5**:392, **10**:758
Parmenides **5**:339
Paros **3**:217
Parsa region **1**:18
Parsees **10**:795, **10**:*796*,
  **10**:799
Parthava **8**:591
Parthenon (Athens) **1**:20, **1**:*21*,
  **1**:74, **2**:99, **2**:101, **8**:598
Parthia **1**:56, **6**:475
Parthians **2**:87, **8**:591–593

Arsacid kingdom **8**:591
  government **8**:591
Parvati **5**:367
Pasargadae **3**:*220*, **3**:221,
  **10**:796
  tomb of Cyrus the Great
    **3**:*220,* **8**:600
Pashedu, tomb of **1**:71
Passover **6**:427
pastoral **1**:79
pastoralism **2**:122, **2**:159
Pataliputra **5**:341, **5**:342,
  **7**:494, **7**:*495*, **7**:496,
  **8**:594–595
Patanjali **5**:396
paterfamilias **4**:282
Patna **8**:594–595
patriarchy **7**:491–493, **10**:781,
  **10**:799
patrician **9**:706, **9**:719
Patrick, Saint **2**:155
Patroclus **5**:393, **10**:759
patron **1**:79
Patti-hegali canal, Calah **2**:142
Paul of Tarsus, Saint **3**:185,
  **3**:212, **8**:596–597, **9**:701
  Epistles **8**:597
Pausanias **8**:605
*pax Assyrica* **9**:690, **9**:691
Pazuzu **2**:92
Pazyryk culture **7**:539
peasants **9**:700
peat bogs **7**:539, **7**:559, **9**:667
  Irish **7**:523
Peisistratos **9**:710
Peloponnese **7**:545, **9**:711
Peloponnesian War **5**:324,
  **5**:325, **9**:712
Penelope **5**:393, **5**:394, **8**:582
Pentateuch **6**:430
pentathlon **8**:588
percussion instruments **7**:541,
  **9**:*718*
perfume **3**:200
Periander **3**:212
Pericles **1**:20, **1**:21, **2**:102,
  **8**:598–599
*perioikoi* **9**:712
Peripatetics **1**:68
permafrost **7**:539, **7**:559
persecution **7**:557–558, **8**:597,
  **8**:630, **9**:678, **9**:719, **10**:732
Persephone **3**:230, **5**:333,
  **5**:*334*
Persepolis **1**:*66*, **3**:222, **3**:223,
  **4**:290, **8**:600–601
  Apadana **3**:223, **8**:601

Gate of All Nations **8**:600
Persian palaces **8**:590, **8**:600
  royal palace **1**:29, **10**:*787*,
    **10**:796
Perseus **2**:98, **5**:335
Persia **9**:678
Persian Empire **1**:18–19,
  **3**:220–223, **4**:268, **5**:324,
  **6**:417, **6**:470, **8**:600, **10**:764,
  **10**:786
Persian Gulf **1**:18, **7**:509
Persian royal road **9**:644
Persians **1**:18–19, **1**:28–29,
  **2**:100, **2**:113, **2**:117, **2**:120,
  **2**:125, **3**:220, **3**:222–223,
  **3**:235, **5**:325, **5**:357, **5**:358,
  **7**:510, **7**:517, **8**:564, **8**:565,
  **8**:598, **8**:608, **10**:775,
  **10**:792
  conquered by Alexander the
    Great **1**:38
  religion **1**:28–29, **4**:290,
    **10**:795–798
  sack of Athens by **1**:18,
    **1**:19, **1**:20
Peru **1**:71, **1**:72, **3**:164,
  **7**:524–527, **7**:540, **8**:577,
  **8**:626, **9**:703
Peruvians, pottery **8**:617
Peseshet **10**:782
Peter, Saint **3**:187, **5**:383,
  **5**:384, **8**:597
Petra **8**:602–603
  Deir Mausoleum **8**:603
  mausoleums **8**:603
Petrie, William Matthew
  Flinders **1**:63
petroglyphs **1**:15
Peutinger's Tabula **4**:*305*
Phaistos **7**:520, **7**:*521*
phalanx **8**:604
pharaohs **1**:46, **4**:253–254,
  **4**:261–262
  Egyptian **8**:572, **8**:633
  female **3**:196, **5**:349, **7**:555,
    **10**:781, **10**:*782*
  pyramids **8**:626
  as semidivine **8**:590
  and slavery **9**:700
  tombs of **4**:256–258,
    **4**:309–311, **7**:556,
    **10**:770–772
Pharisees **5**:357, **6**:425, **6**:431,
  **6**:479
Pharsalus **2**:140
Phidias **1**:20, **1**:21, **8**:587
Philip III (Arrhidaeus) **6**:469

Philip II of Macedon **1**:37,
  **1**:68, **5**:325, **6**:469,
  **8**:604–605
Philippi, Battle of **1**:56, **2**:107
Philippines **7**:514
Philippus I **9**:679
Philistines **3**:224, **3**:225, **5**:356
Philo of Byzantium **2**:114
Philodemus of Gadara **5**:361
philosophy **5**:336, **5**:395
  Chinese **3**:180–183,
    **3**:203–206
  Greek **1**:67–69, **2**:101,
    **2**:102, **2**:106, **3**:180,
    **5**:326, **5**:336–339,
    **8**:610–611, **9**:652,
    **9**:707–708, **10**:782
  Japanese **6**:413
  Platonic **8**:610–611
  Roman **9**:652–655
  in Roman life **9**:654–655
Phoenicia **7**:533, **8**:*574*
Phoenicians **2**:150, **8**:606–609,
  **10**:764–765
  alphabet **8**:606, **8**:609
  language **8**:607, **8**:609
  navigation **8**:607, **10**:755
  religion **4**:290, **8**:609
  ships **8**:607, **9**:692, **10**:757,
    **10**:774
  trade and crafts **8**:608
Phrygia **9**:650
Piankhy **8**:576
pictograph **4**:275, **4**:319,
  **7**:*512*, **7**:529
Picts **1**:54, **7**:493
pilgrimage **8**:595
pilgrims **5**:367
piracy **7**:517, **7**:548, **8**:607,
  **9**:700
Piramesse **8**:633
Pisistratus **6**:461
Piso, Lucius Calpurnius **5**:361
*pithoi* **6**:439, **8**:618
Pitjantjatjara **10**:766
planetarium **8**:580
plantain **2**:124, **7**:503
plaques, terra-cotta **8**:619
Plataea, Battle of **1**:18, **1**:19,
  **3**:223, **5**:325, **10**:786
Plato **1**:67, **2**:102, **2**:106,
  **4**:301, **5**:326, **5**:329, **5**:336,
  **5**:337, **5**:339, **7**:522,
  **8**:610–611, **8**:629, **9**:652,
  **9**:655, **9**:707, **9**:708
  Academy **5**:326, **5**:327,
    **8**:609

*Apology* **8**:610
*Crito* **8**:610
*Phaedo* **8**:610, **8**:611
*Republic* **5**:337, **8**:611
Platonism **8**:610–611
Plautius, Aulus **3**:194
Plautus **9**:663
plaza **8**:584, **10**:788
plectrum **9**:675
Pliny the Elder **1**:71, **1**:74, **6**:423, **9**:685
*Historia Naturalis* **9**:685
Pliny the Younger **8**:616
Plotinus **9**:655
plows **4**:287, **5**:*329*
Plutarch **1**:57, **3**:197, **7**:495, **9**:683
Pluto **3**:230, **10**:793
pneumatics **10**:736
Pnyx, Athens **2**:100
poetry **6**:463–464
Greek **9**:674–675
Indian epic **8**:631–632
Latin **2**:109
Pohnpei **7**:515, **7**:516
*pok-ta-pok see palla*
politics, women in **10**:781–782
Pollio, Marcus Vitruvius **1**:59
Polycletus the Younger **4**:273
polygamy **7**:484, **7**:486
Polygnotos of Thasos **1**:74
polygons **10**:740
Polynesia **6**:456, **7**:518
Polynesian culture **7**:517, **8**:612–614
Easter Island **8**:612, **8**:614
food and homes **8**:612
magic and cannibalism **8**:614
myths **7**:551
navigation **8**:613, **9**:694, **10**:755
society **8**:612–613
Polynesian languages **7**:503
Polyphemus (the Cyclops) **5**:393, **5**:394
Pompeii **3**:169, **5**:360, **5**:*378*, **8**:*611*, **8**:615–616
Cicero's villa **7**:*544*
destruction of **8**:615, **9**:657
rediscovery (1748) **8**:616
Pompey the Great (Gnaeus Pompeius Magnus) **2**:139, **2**:140, **2**:*141*, **3**:189, **5**:359, **6**:469, **9**:714
Pons Aemilius **9**:*646*

Pontius Pilate **6**:421
Porphyry **9**:655
Poseidon **1**:21, **2**:98, **3**:212, **5**:333, **10**:793
potassium-argon dating **1**:63, **1**:79
potsherd **1**:61, **1**:79, **4**:277, **4**:319
potter's wheel **8**:618, **10**:728
pottery **1**:72, **3**:165, **3**:166, **3**:169, **3**:239, **8**:617–619
Anglo-Saxon **1**:55
Aryan **1**:78
Athenian **2**:102, **8**:619
Babylonian **8**:617–618
Bantu **2**:122–123
black-figure **3**:212, **3**:239, **5**:330
Chavín **3**:165, **3**:166
color of **8**:617–618
combware **6**:441, **6**:443
Corinthian **3**:212
Cycladic **3**:217
discovery of **9**:681
Egyptian **8**:618
firing **8**:617
first **8**:623
from Eridu **4**:277
Greek **3**:*230*, **5**:330, **8**:618–619
Harappan **6**:406, **6**:*408*
Hopewell **5**:*374*
Japanese **8**:617, **8**:622
Jomon **6**:413
Lapita culture **6**:458
La Tène style **2**:*154*
Melanesian **7**:504
Mesopotamian **8**:617
Mimbres style **1**:52
Moche **7**:524, **7**:525, **7**:526
Mogollon **1**:52
Neolithic **2**:152
Nok culture **8**:566, **8**:568–569
Olmec **8**:586
painted gray ware **1**:78
Peruvian **8**:617
red-figure **3**:169, **5**:330
Roman **8**:619
Samian ware **8**:619
Shang **5**:379, **5**:380
Spartan **9**:711
Turkey **8**:617
power technology **10**:734–736
Praetorian Guard **1**:79, **3**:239, **7**:*506*, **7**:557, **7**:558, **7**:559
Praktri **5**:396

*prandium* **4**:296
Prasutagus, King **2**:129
prehistory **2**:110–111, **8**:620–623
arrival of writing **8**:623
early communities **8**:622–623
first farmers **8**:621–622
men and women in **7**:506
Orkney **9**:697–698
Priam **7**:*518*, **10**:758, **10**:759
priests **3**:169, **7**:506, **7**:511, **7**:549, **9**:703, **10**:737, **10**:779
hygiene of **5**:391
medicine **5**:351
and priestesses in Egypt **4**:254, **4**:261
Prinsep, James **2**:84
Priscus **5**:381
procurator **7**:559
professionals **7**:544
Prometheus **10**:794
propaganda **1**:33, **1**:34
prophets **3**:214, **3**:239, **5**:358, **6**:429
Propylaia **1**:21
prose fiction **6**:465
*proskenion* **4**:273
Proto-Indo-European **6**:450
Psalm 48 **6**:418
*Psalm of Marduk* **6**:478
Psalms, Book of **3**:225
Pseudo-Xenophon **9**:702
Psyche **5**:334
Ptolemaic system **2**:97, **8**:624–625
Ptolemies **5**:357
Ptolemy, Claudius (of Alexandria) **2**:96–97, **6**:470, **8**:624–625
*Almagest* **2**:97, **8**:624, **8**:625
astronomical work **8**:624
*Geographia* **4**:305, **4**:306, **8**:625
*Harmonica* **8**:625
*Optics* **8**:625
Ptolemy (Cleopatra's brother) **2**:141
Ptolemy I **6**:462
Ptolemy II **1**:40
Ptolemy III **1**:40, **6**:462
Ptolemy XII **3**:196
Ptolemy XIII **3**:196
Ptolemy XIV **3**:196
Ptolemy Soter **1**:40
Pu-Abi **3**:228, **10**:747

Pueblo I **1**:51, **1**:53
Pueblo II **1**:51, **1**:53
Pueblo III (classic period) **1**:51, **1**:53
Pueblo Bonito **1**:50, **1**:53
pueblo peoples **1**:50–53
pulley **10**:733
compound **10**:736
pumice **5**:399, **7**:522, **7**:559, **8**:615, **8**:616
Punic Wars **5**:347, **5**:399, **9**:658, **9**:693
First (264–241 BCE) **5**:347
Second (218–201 BCE) **5**:347
punishment
Babylonian **9**:706
capital **5**:370
crime and **3**:213–216
of slaves **9**:700, **9**:*701*
Punjab **1**:75, **1**:77, **7**:494
Punt **5**:350, **5**:399
puppets, Indonesian **6**:*473*
purple dye **3**:200, **8**:606, **9**:703, **10**:731
Purusa **5**:396
Purushapura **6**:446
Pushyamitra Shunga **7**:497
Pygmalion **2**:150
Pylos **7**:548
palace at **7**:546, **7**:*547*
Pyon-han **6**:442, **6**:443
pyramids **1**:45, **1**:64–65, **4**:258, **4**:309–311, **8**:626–628
of the Americas **8**:626–628
building **4**:309–311, **10**:733
complexes **4**:309
Egyptian **8**:626, **10**:748
Mayan **7**:498, **8**:628
Olmec **8**:585
size of **4**:311
stepped **10**:737
*see also* ziggurats
Pyramid of the Sun **10**:741, **10**:742
Pyramid Texts **2**:127
Pyramus **9**:651
Pythagoras **2**:96, **2**:97, **4**:304, **8**:579, **8**:629–630, **9**:682
*Elements* **8**:*630*
theorems **8**:630
Pythagoreans **8**:629
Pythagoria **5**:389
Pythia **3**:234
Pythian games **3**:234
Python **3**:234

Qin **3**:167
Qin dynasty **2**:157, **2**:158,
  **3**:167–168, **3**:173, **3**:175,
  **3**:204–205, **4**:316, **4**:317,
  **4**:318
quetzal **7**:500, **7**:502
Quetzalcoatl **10**:742
Qufu, Shandong Province
  **3**:*204*
Quin (Ireland) **5**:*375*
quipu **8**:577
Quirigua **3**:210, **7**:500
Quirinus **9**:649
Qumran **3**:226, **3**:*227*, **6**:*430*
quoit **8**:639
Qurna **10**:744

Ra **1**:45, **1**:46, **4**:254, **4**:262,
  **4**:263, **4**:264
rabbi **6**:431, **6**:479, **8**:596,
  **8**:639
Rabgi **7**:551
radiocarbon dating **1**:63, **1**:79,
  **8**:639
rafts **3**:237, **10**:755
*rai* **7**:515
Rainbow Serpent **6**:433
*raja* **1**:76, **1**:77
Rakhigari **6**:405
Rama **8**:631, **8**:632
Rama Gupta **5**:341, **9**:670
*Ramayana* **4**:251, **6**:435,
  **6**:463, **8**:631–632
Rameses **7**:538
Ramses II **4**:255, **5**:369, **7**:556,
  **8**:576, **8**:633–634
  and the Bible **8**:634
Ramses III **5**:389, **7**:517,
  **8**:589, **9**:716
Ramses VI (tomb) **10**:*772*
rank
  in European tribes
    **9**:704–706
  responsibilities of **9**:706
  signs of **9**:703–704
Rano Raraku **8**:614
Ravana **8**:631, **8**:632
Ravenna **9**:660
Red Sea, Moses crossing the
  **6**:*427*, **7**:*519*, **7**:*536*, **7**:*537*,
  **8**:634
refugees **1**:79, **7**:517
regent **5**:349, **10**:762, **10**:791
reincarnation **2**:134,
  **5**:364–365, **9**:705, **9**:719
Reisner, George Andrew **8**:627
relics **9**:673

reliefs **8**:601
religion **8**:635–638
  ancient Egyptian **8**:636
  ancient Greek **8**:636–637
  ancient Roman **8**:637,
    **9**:662–663
  and art **1**:71
  Aryan **1**:76
  Babylonian **6**:477–478
  earliest idea of God **8**:635
  of Germanic tribes **1**:55
  holy scriptures **8**:638
  Japanese **6**:413
  and language **6**:450
  and literature **6**:464
  numbers and magic **8**:579
  and philosophy **5**:395,
    **6**:413
  Sumerian **8**:636
  and warfare **10**:773
Remus **9**:648–649, **9**:664
Renenutet **4**:288
*Republic* (Plato) **5**:337, **8**:611
resin **4**:257, **4**:319
Resina **5**:361
resist style of painting **3**:165
restitution **3**:215
resurrection **3**:188, **3**:230–231,
  **4**:293, **4**:319, **6**:421
retaliation, law of **3**:213
revenge **3**:215
*Revolving Spheres* (Sosigenes of
  Alexandria) **2**:146
Rhea **5**:332, **8**:587, **9**:650,
  **10**:793
Rhea Silva **9**:648
rhetor **10**:731
rhetoric **2**:105, **2**:106, **2**:159,
  **3**:170, **3**:239
Rhind papyrus **8**:*578*
Rhodes **9**:*684*
rhyton **7**:*522*
rice **1**:43, **3**:174, **3**:236, **4**:286,
  **6**:412, **6**:442, **6**:443
Rig Veda **8**:638
  Creation Hymn **5**:395
Ring of Brodgar **9**:698
rings (finger) **6**:423
rites of passage (male coming
  of age) **7**:506
ritual **8**:639, **10**:737
roads **9**:644
  Chinese **3**:176, **9**:645
  construction **9**:646
  news via **9**:645
  Roman **9**:644, **9**:645,
    **9**:646, **9**:647, **10**:757

and soldiers **9**:645–646
Roman architecture **9**:663
Roman army **9**:657
Roman Catholic Church **3**:186
Roman children **9**:662
Roman cities **3**:193,
  **9**:661–662
Roman culture **9**:663
Roman education **3**:170,
  **4**:*252*, **9**:654
Roman Empire **2**:103, **2**:107,
  **2**:147, **3**:194, **3**:207, **4**:288,
  **5**:343, **8**:597, **8**:603, **8**:606,
  **8**:637, **9**:656–663,
  **9**:665–666, **10**:791, **10**:792
  and the Celts **2**:154
  Christianity in **2**:105–106,
    **3**:184–185, **3**:186, **3**:202,
    **3**:207, **8**:638, **10**:740
  Egypt and the **1**:41, **1**:47,
    **3**:196–197
  frontier in Britain
    **5**:345–346
  Hun invasion **5**:381,
    **5**:382–383
  *see also* Eastern Roman
    Empire; Western Roman
    Empire
Roman games **4**:301, **9**:716
Roman history **10**:731–732
Roman law **3**:216, **8**:597
Roman literature **9**:651, **9**:663
Roman mythology **9**:648–651
Roman philosophy **9**:652–655
Roman Republic **1**:56–57,
  **2**:139, **3**:239, **4**:278, **4**:279,
  **9**:656–663, **9**:665
Romans **2**:103, **3**:185, **5**:360,
  **8**:608, **8**:615–619
  aqueducts **1**:59
  bathing **5**:389, **5**:390
  bridges **9**:663
  burial customs **3**:229,
    **3**:230, **10**:750
  calendar **2**:145
  central heating **5**:378
  clothes **3**:171, **3**:200
  conquest of Palestine **5**:357,
    **5**:359
  cosmetics **3**:199, **3**:200
  drama **4**:244
  families **4**:282, **4**:284
  farming **4**:288
  fishing **5**:386
  food **4**:296–297
  geographers **4**:304–306
  and Goths **4**:312

housing **5**:378
invasion of Britain
  **2**:129–130, **3**:194
jewelry **6**:423–424
legions **10**:774
libraries **6**:461
marriage **7**:486
masks **7**:489, **7**:490
measures **10**:776, **10**:778
medicine **5**:352
men and women **7**:508
music and dance **7**:544
Ninth Legion **2**:130
numbers **8**:578
poetry **1**:22–23, **2**:109
pottery **8**:619
religion **4**:283, **4**:290,
  **8**:637, **9**:650, **9**:662–663
roads **9**:644, **9**:645, **9**:646,
  **9**:647, **10**:757
rule in Palestine **5**:359
sanitation **5**:390, **5**:391
and Sasanians **9**:679
ships **9**:693–694
social classes **9**:661
temples **10**:740
toys **3**:171
wheeled vehicles
  **10**:756–757
Roman women **9**:662,
  **10**:781–782
Rome, city of **1**:22, **2**:104,
  **2**:109, **2**:139, **2**:149, **9**:654,
  **9**:664–666
  Arch of Constantine **3**:*208*
  Arch of Titus **9**:*666*
  Cloaca Maxima **5**:388
  Colosseum **3**:201–202,
    **3**:*201*, **9**:666, **9**:716
  death penalty **3**:216
  Epicureanism in **9**:654
  Forum **3**:*193*
  Forum of Augustus **2**:109
  forum Romanum **9**:664,
    **9**:665
  Great Fire **3**:186, **7**:557,
    **9**:657
  and Macedonia **6**:471
  origin myth **9**:648–649,
    **9**:664
  Palatine Hill **8**:589, **9**:665
  Pantheon **1**:*65*, **9**:665,
    **9**:666
  plagues **4**:273, **5**:391
  public baths **5**:389, **5**:390
  sack of **4**:313, **4**:314, **4**:315,
    **9**:657, **9**:666

Saint Peter's Church **3**:*187*
sanitation **3**:193
Second Triumvirate **1**:56
seven hills **9**:656
sewers **5**:390
slaves **9**:701
Stoicism in **9**:652–653
Temple of Apollo **2**:109
Temple of Mars Ultor **2**:109
Temple of Venus Felix and
    Roma Aeterna **9**:*664*
Romulus **7**:537
    and Remus **9**:648–649,
    **9**:657, **9**:664
*rongo-rongo* **8**:614
Rosh Hashanah festival **7**:543
Roxana **1**:39
Rubicon, crossing the **2**:140
rudder **3**:178, **10**:756
Rufus, Lucius Verginius
    **10**:732
Rugila **2**:103, **5**:382
Russia **7**:519

Sabbath **6**:427, **6**:479
Sabines **9**:649
Sabinus, Nymphidius **7**:558
sacred **8**:587, **8**:638, **8**:639
sacred groves **10**:737
sacred sites, aboriginal **1**:15,
    **1**:16
sacrifice **1**:76–77, **4**:293,
    **6**:428, **7**:502, **8**:588, **8**:636,
    **8**:637, **9**:667–669, **10**:737
    animal **5**:364, **5**:365, **8**:621,
        **9**:662, **9**:668, **10**:737
    Christian **9**:669
    crop **9**:668–669
    horse **1**:78
    human **1**:55, **2**:150, **2**:156,
        **9**:667–668, **9**:689, **10**:746
    Moche **7**:526
    Persian **1**:29
    Scythian **9**:689
saddle with stirrups **10**:774
Sadducees **5**:357, **6**:425,
    **6**:431, **6**:479
saffron **4**:296, **4**:319
Sagburro **4**:275
Saguntum **5**:347
Sahara Desert **2**:122, **8**:566,
    **8**:571
Saint Albans *see* Verulamium
Saka **9**:686, **9**:687
Sakya clan **2**:131
Salamis, Battle of **1**:18, **1**:19,
    **2**:100, **4**:245, **4**:246, **5**:325,

**10**:786
*salarium* **4**:296
Salem **6**:416
Salisbury Plain **10**:724–725
Samhain **4**:292, **4**:293
Sam Han *see* Three Hans
Samian ware **8**:619
Samkhya **5**:396
Sammonicus, Serenus **6**:462
Samnites **5**:360, **8**:615
Samoa **6**:456, **6**:457, **8**:612,
    **9**:694
Samos **1**:66, **6**:461, **8**:629
    tunnel of Eupalinos **1**:66,
        **5**:389
samsara **2**:134
Samudra Gupta **5**:340, **5**:341,
    **9**:670–671
    coins **9**:670
    inscriptions **9**:671
Sanchi **9**:672–673
    Ashoka's Great Stupa **7**:*497*,
        **9**:672–673
Sangha **9**:673
sanitation **5**:388–391
    and health **3**:193
San Lorenzo **8**:583, **8**:585
Sanskrit **1**:77, **1**:78, **6**:435,
    **6**:450, **6**:479, **8**:632, **9**:673
    and Hinduism **6**:450
Santorini *see* Thera
Sappho **9**:674–675
Saqqara **4**:258, **9**:*717*
sarcophagus **1**:38, **3**:230,
    **3**:*231*, **3**:239, **4**:*279*, **8**:*638*,
    **9**:*694*, **10**:749, **10**:799
Sardis, Battle of **3**:220
Sargon of Akkad **1**:30–31,
    **1**:32, **1**:*33*, **7**:509,
    **9**:676–677, **10**:727
Sargon II **2**:91, **2**:92, **2**:94,
    **2**:143, **9**:690
    palace at Khorsabad **2**:*91*,
        **4**:*308*
*sarissa* **8**:604
Sarmatians **9**:687, **9**:688
Sarnath **2**:132, **2**:133
sarsen **10**:*724*, **10**:725, **10**:799
Sasan **9**:678
Sasanian kings **1**:29
Sasanians **4**:271, **6**:446–447,
    **9**:678–680
    coming of Islam **9**:680
    enemies of Rome **9**:679
    religion **9**:678, **10**:795,
        **10**:798
*sascab* **5**:377

satrap **1**:19, **1**:79, **3**:222
Saturn **8**:625, **9**:650
Saturnalia **4**:293, **4**:301
Saul **3**:224, **5**:356
Saxons **1**:54–55
scales, balance **10**:*776*, **10**:777
scalping **9**:689
scarab **1**:44, **4**:263, **10**:*744*
scepter **10**:799
Schliemann, Heinrich **1**:61,
    **7**:545, **7**:547, **10**:759
schools
    gladiator **9**:713, **9**:716
    Greek **4**:251–252
    public Roman **9**:662
    scribe **4**:249
    Sumerian **10**:728
science **9**:681–685
    materials **9**:681
Scioto River **5**:372, **5**:373
Scipio Africanus **5**:348, **10**:775
Scotland **2**:155, **5**:345, **7**:493
screw **10**:733
    Archimedes' **1**:40, **4**:288,
        **4**:319, **8**:580, **9**:683
scribes **1**:40, **1**:44, **1**:45, **2**:159,
    **3**:209, **4**:249, **4**:259, **7**:511,
    **7**:512, **10**:785
    schools **4**:249
script, Linear A and B **7**:548
scriptorium **3**:*227*
scriptures, holy **8**:638
scrolls **3**:170, **3**:226
    copper **3**:*226*
sculpture
    Cycladic marble **3**:217–219
    Greek bronze **1**:73
Scylla **5**:393, **8**:582
Scythia **8**:591, **9**:686
Scythians **1**:19, **9**:686–689
    customs **9**:688–689
    horsemanship **9**:687
    Persian war with **3**:223
    Royal **9**:686
Sea of Galilee **6**:419
Sealand dynasty **6**:436, **6**:437
sealing wax **6**:423
seals
    Assyrian **6**:*410*
    glass **9**:681
    Indus valley **6**:407
    Sumerian **10**:*727*
Sea People **5**:369, **5**:371, **7**:517
Sebeknefru **10**:781
Second Temple **6**:431
secret societies **7**:490
sediment **10**:766

Seip **5**:373
seismograph **9**:685
seismoscope **3**:179
Sekhmet **8**:575
Seleucia **2**:120
Seleucid Empire **8**:591, **10**:765
Seleucids **5**:357
Seleucus **6**:470, **6**:471, **7**:554,
    **8**:594
Seleucus Nicator **7**:494–496
Semitic languages **1**:31, **2**:115,
    **2**:159, **8**:609, **10**:785
senate **1**:56, **1**:79, **2**:108,
    **2**:139, **2**:159, **3**:194, **5**:344,
    **9**:658, **9**:*659*, **9**:660
senators **9**:657, **9**:703, **10**:731
Seneca **1**:27, **5**:389, **7**:557,
    **9**:653, **9**:654, **9**:655, **9**:661
*senet* **4**:301
Sennacherib **1**:58, **2**:91, **2**:93,
    **2**:117, **8**:564, **9**:690–691
    aqueduct of **1**:58
    palace at Nineveh **8**:565
Sennedjem **4**:259
Sennefer **7**:*508*
Senustris III **8**:573
Serapis, temple at Alexandria
    **1**:41
serpentine **7**:513
Seshat **10**:*785*
Seth **4**:264, **4**:265
Sethlans **4**:280
Seven Wonders of the World
    **2**:159, **3**:201, **8**:587, **8**:639,
    **10**:749, **10**:794
    lighthouse at Alexandria
        **1**:40
    Mausoleum at Halicarnassus
        **5**:*363*
    statue of Zeus **1**:21
    Temple of Artemis **4**:270
Severus, Septimius **4**:284
sewage systems **1**:65, **5**:388
    Roman **5**:390–391
sexagesimal **7**:513, **7**:559
*shabtis* **2**:128
shadoof **4**:288, **4**:319, **10**:734,
    **10**:799
Shahenshasi **6**:447
Shalmaneser I **2**:91, **2**:142
Shalmaneser III **2**:143
shaman **5**:373, **7**:549, **7**:559
Shamash **2**:120, **3**:213, **3**:214
Shamash-shum-ukin **2**:88
Shamshi-Adad I **2**:91
Shandong Province **3**:205
Shang dynasty **3**:172, **3**:173,

Shang dynasty (cont.)
  3:175, 3:177, 3:178, 4:291,
  5:380, 7:543, 9:700,
  10:784
Shankara 5:397
Shaolin Monastery (near
  Zhengzhou) 2:138
Shapur I 9:678, 9:679, 10:792
Shapur II 9:679
Shavuot festival 4:291, 9:669
shekel 3:215, 3:239
shells 7:531, 10:751
shih 10:778
Shimon Bar Kokhba 5:344,
  5:359
Shinto 1:42–43, 2:138, 6:413
ships 9:692–694, 10:755
  building 10:756
  Egyptian 9:692, 10:756
  Greek 9:693
  Phoenician 8:607, 9:692,
    10:757
  Roman 9:693–694
  use in fishing 5:386
Shiva 5:342, 5:366, 5:367,
  8:635, 8:638
shofar 7:543
shophen 3:232
Shortugai 6:404
shrines 4:261, 10:779
  Vietnamese 10:761
shroud 10:799
Shu 4:264, 8:575
Shulgi 4:266, 6:409,
  9:695–696, 10:729, 10:769
  royal hymns 9:695, 9:696
Shungas dynasty 7:497
Shutruk-Nahhunte 6:438
Siberia 7:539
sibyl 9:650, 9:719
  of Cumae 9:650
Sicarii 7:487
Sicily 2:102, 2:149, 3:211,
  5:347, 7:517, 8:580, 9:674,
  9:714
sickle 4:285, 4:287
Siculus, Diodorus 2:156
Siddhartha Gautama see
  Buddha
Sidon 1:38, 8:606, 8:607,
  8:608
Siduri 4:308
siege 10:774–775
siege engines 4:312, 4:319,
  10:775
siege tower 7:487
signet ring 6:423

sikhlu 2:88
silk 3:178, 3:179, 5:379,
  9:681, 10:752
Silk Road 2:138, 2:158, 3:172,
  3:178, 3:183, 4:247–248,
  6:447, 8:591, 10:752
Silla 6:444, 6:445
silted up 4:319
Silva, Flavius 7:487
Silvanus 4:298
silver 6:422
Similaun Man 7:540
Simon see Peter
Sinai 5:350, 5:399
Sinai Desert 7:536, 8:602
Sind 7:528
Sin 2:125
Sino-Tibetan languages 6:450
Sipan, Lord of 7:525, 7:527
sipapuni 1:51
Sippar 3:214
sirens 5:394, 10:748, 10:799
Sirius 2:144
sistrum 7:542
Sita 8:631
Sivan 4:291, 4:319
Skanda Gupta 5:340, 5:341,
  5:342
Skara Brae, Orkney 1:64,
  9:697–698
  buildings 9:697
  everyday life 9:697–698
skene 4:244, 4:273
skins, animal 3:198
Skipshelleren, Norway 5:386
Skythai 9:686
slavery 9:661, 9:699–702
  Babylonian 2:115
  and civilization 9:699
  in Egypt 9:700
  in Greece and Rome 9:661,
    9:701
  in India and China 9:700
slaves 4:288, 7:508
  Greek 5:331
  Roman 9:661
  Spartacus frees the
    9:713–714
  trade in 10:752
  treatment of 9:701, 9:702
slip 5:330, 8:568
smelting 8:567, 10:734
Smenkhkare 7:556, 10:762
Smith, Edwin 5:353
Smoking Frog 10:745
snake game 4:301
Snaketown 1:52

Sneferu 8:626, 8:627, 10:748
soapstone 8:639
  seal at Mohenjo Daro 8:635
Sobek 4:262
Sobekemsaf II 10:772
social classes
  Athenian 9:710
  Roman 9:661
social hierarchy 9:661,
  9:703–706
  rank in European tribes
    9:704–706
  responsibilities of high rank
    9:706
  signs of rank 9:703–704
  see also caste system
Society Islands 8:612
Socrates 1:69, 2:101, 5:325,
  5:326, 5:336–337, 5:339,
  7:517, 8:610, 9:707–708
  death of 9:708
  dialogues of 5:337
  teaching of 9:707
solar year 5:341
soldiers, roads and 9:645
solidi 9:704, 9:706
Solomon 5:356, 6:416, 6:428,
  9:693
Solomon Islands 7:503, 7:504
Solon 2:100, 9:674,
  9:709–710
Son River 8:594
Sophocles 2:101, 4:245, 5:330,
  5:332
Sosurim 6:445
South African horn music
  7:543
South America 7:518, 10:734
South American languages
  6:451
Southeast Asia 2:137, 3:183,
  3:237
Spain 2:153, 4:314, 5:347
Spanish conquistadores 3:210
Sparta 5:324, 5:325, 5:392,
  7:508, 9:711–712, 10:758
  Athenian war with 2:102
  education 3:170
  government 9:712
  and Greece 9:712
Spartacus 2:141, 9:657, 9:702,
  9:713–714
Spartan regime 9:711–712
Spartans 1:18, 8:599, 10:786
  education 5:328
  Equals 9:711, 9:712
  men and women 9:712

pottery 9:711
Spartan words 9:712
spells, Egyptian 4:265
Sphinx 4:309, 4:311
spices 4:296, 8:602, 10:751
spindles 3:198, 3:199
Spitama clan 10:797
sports 4:300, 6:465,
  9:715–718
  ancient Egyptian 9:717,
    9:718
  hunting and fighting 9:715
  racing with horses 8:570,
    9:716
  weaponless combat sports
    9:715–716
spring festivals 4:291–292
  Mayan ball games 9:718
Sri Lanka 2:136, 2:137, 3:183,
  8:595
  see also Lanka
stadium 1:66, 8:588
standing stones 10:724–725
  Orkney 9:698
  see also stone circles
Stanegate 5:345
stars 5:341
  magnitude of 8:624, 9:684
star worship 4:268
states, emergence of 10:751
steam power 10:736
steatite 6:407
stele 1:32, 3:209, 5:370,
  7:498, 7:559, 10:746,
  10:790
  Mayan 7:498, 7:500
Stephen, Saint 8:596
Stephens, John Lloyd 3:210,
  7:499
steppe 9:686, 9:719
steppe nomads 8:570–571
Step Pyramid 8:626
stern 9:692, 9:693, 9:719
stirrups 10:774, 10:775
stirrup spout vessel 3:165
stoa 1:74, 1:79
Stoa Poikile 9:652
Stoicism 6:476, 9:652–653
Stoics 5:338
Stone Age 2:124, 5:385,
  5:387, 8:572, 8:621–622
  animal masks 7:489
  cave paintings 5:387
  fishing 5:386
  horn music 7:543
  hunters 5:385–387
  jewelry 6:422

Middle (or Mesolithic)
   **5**:385, **8**:621
New (or Neolithic) *see*
   Neolithic era
Old (or Paleolithic) *see*
   Paleolithic era
tools **1**:62
water transport **10**:754–755
weapons and tools **5**:385
stone circles,
   British Isles **2**:111
   Orkney **9**:698
Stonehenge **2**:110,
   **10**:724–725
   Heel Stone **10**:724, **10**:725
stonemasons **1**:52
stone-money island *see* Yap
Stones of Stenness **9**:698
storytelling **6**:451
Strabo **7**:492
   *Geographia* **4**:305
stratigraphy **1**:61, **1**:79
stupas **9**:672–673, **9**:719
stylus **1**:32, **2**:120, **2**:159,
   **3**:170, **4**:*251*, **5**:328, **5**:399,
   **7**:512, **7**:559, **10**:*732*
Styx, River **3**:230, **3**:*231*
suckle **9**:649, **9**:664, **9**:719
Sudan **8**:566, **8**:572
Suddhodhana **2**:131
Sudras **1**:76, **4**:252, **9**:705
Suetonius **1**:27, **2**:107, **2**:109,
   **2**:148, **3**:195
Suetonius Paullinus **2**:130
suicide **7**:488, **9**:653, **9**:708,
   **10**:761
Sui dynasty **2**:158, **3**:173,
   **3**:174, **4**:247, **4**:316, **4**:318
Sukkoth **4**:292, **4**:*293*
Sulla **9**:659
Sumer **3**:192, **3**:221, **3**:228,
   **4**:266, **4**:274, **4**:275, **4**:276,
   **8**:623, **8**:636, **8**:637,
   **10**:726–730, **10**:768,
   **10**:774, **10**:779
   conquest of **10**:727–728
   growth of cities
      **10**:726–727, **10**:729
   weights and measures **8**:579
Sumerian language **1**:31, **1**:32,
   **2**:89, **2**:159, **7**:511
Sumerian religion **4**:290,
   **4**:295, **6**:409, **8**:636
Sumerians **1**:30, **1**:33, **2**:115,
   **2**:119, **2**:120, **4**:266, **4**:274,
   **7**:509–513, **9**:676,
   **10**:726–730

arts and crafts **10**:729–730
clothes **3**:198
cuneiform **9**:*696*
drink **4**:297
dynasties **10**:768
game boards **10**:*729*,
   **10**:730
irrigation **10**:734
jewelry **6**:422, **6**:424,
   **10**:*728*, **10**:729–730,
   **10**:*768*, **10**:769
kingship **10**:727
law codes **10**:729
literature **4**:307, **6**:451,
   **10**:730
mythology **7**:550, **7**:551
sports **9**:716
writing **8**:623, **10**:728,
   **10**:783
ziggurats **8**:628, **8**:636
sumo wrestling **9**:716
sun **2**:97, **2**:144, **5**:326, **5**:336,
   **5**:341
   and myths **4**:263
sundials **8**:625
surgery **5**:351, **5**:*352*, **9**:682
Surus **5**:347
surveying techniques **4**:303,
   **4**:304
Susa **2**:88, **2**:91, **4**:266, **4**:267,
   **4**:268, **6**:478, **8**:600, **8**:601,
   **8**:617, **10**:787
   Iran **3**:213, **3**:222
   royal palace **10**:*795*
Susano-wo **1**:42
Su Ting **10**:760
sutras **2**:159, **4**:252, **5**:396
swords **10**:774
symposia **5**:327
*Symposium, The* (Xenophon)
   **5**:325
synagogue **6**:431, **6**:479
syntax **10**:783, **10**:799
Syracuse **2**:102, **2**:149, **8**:580,
   **9**:674, **9**:683
Syria **3**:215, **5**:343, **5**:369,
   **7**:553, **8**:602, **8**:606, **8**:608,
   **9**:676, **9**:679, **9**:688, **9**:690,
   **10**:735, **10**:791
Syros **3**:217
Syrus **8**:624

Tabasco **8**:627
tabernacle **7**:536
tablet **7**:512, **7**:546–547,
   **7**:*548*, **7**:559
Tacitus **3**:215, **7**:558,

**10**:731–732
*Annals* **10**:732
*Histories* **10**:732
*Life of Julius Agricola* **10**:732
*Origin of the Germans*
   **10**:732
Tadius, Spurius **1**:71
T'aehak **6**:445
Tahiti **8**:612, **8**:613
Taklamakan Desert **7**:539
*Tale of Sinhue* **6**:465
Talmud **6**:431
tambourines **7**:542
*tan* **10**:778
*tanbo* **6**:412
Tang dynasty **1**:48, **2**:158,
   **6**:445
Tan'gun legend **6**:442
Tanit **2**:150, **8**:609
tannic acid **7**:539, **7**:559,
   **9**:667
Tao **3**:181
Taoism **2**:138, **3**:173, **3**:178,
   **3**:180, **3**:181–182,
   **6**:453–455
   Celestial Masters movement
      **6**:455
   and Confucianism **6**:455
*Tao Te Ching* **3**:181, **3**:182,
   **6**:453–454
tapestry, French **3**:*225*
*tapu* **8**:613
Tarhun **5**:370
taro **7**:503, **7**:514, **7**:559
Tarpeian Rock **3**:216
Tarquins **4**:278, **4**:279
Tarquin (Tarquinius Superbus)
   **4**:279, **9**:650, **9**:656, **9**:657
Tarsus **8**:596
Tartaros **3**:230, **10**:793
Taru **5**:370
Taruga **8**:567
Tasman, Abel **7**:504
Tassili caves, Sahara **1**:72
Tawa **1**:51
Taweret **4**:264
taxes **7**:530, **9**:680, **10**:760
Taxila **6**:446, **8**:591
Tayma **2**:125
Tebtunis **5**:391
*techne* **1**:70, **1**:71, **1**:73, **10**:733
technology **10**:733–736
   iron making **2**:122–123,
      **8**:566, **10**:734
   irrigation **10**:734
   power **10**:734–736
   simple machines **10**:733

smelting **8**:567, **10**:734
Tefnakht **8**:576
Tefnut **4**:264, **8**:575
Teiresias **2**:99
Telemachus **5**:393, **5**:394,
   **8**:582
*tell* **6**:479, **7**:510
*temenos* **4**:272
Temple of the Jaguar **10**:746
temples **1**:64–65, **1**:79, **3**:214,
   **4**:261, **10**:737–740
   Christian **10**:740
   Egyptian **10**:738
   Greek **10**:738
   Indian **10**:739
   Mesopotamian **10**:737
   Roman **10**:740
Ten Commandments **3**:214,
   **3**:224, **3**:239, **7**:536
Tenth Legion **7**:487
Teotihuacán **1**:65, **7**:534,
   **10**:741–742, **10**:790
   arts and crafts **10**:741–742
   Palace of Tepantitla **10**:742
   Pyramid of the Sun **8**:628,
      **10**:741, **10**:742
   Street of the Dead **10**:741
Teotitlan del Valle **10**:788
Terminus **9**:650
terra-cotta **5**:329, **5**:376,
   **5**:399, **7**:*502*, **7**:*511*, **8**:568,
   **8**:619, **8**:639
   Greek **9**:*700*, **10**:*781*
Terra-cotta Army **3**:168
Tertullian **3**:186
Teumman **8**:565
Teutates **9**:*667*
textbooks, Egyptian **4**:250
Thailand **2**:137, **3**:237, **8**:622
Thales **5**:336, **8**:629
Thanh Haa **3**:238
Thargelia **4**:292
Thebans **9**:712
Thebes (Egypt) **1**:44, **1**:46,
   **2**:88, **7**:556, **8**:589, **8**:590,
   **10**:743–744, **10**:770,
   **10**:772
   tomb of Pashedu **1**:71
Thebes (Greece) **7**:546, **8**:604
Themis **10**:793
Theocritus **1**:41
Theodora **8**:576
Theodoric the Great **4**:313,
   **4**:314, **9**:*706*
Theodosius I **1**:41, **3**:184,
   **3**:235, **6**:462, **8**:588, **8**:638,
   **10**:794

Theodosius II **2**:103, **5**:382, **5**:*383*

Theon the Mathematician **8**:624

theorem **8**:630, **8**:639

theories, scientific **9**:681

Thera (Santorini) **1**:72, **3**:218, **3**:219

explosion on **7**:518, **7**:522, **7**:523

wall painting **9**:*693*

Theravada Buddhism **2**:136, **2**:137

Thermopylae, Battle of **1**:18, **5**:325, **9**:*711*, **9**:712, **10**:786

Theseus **5**:334–335, **7**:492

Thesmophoria festival **4**:292, **7**:493

Thespis **7**:489

Thessalonika **6**:468

Thessalonika, Battle of **4**:312

Thessaly **3**:215

Third Buddhist Council **8**:595

Thirty Tyrants, Athens **9**:708

Thisbe **9**:651

*tholos* **4**:273

Thomsen, Christian **1**:62

Thor **1**:55, **2**:145

Thorismund **2**:*104*

Thoth **2**:127, **4**:262, **4**:265, **6**:449

Thrace **3**:223, **9**:713

thread pump **1**:40, **1**:79

Three Age System **1**:62

Three Hans **6**:442–443

Three Kingdoms period **6**:443, **6**:444–445

thresh **4**:287, **4**:319

Thucydides **8**:599

Thuria **5**:362

Thutmose (sculptor) **7**:555

Tiamat **6**:477

Tiberius **2**:108, **2**:147, **7**:*484*, **7**:485

Tiber River **5**:388, **5**:390, **9**:664

Tibet **2**:138, **3**:183

Tibur **5**:344

Ticinus, Battle of **5**:348

Tiglath-Pileser I **2**:87, **2**:91

Tiglath-Pileser III **1**:72

Tigris River **2**:90, **2**:93, **2**:142, **7**:509, **8**:565, **8**:591, **8**:621, **9**:692

Tikal **7**:498, **10**:745–746

acropolises **10**:745–746

Temple of the Jaguar **8**:*627*,

**10**:746

timber **10**:751

tin **10**:753

Tinia **4**:280

Tir **1**:55

Tiryns **7**:546, **7**:548

Tishri **4**:319

Titans **5**:332, **10**:793

Titus **9**:666

Tiy **8**:590

Tjuiu **5**:*377*

toga **3**:200, **9**:703, **9**:719

purple **9**:703, **10**:731

Tollund Man **7**:539

tombs **3**:228, **10**:747–750

builders **10**:771

Egyptian **10**:748

graves of Ur **10**:747, **10**:768–769

guards **10**:747

inscriptions **10**:750

Nabataean **8**:*602*

robbers **10**:748, **10**:770–771, **10**:772

writings inside **2**:127–128

Tonala River **8**:583

Tonga **6**:456, **6**:457, **8**:612, **9**:694

tools

flint **8**:*621*

prehistoric **8**:*621*, **8**:*622*

Stone Age **5**:385

Three Age System **1**:62

Torah **3**:214–215, **6**:430, **6**:431, **7**:536

*toran* **9**:715

*torana* **9**:672

torcs **2**:*130*, **2**:159

Tower of Babel **2**:113, **6**:*449*

towns **5**:388

plans **3**:175

walled **1**:64

toys **3**:170–171, **4**:302

Egyptian **3**:170–171

Indus valley **3**:170, **6**:408

Roman **3**:171

trade **10**:751–753

Babylonian **2**:117

and barter **7**:530

Chinese **4**:247–248

Egyptian **4**:258–259

Ephesian **4**:270

the first **10**:751

first merchants **10**:752–753

goods of **10**:751–752

in luxuries **10**:751–752

Mesopotamian **2**:86

money and **7**:533

Mycenaean **7**:545

Neolithic **2**:151

and roads **9**:644

tin and copper **2**:90

by water **9**:694

tragedy **4**:244, **4**:245–246

Trajan **5**:343, **8**:603, **9**:666

Transalpine Gaul **2**:154

transportation **10**:754–757

early water **10**:754–755

land **10**:752, **10**:756–757

using animals **10**:754

Trasimene, Battle of **5**:348

travois **10**:754

Trebia, Battle of **5**:348

Tres Zapotes **8**:583

tribal clans, Korea **6**:442

tributary **10**:768, **10**:799

tribute **1**:44, **1**:72, **2**:159, **5**:340, **5**:399, **8**:598, **8**:639, **10**:751, **10**:764, **10**:799

trigonometry **9**:*684*

trilithon **10**:725, **10**:799

Trinovantes **2**:129

trireme **9**:692, **10**:757, **10**:799

Trojan War **1**:24–25, **2**:98, **2**:99, **4**:246, **5**:392–393, **8**:581, **10**:758–759

Troy **5**:325, **7**:518, **10**:758–759

excavation of **1**:*61*, **10**:758–759

the fall of **1**:22

wooden horse of **1**:25, **10**:758, **10**:*759*

*see also* Trojan War

Trujillo **7**:524

Trung sisters **10**:760–761

Trung Nhi **10**:760–761

Trung Trac **10**:760–761

*tsu* **4**:282

Tsuki-yomi **1**:42

tuberculosis **1**:16, **1**:79

Tu Fu **9**:647

tumulus **9**:689

Tuna-el-Gebel **10**:*735*

tunica **3**:200

Tunisia **8**:607

Tunnel of Eupalinos, Samos **1**:66, **5**:389

Turkey **2**:151–152, **2**:153, **9**:676, **10**:758–759

pottery **8**:617

Turks **9**:680

Tushratta **1**:44

Tutankhamen **1**:47, **3**:*198*,

**7**:*485*, **7**:555, **7**:556, **10**:744, **10**:762–763

tomb of **4**:301, **10**:*744*, **10**:762–763, **10**:*784*

Tuthmoses **7**:538

Tuthmosis I **5**:349, **7**:486

Tuthmosis II **5**:349

Tuthmosis III **5**:349, **5**:350

Tuthmosis IV **9**:*701*

Twelve Apostles **6**:420, **6**:421

tyranny **5**:325

Tyre **8**:606, **8**:607, **8**:608, **8**:609, **10**:764–765

colonies **10**:764

commerce **10**:765

history **10**:764–765

religion **10**:765

temple to Melqart **10**:765

Tyr **2**:145

Tyrolean Alps **7**:540

Uaxactun, Battle of **10**:745

Ubaidians **10**:726, **10**:727

Ugarit **8**:607

Ujjain **8**:595

Ukraine **5**:385, **7**:541, **8**:571, **9**:685, **9**:686

Ulam-Buriash **6**:436, **6**:437

Ulfilas **4**:313

Ulster **7**:550

Uluru **10**:766–767

rock art **10**:767

umbrellas **3**:177

underworld **1**:22, **1**:50, **4**:255, **4**:265, **5**:333, **6**:410, **7**:550, **7**:551

Uni **4**:280

university, Chinese **3**:206

Untash-Gal **4**:267, **4**:269

"untouchables" **5**:365, **9**:705

Upanishads **5**:395–397

Upper Zab River **2**:142

Ur **1**:30, **1**:64, **3**:228, **4**:266, **4**:267, **4**:275, **4**:301, **5**:355, **6**:409, **6**:422, **7**:510, **7**:511, **7**:541, **9**:677, **9**:695–696, **10**:726, **10**:727, **10**:728, **10**:729, **10**:730, **10**:768–769

royal graves of **10**:747, **10**:768–769

Ziggurat of Ur-Nammu **7**:*513*, **10**:769

Urarta **9**:690

Ur-Nammu **9**:695, **10**:729, **10**:768, **10**:769

Ziggurat of **7**:*513*, **10**:769

Urnfield Culture **2**:153, **2**:155

Uruk see Erech
usury 7:532, 7:559
Utica 8:607, 9:661
Utnapishtim 4:308
Utu 4:275, 6:409
Uxmal 7:499
Uzume 1:42

Vaisheshika 5:396
Vaisyas 1:76, 4:252, 9:705
Valens 4:313, 4:314
Valerian 9:659, 9:679, 10:792
Valley of the Kings 4:256,
    4:259, 5:350, 10:743,
    10:744, 10:748, 10:762,
    10:763, 10:770–772
    reburied mummies 10:772
    tomb builders 10:771
    tomb robbers 10:748,
        10:770–771
Valley of the Queens 4:256,
    10:744, 10:770
Valmiki 8:631
Vanuatu 7:503, 7:504
Varahram II 9:678
Varahram V 9:679
Varanasi (Benares) 5:367
Varuna 1:76
Vasio 10:731
vassal 1:79, 9:719
Vatican 3:186
Vedanta 5:397
Vedas, the 1:75, 1:78, 4:251,
    4:252, 5:364, 5:395, 5:397,
    6:464, 9:705
Vedic hymns 4:244
Vedic religion 7:519
venationes 9:716
Ventris, Michael 7:548
Venus 2:120, 7:549
Venus (planet) 7:502, 8:625
Vercingetorix 2:139
Vergina 6:469
Verulamium (Saint Albans)
    2:130
Verus, Lucius 6:475, 6:476
Vespasian 3:201, 6:425, 6:426,
    9:666, 10:731
Vesuvius, Mount 5:360, 8:615,
    9:657, 9:685, 9:713
    eruption of 8:615–616
Vidisha 9:673
Vietnam 3:236–237
    Chinese occupation
        10:760–761
villa, Roman 5:378
Vindolanda writing tablets

5:346
Virgil 1:22–23, 2:109, 5:332,
    9:663
    Aeneid 1:22–23, 9:649,
        9:651
    Eclogues 1:23
    Georgics 1:23
Vishnu 5:366–367, 6:473,
    8:631, 8:638, 9:670
Vishtaspa 10:797
Visigoths 2:103–104, 4:298,
    4:299, 4:312, 4:314, 4:315,
    4:319
    art of 4:314
    map of kingdom 4:312
Vitiges 1:59
volcano 5:360, 7:522–523,
    8:615
Voltumna 9:650
Volturnus 9:650
volume 9:682, 9:683, 9:719
votive offering 8:639
Vouillé, Battle of 4:314
Vulcan 4:319
Vulgate Bible 7:538

wadis 8:603
Wahballet 10:791
Wales 2:155, 7:550
wall paintings,
    Minoan 7:522
    Neolithic 2:152
wampum 7:531, 7:559
Wang Mang 6:467
war
    causes of 10:773
    Huns in 5:383
    and migration 7:517–518
    theory and organization
        10:775
war chariots 10:756–757,
    10:774, 10:775
    Egyptian 4:260
warfare 10:773–775
Warka see Erech
war machines 9:683
warp-ikat 3:237
Warring States period 3:173,
    3:180, 3:204
warships 10:774
water management, Indus
    valley 6:406, 7:528
water mills 10:735
water power 10:735
water supply 5:389
water transport 4:277, 7:516,
    10:754–755

waterwheels 10:735
Way of the Heavenly Teacher
    3:182
weapons 10:773–774
    aboriginal 1:17
    bronze 10:773
    Chinese 3:178
    copper 10:773
    iron 5:368
    prehistoric 8:621
    in sports 9:715
    stone 10:773
    Stone Age 5:385
weaving 3:199
    Moche 7:524
wedge 10:733
week 2:144
    days of the 1:55
Wei Fu-Jen 10:782
weights 8:579, 10:776–778
    devices 10:777
    early methods 10:776–777
weiqi 4:301
Welsh myths 7:550
wergild 9:704, 9:706
West Africa 8:566–568
    horn music 7:543
West African language group
    2:123
Western Roman Empire 9:660
    see also Roman Empire
whale hunting 5:386
wheel 4:275, 4:288, 9:645,
    10:733, 10:756
wheelbarrows 3:177
wheeled vehicles 9:644,
    10:728, 10:756–757, 10:774
White Huns 5:341, 5:342,
    9:680
wigs 3:199
William the Conqueror 1:55
windmills 10:736
wind power 10:736
wind rose 10:755
wine 4:287, 4:295, 4:297,
    9:669
witchcraft 7:504
Woden 1:55, 2:145
Wolters, Paul 3:219
women 10:779–782
    admission to school 9:653
    authors 9:677
    Babylonian 2:116
    charioteers 9:716
    Chinese 7:492
    doctors in Egypt 10:782
    Egyptian 7:507, 7:508

Etruscan 4:280
    goddesses 10:779
    Greek 5:327, 7:492, 7:508
    Jewish 7:493
    and men 7:508
    as mistresses of the
        household 10:780
    poets 9:674–675
    in politics 10:781–782
    prestige 7:493, 7:555
    priestesses 10:779
    role among Israelites 3:233
    Roman 1:26, 7:492, 7:508,
        9:662
    Scythian 9:688
    in society 10:781
    Spartan 9:712
    see also matriarchy
wool 3:198
words, magical 6:449
worship 8:635
wrestling 5:327, 9:716, 9:717,
    9:718
writing 10:783–785
    arrival of 8:620, 8:623
    Chinese 3:179, 5:380,
        10:784
    Chinese in Japan 6:412
    and civilization 10:783,
        10:785
    cuneiform 1:32, 6:479,
        8:577, 8:609, 8:623,
        9:696, 10:783, 10:784
    Dorian 9:711
    Egyptian 2:127, 4:249,
        4:259, 10:784
    Etruscan 4:280
    and Greek philosophy 5:339
    Indian 1:75, 1:78
    Indus valley 6:406
    Kassite 6:438
    and male power 7:506
    materials 10:784–785
    Mayan 7:500
    Mesopotamian 7:511, 7:512
    Minoan 7:521
    Phoenician 8:609
    proto-cuneiform 4:274
    Roman 5:346
    Roman materials 10:732
    science and 9:681
    Sumerian 10:728, 10:783
    words 10:784
    Zapotec 10:789
writing tablet 5:346, 5:399
Wu Di 3:173, 3:175, 3:206
Wurusemu see Arinna

Xenophanes **5**:336, **5**:337, **5**:339

Xenophon
  *Cyropaedia* **2**:126
  *The Symposium* **5**:325

Xerxes **1**:18, **1**:19, **1**:28, **1**:29, **8**:601, **8**:608, **10**:786–787

Xia kings **5**:380

Xi'an **2**:157

Xianyang **2**:157, **3**:167, **3**:175

Xin (Hsin) dynasty **6**:466, **6**:467

Xionghu **5**:381

Xi Wangmu **3**:179

Xunzi **1**:47, **3**:204

Yagul **10**:788, **10**:789

Yahweh **6**:427–429, **6**:450, **9**:691, **10**:765
  *see also* God

*yaksha* **6**:*435*, **6**:479

Yamato culture **1**:43, **6**:411, **6**:412, **6**:413

Yam, kingdom of **8**:573, **8**:575

yams **2**:124, **5**:354, **7**:503, **7**:514

yang **3**:182, **5**:354, **6**:454

Yankunytjatjara **10**:766

Yap (the stone-money island) **7**:515

Yasodhara **2**:131

Yax K'uk Mo' **3**:209

Yax-Pac **3**:210

Yax Pasah **3**:210

Yazd, Tower of Silence **10**:797, **10**:*798*

Yazdagird III **9**:679, **9**:680

years **2**:144

Yellow Emperor *see* Huangdi (Huang-ti)

Yellow River (Huang He) **3**:172, **5**:380

yin **3**:182, **5**:354, **6**:454

Yoga **5**:396, **5**:*397*

Yom Habbikurim **4**:291

Yom Kippur **6**:427

Yoruba people **8**:568

Yosef ben Mattityahu *see* Josephus, Flavius

Yueh-Chi **6**:446, **6**:447

Yu Huang Shang Di **3**:179

yurt **8**:*571*

Zagros Mountains **6**:436

Zama, Battle of **5**:348, **10**:*774*

Zambia **2**:122

Zapotecan languages **6**:451

Zapotecs **7**:534–535, **10**:788–790
  ball game **4**:*245*
  calendar **10**:790
  carvings **10**:788–789
  religion **10**:788
  stelae **10**:790
  writing **10**:789

Zarathustra **1**:28, **10**:795–796, **10**:797

Zarpanitum **6**:477

Zedekiah **7**:553, **7**:554

Zen **2**:138

Zend Avesta **10**:796

Zengzhou **3**:175

zeniths **10**:790

Zeno **9**:652

Zenobia **10**:791–792

zero **3**:210, **5**:341, **7**:502, **8**:580, **9**:684

Zeus **1**:21, **1**:47, **2**:98, **3**:215, **5**:326, **5**:332, **5**:333, **5**:334, **5**:335, **5**:359, **6**:417, **6**:468, **7**:506, **8**:587, **8**:588, **8**:637, **9**:648, **9**:668, **10**:779, **10**:793–794
  statue at Olympia **1**:71

Zeus-Ammon **1**:47, **8**:605

Zhang Daoling **6**:455

Zhang Heng **3**:179

Zheng *see* Cheng

Zhongguo (Middle Kingdom) **3**:172

Zhou dynasty **2**:157, **3**:172, **3**:173, **3**:203

*Zhuangzi see Chuang-tzu*

ziggurats **1**:65, **2**:86, **2**:113, **2**:142, **2**:159, **3**:192, **4**:*269*, **4**:276, **7**:510, **7**:512, **8**:628, **10**:769
  Babylonian **9**:667
  Mesopotamian **8**:628
  Sumerian **8**:636

Zion **6**:416

zodiac **2**:96, **2**:*97*, **2**:159

zoology **1**:69

Zoroaster *see* Zarathustra

Zoroastrianism **9**:678, **10**:795–798
  customs **10**:796–797
  funeral practices **10**:797–798

Zuni tribe **7**:551